Bureaucracy at War

Also of Interest

†*The Second Indochina War: 1954–1975*, William S. Turley

The U.S. in Vietnam: War Without Fronts, Thomas Thayer

†*Vietnam: Nation in Revolution*, William J. Duiker

The Communist Road to Power in Vietnam, William J. Duiker

The Third Indochina Conflict, David W. P. Elliott

The Two Vietnams: A Political and Military Analysis, Bernard B. Fall

Communist Revolutionary Warfare: The Vietminh in Indochina, George K. Tanham

The United States After Empire: Policy Toward the Third World in the 1980s, Thomas Perry Thornton

War of Ideas: The U.S. Propaganda Campaign in Vietnam, Robert W. Chandler

Communist Indochina and U.S. Foreign Policy: Postwar Realities, Joseph J. Zasloff and MacAlister Brown

A History of Cambodia, David P. Chandler

The Rise and Demise of Democratic Kampuchea, Craig Etcheson

†Available in hardcover and paperback.

About the Book and Author

This study is one of the first analyses by a senior participant that examines why, despite their enormous superiority, the U.S. and its South Vietnamese allies performed so poorly in the Vietnam War. Ambassador Komer provides a systematic assessment of the crucial factors that largely determined what the U.S. could and could not accomplish in the unique circumstances it confronted. He focuses particularly on how a set of typical bureaucratic responses by U.S. military actors made it virtually impossible to adapt to a highly atypical conflict environment.

Robert W. Komer's distinguished career in foreign policy and national security included the post of Deputy to the Commander, U.S. Military Forces, Vietnam. As chief pacification advisor, he was responsible for civil operations and revolutionary development support. During the Carter administration he was undersecretary for policy in the Department of Defense. He is currently a visiting professor at George Washington University and a consultant to the RAND Corporation.

Bureaucracy at War
U.S. Performance
in the Vietnam Conflict

Robert W. Komer

Foreword by William E. Colby

Westview Press / Boulder and London

Westview Special Studies in National Security and Defense Policy

Copyright © 1986 by Robert W. Komer

Published in 1986 in the United States of America by Westview Press, Inc.; Frederick A. Praeger, Publisher; 5500 Central Avenue, Boulder, Colorado 80301

Library of Congress Cataloging-in-Publication Data
Komer, R. W.
    Bureaucracy at war.
    (Westview special studies in national security and defense policy)
    1. Vietnamese Conflict, 1961–1975—United States.
2. Bureaucracy—United States. I. Title. II. Series.
DS558.K66 1986   959.704′33′73   85-22718
ISBN 0-8133-0237-4

Composition for this book was provided by the author
Printed and bound in the United States of America

10   9   8   7   6   5   4   3   2   1

CONTENTS

vii

FOREWORD

For many of us who served in Vietnam, as well as dealt with it from Washington, it always appeared as a complex revolutionary struggle, a "people's war" which only in its later stages became overlaid with an increasingly conventional conflict. However, not until 1966-1967, when hundreds of thousands of U.S. troops were already in the country, did the U.S. mount an effort to cope with this aspect of the contest on a scale commensurate with the need. The chief architect of that effort, as all who dealt with him would agree, was Robert W. Komer, the author of this book.

The long history of American involvement in Vietnam certainly had many turning points, bad as well as good. But one of the more significant ones was when President Johnson became exasperated in 1966 at what he considered bureaucratic foot dragging against his insistence that greater attention be given to what he called the "other war," the challenge of economic, social and political development in South Vietnam. Johnson's motive was partly to counter the nightly TV and other media images of death and destruction resulting from the military clashes there, but his actions proved to be critical for the direction of the war effort.

President Johnson removed Bob Komer from the area he knew and loved, the Middle East, and made him a Special Assistant to supervise U.S. support for the "other war" among the many agencies in Washington which had a potential contribution to make. Komer rapidly earned the nickname, and it was not wholly complimentary, of "Blowtorch," from the heat he put on recalcitrant or parochial civil servants resistant to his pressure for faster action or broadening of narrow programs.

Komer did more than move the government machinery; he thought about the strategy of the war itself. And he soon concluded that the American and South Vietnamese approach to the war was badly out of proportion to the situation on the ground and the strategy of the enemy. It seemed that we insisted on fighting our kind of "soldier's war" while the enemy made it very clear that he was fighting a "people's war." Komer saw the challenge to be raising the "other" war to equivalence to the military war. This immediately embroiled him in the bureaucratic politics and institutional prerogatives of all the agencies concerned with Vietnam: the Department of State, the Agency for International Development, the United States Information Agency, the Central Intelligence Agency, and of course the Department of Defense and its many elements. Each of these had its own ideas as to how it could best advance American interests—and sometimes its own role—in Vietnam. And each had the responsibility and incentive to report directly to the Congress on its activities and programs to ensure that Congress would provide it the appropriations needed to continue and even hopefully enlarge its activities in Vietnam and, in consequence, in Washington.

Milder men faced with such a situation might have turned to the magic word "coordination" in order to limit their exposure to the crossfire that an active and forceful intervention would encounter in such a contest of interest, conviction and ambition. But Komer is not a mild man. He dove into the fray with gusto, demanding reports as to what the various agency programs were actually accomplishing for the war effort, insisting on reviewing the competence of the agencies' career officers at work there and requiring that the programs of the different agencies be reviewed together rather than separately. He looked for and exposed contradictions and conflicts among them to ensure that they contributed to an overall strategy rather than to the parochial interests or convictions of a particular agency. He was not popular, but he brought a new unity to the enterprise.

Komer soon saw that the single point of direction he had provided in Washington needed to be moved closer to the action in Vietnam. Because of his success in changing the stripes of the Washington problem, President Johnson sent him to do the same in Vietnam. But Komer had to determine how this could be accomplished within the bureaucratic realities of the American government structure. He knew that the military insisted on the principle of unity of command, which meant to them that all matters military had to be directed by a single commander. He also realized that the civilian agencies believed that their operations would be frustrated if they were subordinated to a military commander focussed on striking the enemy rather than building the economic, social and political structures they believed so critical to creating a self-reliant nation.

To cut through this dilemma, Komer came up with an ingenious practical solution: the U.S. advisory and support effort would be integrated under a civilian director who would hold the rank of deputy to the military commander. In compensation, the director would have authority over U.S. military support of the GVN local security forces, so that the U.S. had leverage to press for a fully integrated pacification program in the rural countryside, rather than having the various U.S. agencies each "do their thing" there.

Komer then took on the task of making this new machine work, and the same force and drive he displayed in Washington produced results in Vietnam. He pulled the military and civilian advisors together in the provinces, a military officer commanding one, a civilian official in another. He insisted on combined plans for the pacification campaign at all levels, so that the economic development projects so important to the villagers were accompanied by new local security units to protect them from enemy assault. And he worked with the Vietnamese government from President Thieu down to village chiefs to devote their full attention to bringing security and development to the countryside.

His drive irritated some, but it established the pacification campaign as the primary means of building strength behind the military shield, so that the American forces could be phased out of the war and yet leave Vietnam to develop and protect itself, with American help but without American soldiers on the ground. Komer left Vietnam in November 1968, but the program and the machinery he started continued to reflect his ideas and his drive as it effectively won the "people's war" against the Communists over the next several years. The fall of Vietnam in 1975 was a defeat by a massive North Vietnamese military force, not a guerrilla movement, with the United States withholding the support which had been promised in such a case.

Komer was an analyst as well as a leader. After joining RAND in late 1969, he sought to analyze why the U.S. and South Vietnam could not seem to accomplish more despite the cumulatively enormous human and material resources they were investing. This book is the fruit of that analysis. It is deliberately focussed on performance rather than policy. It dwells chiefly on a wide range of bureaucratic constraints which long seriously impeded the execution of U.S. policy in the field. For the most part, I regard his analysis and conclusions as eminently sound. He shows clearly why we couldn't "win" the war the way we fought it, yet turned American opinion against it as a result, to the extent that in the end we rejected even the small support which might have enabled Saigon to withstand the enemy.

On one matter, I do find some disagreement with Komer's study. He speaks of the "flawed nature of our chosen instrument," the Government of South Vietnam, and stresses how we should have gotten "better performance" out of it. This was a frequently aired subject during our years in Vietnam, particularly in the earlier ones. It led to some of our more ill-advised actions there, such as the American connivance in the overthrow of President Ngo Dinh Diem in 1963 and the tendency of our military—and some civilians—to push the Vietnamese aside and take the war over from them. A 1963 policy document spoke of using "persuasion and pressure" against the Vietnamese government, but in my view the American tendency, then and later, was to stress the latter. The cost in many cases was Vietnamese passivity, a wound to nationalist credentials or just plain error, as in Kissinger's compulsion of President Thieu to accept the continued presence of North Vietnamese troops in South Vietnam in the "peace treaty" of 1973.

In some other cases when the Vietnamese were given full U.S. support, they performed admirably, such as in the execution of the pacification campaign from 1969 to 1972 and in repelling the North Vietnamese spring offensive of 1972. Alliance relationships are delicate in all situations, but particularly when one ally is clearly dependent on another. In most such cases, more can be gained by "persuasion" than "pressure." I suspect that Komer would agree with this, but his very enthusiasm and drive require a reminder of it.

This is only a footnote to a book which is not only a critique of the past but full of useful lessons for the future. In that Achilles heel of so many fine policies, their execution, it points up valuable lessons of organization and control. These should have been dealt with at the outset of our effort in Vietnam, rather than coming so late in the war that the obstacles to success were so much higher and—a critical factor—the support of the American people had diminished out of frustration that our "soldier's war" seemed to have such little effect on the enemy's "people's war." In this respect his study is a valuable reminder of actions needed as the United States faces other challenges to its interests and its friends in the world. The program of assistance to El Salvador and the report of the Kissinger Commission on Central America suggest that these lessons have been at least partly heeded, but other policies and programs make clear that they have not.

William E. Colby

PREFACE

Unlike most analyses of our tragic Vietnam entanglement, this book focuses chiefly on U.S. and South Vietnamese performance rather than policy. It addresses a still neglected dimension of the Vietnam conflict: Why, whatever our purposes, did our massive intervention accomplish so little for so long—until finally the U.S. turned its back on Vietnam?

This issue increasingly concerned me during my three years of Vietnam service at the height of the U.S. intervention (1966–1968). Later as a consultant at the RAND Corporation, I seized the opportunity to examine it systematically as part of a study of counterinsurgency responses in Southeast Asia sponsored by the Defense Advanced Research Projects Agency. The result was my August 1972 RAND Report entitled *Bureaucracy Does Its Thing: Institutional Constraints on U.S./GVN Performance in Vietnam*. It drew heavily on the so-called *Pentagon Papers*, because this official report so extensively quoted actual documents and message traffic as to be practically a primary source.

The present volume is an updating and revision of my RAND report to incorporate both what happened up to 1975 and many of the relevant studies published since my original RAND work was done. This updating actually strengthens my original case, because in a real sense South Vietnam's 1975 collapse offered a final demonstration of its inability, and that of its U.S. ally, to win a revolutionary war the way we fought it.

In writing as a one-time participant in that war, I can hardly escape at least some parochialism, especially about the "new model" GVN pacification effort to which I became in effect chief U.S. advisor during 1967-1968. I stress the term "advisor" because, unlike the so-called "big-unit" war which the Americans largely took over, the American role in pacification was confined to advice and support. It remained a Vietnamese program at all times. In any case it is doubly difficult to be objective about what was partly one's own performance. However, having been a participant can also produce invaluable insights as to what really happened. My own experience at the top management level—both in Washington and in the field—showed me as nothing else could the operational and bureaucratic difficulties in translating policy into real-life performance. And my close relationship with our Vietnamese colleagues as their senior advisor gives me a lively sympathy for the constraints under which they labored too.

Any book which tries to help explain how we lost a war is necessarily critical of our performance and that of our South Vietnamese allies. My contention is, however, that underlying institutional constraints contributed at least as much as any faults of leadership. Unless we fully grasp the nature of these constraints, we will not grasp why we lost the war. Even so, this book does not pretend to be a comprehensive analysis of our Vietnam disaster, only an explanation of how various institutional constraints so powerfully affected what we could and could not do.

Finally, my great appreciation to those who helped make this book possible—Stephen Hosmer, George Tanham and Guido Ianiero. Above all, my thanks to Leslie Harrington, who rendered my scribblings into reasonably readable prose.

Robert W. Komer
Washington, D.C.
May 1985

ACRONYMS

AID	Agency for International Development (also USAID)
APC	Accelerated Pacification Campaign
ARVN	Army of the Republic of Vietnam
BAM	British Advisory Mission
CAP	Combined Action Platoon
CG	Civil Guard (later Regional Forces)
CIDG	Civilian Irregular Defense Group(s)
CINCPAC	Commander-in-Chief, Pacific
CIP	Counter-Insurgency Plan
COMUSMACV	Commander, U.S. Military Assistance Command, Vietnam
CORDS	Civilian Operations and Revolutionary Development Support
DCPG	Defense Communications Planning Group
DMZ	Demilitarized Zone
DPM	Draft Presidential Memorandum
DRV	Democratic Republic of (North) Vietnam
FEC	French Expeditionary Corps
GVN	Government of (South) Vietnam
JCS	Joint Chiefs of Staff
JGS	Joint General Staff

JUSMAG	Joint U.S. Military Advisory and Planning Group
JUSPAO	Joint U.S. Public Affairs Office
KMAG	Korean Military Advisory Group
LOC	Line of Communication
MAAG	Military Assistance Advisory Group
MACV	Military Assistance Command, Vietnam
MALT	Mobile Advisory Logistics Team
MAP	Military Assistance Program
MAT	Mobile Advisory Team
MSUG	Michigan State University Advisory Group
NLF	National Liberation Front
NSAM	National Security Action Memorandum
NSSM	National Security Study Memorandum
NSC	National Security Council
NVA	North Vietnamese Army
OCO	Office of Civil Operations
OSD/ISA	Office of the Secretary of Defense/ International Security Affairs
OSD/SA	Office of the Secretary of Defense/Systems Analysis
PF	Popular Forces
PFF	Police Field Force
POL	Petroleum, Oil, and Lubricants
PROVN	Program for the Pacification and Long-Term Development of South Vietnam
PSDF	People's Self-Defense Forces
RD	Revolutionary Development
RF	Regional Forces

ROK	Republic of Korea
RUSI	Royal United Services Institute for Defense Studies
RVNAF	Republic of Vietnam Armed Forces
SEA	Southeast Asia
SEATO	Southeast Asia Treaty Organization
SDC	Self Defense Corps (later Popular Forces)
SVN	South Vietnam
USAID	U.S. Agency for International Development
USG	U.S. Government
VC	Viet Cong
VCI	Viet Cong Infrastructure

1
VIETNAM WAS DIFFERENT, AND WE KNEW IT

In analyzing the long and costly U.S. entanglement in Vietnam, with its many tragic consequences, it is important to look at performance as well as policy. Whatever the wisdom of U.S. intervention on the side of South Vietnam, the resulting immense disparity in strength and resources between the two sides would have suggested a different outcome—as indeed it did to successive U.S. administrations. Yet why did a cumulatively enormous U.S. contribution—on top of South Vietnam's own great effort—have such limited impact for so long? Why, almost regardless of the ultimate outcome, did U.S. intervention entail such disproportionate costs and tragic side effects?

The reasons are many, complex, and interrelated. They include the unique and unfamiliar—at least in U.S. experience—conflict environment in which we became enmeshed. We repeatedly misjudged the enemy, especially his ability to frustrate our aims by his tactics and to counterescalate at every stage. Another constraint was implicit in the incremental nature of our response, doing only what we believed minimally necessary at each stage.

As heirs to the French, we inherited their colonialist mantle, The Government of South Vietnam (GVN) were portrayed as our puppets— disadvantages which Hanoi and its captive National Liberation Front vigorously exploited. We suffered even more from the sharp contrast between the adversary we faced and the ally we supported—a tightly controlled, ideologically disciplined regime in Hanoi and a revolutionary Viet Cong apparatus versus a weak traditionalist regime barely governing a still half-formed nation in the South.[1]

Thus, any serious analysis of U.S. performance in the Vietnam war must start from explicit recognition of how different it was from any major conflict in previous U.S. experience. Each war is different from the last, but most will concede that Vietnam was much more different from Korea than, say, Korea was from World War II. By

1

almost any standard, Vietnam presented a highly atypical conflict environment to the U.S. and its allies. As Samuel Huntington has pointed out,

> the situational characteristics of our Vietnamese entanglement were in many respects quite unique. The Vietnam problem was a legacy of Western colonial rule, which has just about disappeared from world politics. Vietnam was, in addition, the one European colony in which, for a variety of complex and unique historical factors, communist groups established an early ascendancy in the nationalist movement. In no other European colony—much less any American one—have communism and nationalism been more closely linked. The resulting problems were compounded by a combined heritage of Chinese and French cultural primacy which reinforced each other in emphasizing rule by an intellectual-administrative elite culturally and socially divorced from the mass of the population. The struggle for independence led to a divided country, again a sequence of events which seems unlikely to be duplicated in the future. Finally, the American involvement in Vietnam came at the end of cycle of active American concern with foreign affairs which seems unlikely to be repeated for some time in the future.[2]

Much more could be said about these many special circumstances which made Vietnam so prickly a nettle. Not least among them were all the sheer practical problems of coping with an unfamiliar conflict environment, strange culture patterns, and the like. Almost as unfamiliar was the very nature of the revolutionary conflict in which we became enmeshed: a largely political insurgency war. General Lewis Walt is a refreshingly candid witness on this score: "Soon after I arrived in Vietnam it became obvious to me that I had neither a real understanding of the nature of the war nor any clear idea as how to win it."[3]

Such unique circumstances do much to explain why the GVN, and later the United States, had such difficulty in coping with the threats which they confronted. They posed a whole series of real-life constraints, which largely determined what realistically could and could not be accomplished in Vietnam. Huntington concludes that they also may make Vietnam "irrelevant" as a source of lessons for the future. He warns about the danger of drawing "mislessons" from it.

It is true, of course, that "every historical event or confluence of events is unique" and its characteristics hardly likely to be precisely duplicated elsewhere.[4] But even these circumstances are insufficient to explain why the U.S. and the GVN did so poorly for so long. Why is it that over sixteen years, with a massive investment of over

$330 billion (in today's dollars) and direct intervention with over a half-million troops at peak, the U.S. was unable to devise a more successful response? Herein may lie some useful lessons of wider application.

Moreover, the author is one of those who contend that to a great extent U.S. policymakers realized how different Vietnam was and what difficulties we faced. Undersecretary of State George Ball was one well-known Cassandra, but there were many others. "There were all kinds of warnings that were heard and even listened to at the highest levels of government. At no point could anyone properly say, 'We didn't know it was loaded.'"[5]

Other analysts have also developed the thesis that the U.S. government knew what it was getting into, although more with respect to how the U.S. got progressively more enmeshed in Vietnam than with respect to its performance in the field. Take Leslie Gelb's fascinating "third hypothesis" that four Presidents and many of their advisers realized that the "minimal" steps they took were not adequate to solve the Vietnam problem and that "perseverance more than optimism was the touchstone of each new step." Daniel Ellsberg makes a similar argument, though he carries it to strange lengths.[6] The extensive documents cited in the so-called *Pentagon Papers* provide ample evidence that decisionmakers generally acted with their eyes open at each stage, with no lack of pessimistic advice that the measures decided upon were "long shots," which might not suffice.[7] Even the Nixon Administration's subsequent Vietnam policy during 1969–1972 seems to fit into this mold.

We may have looked on Vietnam too much as an exercise in containing global Communist expansionism, but much evidence exists of realistic analysis and high-level grasp of the nature of the problem we confronted in Vietnam itself. After all, we had plenty of time to learn—including some twenty years between 1945 and our direct intervention in 1965. As far back as the French days, many were pointing out the essentially political nature of what began as an anticolonial struggle, became a revolutionary war, and evolved into more of an outright invasion of South Vietnam as the revolution failed. Even in the early Fifties, the United States persistently urged France to build a legitimized indigenous government as the key to the viability of a non-Communist Vietnam. American stress on building such a government in Saigon after 1954 is another case in point. By the late Fifties it was official doctrine that a major threat to Southeast Asia (SEA) was from externally supported insurgency. In 1957 SEATO's second Annual Report stated that "subversion which has always been a major problem is the main threat we now face."[8]

The *Pentagon Papers* amply document "the persistent pessimism about non-Communist prospects and about proposals for improving them, almost unrelieved, often stark—and in retrospect, creditably realistic, frank, cogent—that runs through the intelligence estimates and analyses from 1950 through 1961."[9] The weakness of the Diem regime and its growing estrangement from the people were repeatedly pointed out. The record is full of perceptive insights, not just from intelligence or outside sources but from inside the U.S. and GVN operating agencies as well. That by March 1964 this realism had permeated the highest echelons in Washington is evident from such somber analyses as that in National Security Action Memorandum (NSAM) 288.[10]

Nor was there any dearth of advice on how to fight insurgency through land reform, rural development programs, paramilitary and police techniques, resettlement (as in Malaya), or other unconventional means. For example, in early 1961 Kennedy saw a report from Brigadier General Edward Lansdale which dissented with vigor from both the strategy of the Military Assistance Advisory Group (MAAG) and its complacency. "Lansdale thought that it was essentially a guerrilla war and that it was going very badly."[11] He was a recurrent source of such advice, as were Rufus Phillips and George Tanham, who headed AID's rural programs in the early Sixties. Sir Robert Thompson and Dennis Duncanson, who for four years (1961–1965) headed a British Advisory Mission in Saigon, gave similar operational advice, based on their Malayan experience, to both the U.S. and the GVN. Even earlier (during 1956–1961) the Michigan State University Advisory Group was making similar suggestions.

The chief actors too—Vietnamese and American—were hardly unaware of the atypical nature of the conflict, the fact that it was not just another conventional limited war. John Kennedy with "counterinsurgency," Lyndon Johnson with his "other war," Robert McNamara in his trip reports, and many others sought broader focus. Harriman, Forrestal, and Hilsman in the early Sixties argued for a more rounded politico-military approach. According to Arthur Schlesinger, the doubters feared that "the more elaborate the American military establishment . . . the more it would be overwhelmed by brass, channels, and paperwork, the more it would rely on conventional tactics, and the more it would compromise the Vietnamese nationalism of Diem's cause. Worse, the growth of the military commitment would confirm the policy of trying to win a political war by military means."[12]

Ambassadors Durbrow, Taylor, Lodge, and Bunker were strong advocates of political reforms and pacification, of strengthening GVN administration, or of going after the Viet Cong political infrastructure. Lodge called the latter the "heart of the matter." All this was more than lip service. It was fully reflected in the policy documents and message traffic of the time.

Of course, one can carry too far assertions about our broad perceptions. Certainly, some were far more perceptive than others, civilians perhaps more so than soldiers, as is hardly surprising in a basically political struggle. But almost from the outset, the civilians let Vietnam be looked at too much as a military problem, which unbalanced our response. While many perceived the essentially political and revolutionary nature of the conflict, we miscalculated both its full implications and what coping with it required. We consistently *under*estimated the strengths of the enemy and *over*estimated those of our GVN allies. We also tended to underestimate the great value of allowing the enemy sanctuaries in Cambodia and Laos.

Politically, we failed to give due weight to the revolutionary dynamics of the situation, the popular appeal of the Viet Cong, the feebleness of the Diem regime, or the depth of factionalism among traditional South Vietnamese elites. We only grasped belatedly the significance of the steady attrition of GVN authority and cadres in the countryside, an enfeeblement of political authority which was directly linked to how the Viet Cong conducted the war. Thus there were serious perceptual delays in our recognition of the extent of the threat.[13] Administratively, neither the fledgling GVN nor its U.S. ally fully realized the crucial importance of effective civil administration to a viable counterinsurgency effort. And however well we eventually perceived the key role of the Viet Cong political infrastructure, our detailed intelligence on it remained exceedingly poor till the end.

Militarily, we underestimated the enemy's guerrilla and terror potential, Hanoi's ability to escalate, and the ability of the Viet Cong (VC) and the North Vietnamese Army (NVA) to frustrate a much larger and better-equipped force by hit-and-run tactics stressing economy of force and evasion. One of our greatest military frustrations in Vietnam was the difficulty of pinning down an elusive enemy. Essentially, Hanoi was able to control the rate of its own losses by hit-and-run tactics, evasion and use of sanctuaries, which led to military stalemate.[14]

Nonetheless—however flawed our understanding of many crucial aspects of the problem we confronted—we grasped the overall nature of the problem itself far better than our accomplishments in dealing with it would suggest. Yet if, by 1960 at any rate, we at least broadly perceived the atypical nature of the Vietnam problem, why were we so slow to give adequate weight to it, to enrich our operational understanding, and to translate this into more responsive efforts of a type and on a scale more commensurate with the need?

NOTES

1. George K. Tanham and Dennis J. Duncanson, "Some Dilemmas of Counterinsurgency," *Foreign Affairs*, October 1969.

2. Samuel P. Huntington, *Military Intervention, Political Involvement, and the Unlessons of Vietnam*, the Adali Stevenson Institute of International Affairs. Chicago, IL, 1968, p. 1.

3. General Lewis Walt, *Strange War, Strange Strategy*, Funk & Wagnalls, New York, 1970, p. 7. Or, on p. 32: "It was a new kind of war, with unique ground rules."

4. Huntington, *Military Intervention*, p. 2.

5. Adam Yarmolinsky, cited in Richard M. Pfeffer (ed.), *No More Vietnams?* Harper and Row, New York, 1968, p. 1.

6. Leslie H. Gelb, "Vietnam: Some Hypotheses About Why and How," and Daniel Ellsberg, "Escalating in a Quagmire." Both papers, prepared for the 66th Annual Meeting of the American Political Science Association in September 1970, were distributed at the time, though their texts were not subsequently published. Gelb and Ellsberg write as insiders with past access to official documents transcending their periods of active involvement.

7. *United States–Vietnam Relations, 1945–1967: Study Proposal by the Department of Defense*, 12 volumes, U.S. Government Printing Office, Washington D.C., 1971 (Hereafter referred to as the *Pentagon Papers*). Chester Cooper, "The CIA and Decision Making," *Foreign Affairs*, January 1972, pp. 228–234, gives a good summary of CIA estimates on Vietnam.

8. Cited in A.A. Jordan, *Foreign Aid and the Defense of Southeast Asia*, Frederick A. Praeger, Inc., New York, 1962, p. 17.

9. Ellsberg in aforementioned APSA paper.

10. *Pentagon Papers*, IV.B.3, pp. 38–41.

11. Arthur M. Schlesinger, Jr., *A Thousand Days*, Houghton Mifflin Company, Boston, 1965, pp. 539–541.

12. Ibid., pp. 984–985. For one example of such perceptive official advice, which foreshadowed many future problems, see the citations from Hilsman and Forrestal's report to the President after a trip to Vietnam in January 1963. (Roger Hilsman, *To Move a Nation*, Doubleday & Company, Inc., New York, 1967, pp. 463–466.)

13. See John Dallas Stempel, *Policy/Decision Making in the Department of State: The Vietnamese Problem, 1961–1965,* University Microfilms, Ann Arbor, MI, 1965, pp. 277–280.

14. This is the key theme of Thomas C. Thayer, *War Without Fronts,* Westview Press, Boulder, CO, forthcoming. See especially Chapter 2.

2

WHY DID WE DO SO POORLY?

Hence, in analyzing our long and costly entanglement in Vietnam, it is important to look beyond why we intervened to the way we went about it. Whatever the wisdom of our intervention, why did we then proceed to deal with the problem so poorly for so long, first as advisors and bankers to the French and then the South Vietnamese, and finally as the latter's senior partner? Even the severest critics of the Vietnam war should be interested in why the way in which we sought to cope with it had such limited impact, while entailing such disproportionate costs and tragic side effects. Harry Summers has asked much the same question:

> From the American professional soldier's perspective, the most frustrating aspect of the Vietnam conflict is that the U.S. armed forces did everything they were supposed to do, winning every major battle of the war, yet North Vietnam, rather than the United States, triumphed in the end. How could U.S. troops have succeeded so well, but the war effort have failed so miserably?[1]

Surely it wasn't for lack of resources—in money, machines, and men. Even allowing for many miscalculations, the disparity in strength and resources between the contending sides would have suggested a different outcome, as indeed it did to successive U.S. administrations. Yet there emerged instead an equally great disparity between the cumulatively enormous U. S. input—550, 000 troops at peak, thousands of aircraft, and some $333 billion (in today's dollars) on top of South Vietnam's own great effort—and the ambiguous results achieved. To cite General Maxwell Taylor, "When one considers the vast resources committed to carrying out our Vietnam policy, the effective power generated there-from seems to have been relatively small."[2]

THE GAP BETWEEN POLICY AND PERFORMANCE

Regardless of what one thinks of U.S. policy in Vietnam, there was also a yawning gap between this policy and its execution in the field. To read the rhetoric enshrined in official statements you might think that those who drafted them were often talking about a different war. But more than rhetoric was involved. It is too simple to conclude that the answer lies mostly in politically motivated, even deceptive, public statements designed to cloak our real purposes. We know enough of the classified documents and message traffic to realize that we meant what we said. Instead, what comes out so strongly in the *Pentagon Papers* is the immense contrast between what high policy called for and what we actually did in Vietnam.

As General Taylor put it from his long Vietnam experience, "One of the facts of life about Vietnam was that is was never difficult to decide what should be done but it was almost impossible to get it done, at least in an acceptable period of time."[3] What high policymakers in Washington and Saigon advocated or directed was often imperfectly executed, or not carried out at all. For example, U.S. policymakers saw very early how the paramount importance of "political" considerations meant that the military "solutions" alone could not suffice. But the resultant U.S. policy stress on such measures as political and socioeconomic reform, land distribution, pacification, and the like called for far greater GVN/U.S. emphasis on such efforts than was ever set in train—at least until very late. This was perhaps the greatest gap between policy and performance; it is examined in Chapter 8.

In these respects at least, Vietnam did prove a "quagmire" into which the U.S. floundered. Those who argue otherwise are talking about the policies we adopted rather than our performance in the field. It may well be that "our Presidents and most of those who influenced their decisions did not stumble step-by-step into Vietnam, unaware of the quagmire. U.S. involvement did not stem from a failure to foresee consequences."[4] While we may have been aware of what we were getting into, however, we did sadly miscalculate our capability at each stage to achieve even the limited results expected from the limited steps we took. We grossly misjudged what we could actually accomplish with the huge resources we eventually invested, and thus became more and more caught up in a war we couldn't "win" the way we fought it. And instead of adapting our response to the atypical situation we confronted, we responded quite conventionally. When this response did not suffice, we escalated and counterescalated with more of the same—right up to the Tet watershed of 1968. Hence our actual performance in Vietnam does indeed seem "marked much more by ignorance, misjudgement, and muddle than by foresight, awareness, and calculation."[5] The "system" may have worked, but in terms of performance at any rate it worked poorly indeed.

Why was it so difficult for both the GVN and the U.S. to carry out effectively real-life programs which would meet the needs that were foreseen? As a perceptive reporter wrote in 1966, "experience has shown that the crucial matter is always execution rather than planning."[6] Roger Hilsman, addressing this question in 1966, also contends that "If Vietnam does represent a failure of the Kennedy Administration, it was a failure in implementation." He sees the reasons why mostly in terms of predilections of the chief Presidential advisers and field commanders, and of the bureaucratic politics involved:.

> A strategic concept of great promise for meeting guerrilla warfare was developed under President Kennedy—a concept that has looked more and more appropriate in the light of subsequent events. But although many people in the Pentagon, in the Special Forces, and elsewhere in the armed services—especially among company and field-grade officers—became enthusiastic believers in the concept as a result of their personal experiences in the field, Secretary McNamara, the Joint Chiefs of Staff, and many general officers were never more than lukewarm. General Harkins, for example, the commander in Vietnam, always acknowledged the importance of winning the allegiance of the people. But he never saw that the central principle of the concept was the need to subordinate military measures to a political and social program. What he apparently believed was not only that a regular war should be fought in Vietnam, but that it could be fought parallel to the necessary political and social program without destroying that program—which was probably a mistake. In any case, General Harkins was content to leave to someone else both the problem of pursuing the political and social struggle and the problem of seeing that military measures did not destroy it. As a result, the strategic concept was never fully implemented and military factors were emphasized over political.[7]

But Hilsman's explanation too seems incomplete. Among other things, it puts excessive emphasis on the existence of a clear counterinsurgency concept easily translatable into program (see Chapter 8). It also leaves out the crucial issues of whether any U.S. strategy, however well conceived and vigorously implemented, could have been effectively carried out by the South Vietnamese or would have led Hanoi to desist instead of escalate. Moreover, it focuses too heavily on personalities.

Granted that many failures of leadership at various times and at various levels marred the checkered history of our involvement in Vietnam. But it is too simple to ascribe our Vietnam travail primarily to bad leadership that failed to come to grips with the unique "situational characteristics" already mentioned. There were yet other factors, which created obstacles difficult for even the most enlightened U.S. leadership to have overcome. Hence we need to probe further to find out why it proved so difficult to translate perception into policy, policy into program, and program into practice in a manner commensurate with felt needs.

The reasons are many, complex, and interacting. Much has already been written about them, none of it sufficiently comprehensive. However, in seeking to add a new dimension to Vietnam critiques, this book too will essay only partial explanations. They lie in the realm of various built-in constraints which greatly inhibited the translation of perception into policy, policy into program, and program into performance.

THE WEAKNESS OF THE SAIGON REGIME

In retrospect, perhaps the greatest single constraint on United States ability to achieve its aims in Vietnam was the comparative weakness of the regimes we backed. In their excessive focus on the American role few critics seem to give enough prominence to the feebleness of the instrument through which the U.S. would have to achieve its aims—and to South Vietnam's consequent vulnerability to insurgent attack. This weakness persisted after U.S. intervention, and once the U.S. withdrew was a major factor in Saigon's 1975 collapse. Robert Osgood, writing ten years after the fall of Saigon, points out how:

> In the final analysis, all of the controversies over how the Vietnam War should have been fought are less significant in explaining defeat or the prospect of victory than the likelihood that no military success could have enabled the government of South Vietnam to maintain independence by its own efforts, or perhaps even with the continued presence of American forces.[8]

Moreover, the insurgents could concentrate singlemindedly on disrupting and destroying the GVN's authority, while the government and its U.S. ally had to pursue dual and often conflicting purposes: defeating the insurgency while simultaneously building a viable modern state. This dualism confronted the GVN and U.S. with a series of painful counterinsurgency dilemmas, as aptly pointed out by Tanham and Duncanson.[9] The constraints imposed by the inability or unwillingness of the GVN to rise to these challenges, and the inability or reluctance of the U.S. to force the GVN to face up to them, are discussed in Chapter 3.

ELLSBERG => 3

THE INCREMENTAL NATURE OF OUR APPROACH

Almost equally important is the wide range of political, financial, and resource constraints—usually arising from deliberate policy choice—which set limits from the outset on how the U.S. chose to deal with the Vietnam problem. They include the many careful limits imposed on out-of-country bombing and other operations, force-level decisions, financial ceilings, and the like. Though crucially important, they are not the subject of this study, hence will be mentioned only briefly.

Whether or not this policy of gradualism was sound is not at issue either, though many critics—particularly among the military—argue that it seriously constricted our Vietnam performance. These critics argue that we should have accepted JCS advice to pound North Vietnam much harder from the air and mine Haiphong harbor early in our intervention. They contend that had we done more sooner (even invaded the enemy's sanctuaries and called up our reserves, as the Joint Chiefs repeatedly suggested), we would have broken the enemy's back. However, others counter that quicker escalation would only have escalated the costs while not forcing Hanoi to abandon its fixed aim.

Whatever the merits of these arguments, there is little doubt that policy constraints led to a cautious and deliberate incrementalism in the U.S. approach to the Vietnam problem. The myth of reckless escalation does not square with the facts. Gradualism was the order of the day, with each step usually long agonized over beforehand. Even our withdrawal begun in 1969 took place gradually over a four year period, while we tried to prepare the GVN through "Vietnamization" and to negotiate a retreat with honor.

As a result, Vietnam hardly appears as a "crusade."[10] An "orphan war," as Philip Geyelin called it, seems more apt.[11] Despite all the defensive rhetoric, it was precisely the opposite of a "great patriotic war" (to borrow the Soviet term). Instead of mobilizing, calling up reserves, whipping up patriotic zeal, successive U.S. administrations took a quite different course.

Gelb has documented the compelling hypothesis that each U.S. President involved "essentially played the role of brakeman . . . Each did only what was minimally necessary at each stage to keep Vietnam and later South Vietnam out of Communist hands."[12] Hence direct U.S. military intervention in 1965 was not an early choice but a late desperate rescue effort. For eighteen years, 1948–1965, it had been U.S. policy not to intervene directly, but rather to use the French and then the fledgling Republic of Vietnam as proxies. We tried for a "Vietnamized" solution under Diem and his successors for an entire decade, placing main reliance on an effort to build a viable South Vietnam able to defend itself. This effort was marked by gradualism, expanding slowly step by step. Direct intervention came only as a last resort when this effort seemed on the brink of collapse and when the NVA was infiltrating to administer the coup de grace.[13] By that time, the U.S. saw little choice but to intervene or permit the VN to collapse.

Even after we intervened the policy of gradualism continued, reinforced by our conscious acceptance of limited war constraints in a nuclear age. Every U.S. administration was agreed on one thing—minimizing any risk of a direct confrontation with Peking or Moscow which might escalate out of all proportion to the stakes in Southeast Asia. Our understandable reluctance to risk widening the war led to great care in avoiding precipitate escalation outside of South Vietnam, but also allowed the enemy the great advantage of safe external sanctuaries. The restrictions on bombing, mining, and blockade in the North and on attacking sanctuaries in North Vietnam, Laos, and Cambodia severely constrained the military strategy the generals preferred.

There are numerous other examples of incrementalism—of doing only what was believed minimally necessary at each stage. Witness the slow and carefully measured expansion of the bombing targets in the North or the careful doling out of each new increment of U.S. troops over a four-year period. Though President Johnson has been severely criticized for escalating the U.S. involvement in Vietnam, it must be recognized that at every stage he and Secretary McNamara carefully pruned the military's requests.

Their policy of gradualism sprang from many motives—a U.S. Government reluctantly opting for direct intervention only after all else had failed, a President striving to balance the domestic demands of a "Great Society" against what he initially hoped would be a modest military commitment and thus anxious not to arouse undue

Congressional or public alarm, an Administration careful to avoid risky confrontation with Peking or Moscow, a Secretary of Defense determined to fight a cost-effective war and concerned (as were the Joint Chiefs of Staff) by the distortions of our global strategic posture forced by a growing conflict in Southeast Asia, principals and advisors at all levels hopeful that yet another *tranche* of U.S. forces or step-up in bombing would turn the tide. At the least, it was wishfully thought that the other side would be intimidated and deterred by each succeeding demonstration of our resolve. But we grossly underestimated the determination of our foe.

Have we here another institutional characteristic, the oft-remarked tendency of both professional analysts and policymakers to assume what has been called a "rational process model" of the adversary's behavior? Didn't we tend to assume that no sensible enemy would continue the unequal battle once the U.S. had committed its enormous power and shown its willingness to escalate? We believed that the enemy would react as we would have if confronted with similarly overwhelming strength. In a sense this did reflect a form of arrogance of power—an implicit conviction, born of our misconceptions, that throwing so much U.S. weight into the balance could not help but make the difference. Stanley Hoffman has commented tellingly on how many forms of *hubris* affected our policies and perceptions vis-à-vis Vietnam.[14]

The GVN's approach to the war was as much characterized by gradualism as that of the U.S. Aside from its feeble administrative capabilities, the fledgling government in Saigon also operated under a series of political constraints. Diem's sense of insecurity made him highly reluctant to delegate responsibility. He proved consistently unwilling to take steps to improve GVN war-winning capabilities that might interfere with his domestic hold on power. Xenophobic nationalism also influenced the policy of Saigon (as it did that of Hanoi), and often spurred rejection of U.S. proposals. The GVN was reluctant to antagonize such backers as the landlords and merchants by vigorous land reform, anticorruption campaigns, or stiff tax and monetary measures. It also regularly advanced political concerns in stalling U.S. suggestions for full manpower mobilization until after the shock of Tet 1968.

THE ROLE OF INSTITUTIONAL CONSTRAINTS

The cautious incrementalism of both GVN and U.S. responses is but one example of how both governments seem all too often to have taken the line of least resistance in dealing with the threat they faced. Looking back, one is struck by how often we Americans in particular did the thing that we had the most readily available capability to do, whether or not it was the most relevant. Whatever overall policy called for, the means available tended to dictate that we actually did. All this is quite understandable (see Chapter 4), but it meant that we often failed to face up to the hard choices until very late in the day.

To oversimplify, our policy called for creating a viable, effective GVN, but when frustrated in this aim we usually settled for living with what we could get, rather than try harder. Or, while initial U.S. policy was to create a GVN internal security capability, this became distorted in practice into building a conventional Vietnamese army (see Chapter 8). When the GVN and ARVN failed miserably in coping with insurgency, we came to their rescue and tried to do the job for them. But we too responded conventionally, and helped convert an insurgency conflict into a quasiconventional war. We employed U.S. air and ground power massively, largely because we had the capability readily available.

Again we must search further for the reasons why. Not even all the mistakes in leadership nor the panoply of constraints already mentioned—the atypical conflict environment of Vietnam, the flawed nature of the regimes we backed, the gradualist approach we took— quite suffice in themselves to explain fully the gap between what we saw was needed and what we did about it. There was still great room to maneuver—to adapt our responses more quickly to the needs we claimed to see. But somehow we did not. What else helped make our responses so conventional, so slow to evolve, and so ineffective for so long?

There needs to be added yet another set of real-life constraints which made it doubly difficult to adjust to the practical problems of coping with an unfamiliar conflict environment, and greatly influenced what we could and could not, or would and would not, do. While by no means the whole answer, these constraints reflected patterns of organizational behavior which did much to make our actions ill-suited to the needs, impeded the translation of policy into practice, and inhibited innovation and adaptation. They helped render the U.S./GVN response to an unconventional insurgency/guerrilla war unduly conventional, expensive, and slow to adapt.

This added perspective—so often missing from critical analyses of U.S. performance—is essential to understanding what was done and why it failed, or succeeded, in Vietnam. Hence this study is essentially a pragmatic inquiry into a so far neglected dimension of the Vietnam war. But the role of institutional constraints in how we dealt with the Vietnam problem so conventionally should not be overdramatized. It was only one of many factors. For example, Goodman points out how "No matter how effective ARVN became, it could never cope with the sanctuaries in Laos and Cambodia . . . Moreover, 'North Vietnam was next door,' while Saigon's ally was 10,000 miles away and anxious to disengage."[15] Nor should the following observations on various institutional aspects of GVN/U.S. performance be taken as advancing any theory of bureaucratic determinism as the prime explanation of our failures in Vietnam.[16]

Moreover, the institutional constraints discussed herein are by no means peculiar to our Vietnam experience. They are characteristics inherent to a greater or lesser degree in the behavior patterns of large hierarchically organized institutions—private or public, civilian or military, American or foreign. If we are to understand their import, we must recognize them for what they are. Though calling such institutions "bureaucracies," their personnel "bureaucrats," and their processes "bureaucratic" has pejorative implications, this is not intended here. Instead such terms are simply used herein to describe large organizations that are organized hierarchically—as most inevitably are—and the way in which they typically behave.

Such institutional behavior patterns are naturally least constraining when organizations are performing familiar roles and missions for which they were designed. They are far more constraining when such organizations confront atypical situations with which they are not designed or equipped to cope. This is what happened in Vietnam. Each organization inevitably tended to make policy conform in practice to that with which it was most familiar—to play out its standard organizational repertoire. Each reflected that fact of institutional life cited by an anonymous White House aide who wrote that "bureaucracy as a form of organization tends to contort policy to existing structures rather than adjusting structures to reflect changes in policy."[17] Vietnam further demonstrates how the way in which an organization will use its existing capabilities is governed largely by its own internal goals, performance standards, and measurement and incentive systems—even when these conflict with the role it is assigned.

The Vietnam experience is also a prime example of how, other things being equal, the larger and/or most dynamic of several institutions will tend to dominate the others, to crowd them to one side. In Vietnam, the U.S. and GVN military were both the largest and the most "can do" organizations involved. Moreover, it reflects yet another hallmark of bureaucracy—resistance to change—and, of course, the larger the institution the greater this inertial force. These constraints are discussed in Chapters 4–5.

Lastly, the institutional constraints created by the way the U.S. Government dealt with the war in largely separate bureaucratic compartments, with little attention to unified management, diluted managerial focus and impeded adaptation to the special circumstances of Vietnam. As Stanley Hoffmann has commented tellingly, such diffusion of responsibility in Washington and the field often leaves the impression of Washington "being in the same position President Truman uncharitably predicted his successor would find himself in—giving instructions, thinking that the policy is being carried out, and then discovering that little is happening."[18] As is illustrated in Chapters 6 and 8, this was unfortunately all too often the case in Vietnam.

Nor were these problems peculiar to the Americans. Most of the same institutional constraints were also at work on the GVN side—civil and military. Underlying them all, of course, were the fundamental GVN inadequacies earlier discussed. If anything, the Vietnamese response to a growing insurgency challenge was even more institutionally hidebound than that of the U.S. Militarily, most ARVN commanders seem to have been even less flexible than their American advisers or, after 1965, than their U.S. counterparts—in strong contrast to an enemy also Vietnamese. In this respect they were powerfully influenced by French and then American training, equipment, and advice. So they too played out the institutional repertoires we gave them, rather than adapting themselves to meeting insurgency in Vietnam.

All this is what Henry Kissinger seems to be getting at in assessing our failures in Vietnam:

It seems to me that many of our difficulties in Vietnam have turned out to be conceptual failures; and almost all of our concepts, the military ones as well as some of the traditional liberal ones, have really failed, and failed for two reasons.

One of these reasons is that many of them were irrelevant to the situation. Secondly, they failed for a reason that requires careful study; the degree to which our heavy, bureaucratic, and modern government creates a sort of blindness in which bureaucracies run a competition with their own programs and measure success by the degree to which they fulfill their own norms, without being in a position to judge whether the norms made any sense to begin with.[19]

NOTES

1. Harry G. Summers, Jr. "Lessons: A Soldier's View," in *Vietnam As History*, University Press of America, Lanham, MD, 1984, p. 109.

2. Maxwell D. Taylor, *Swords and Plowshares*, W. W. Norton & Company, Inc., New York, 1972, p. 402.

3. Ibid., p. 311.

4. Leslie Gelb, "The System Worked," *Foreign Policy*, Summer 1971; see also Daniel Ellsberg, "The Quagmire Myth and the Stalemate Machine," *Public Policy*, Spring 1971.

5. A. Schlesinger, Jr., "Eyeless in Indochina," *New York Review of Books*, October 21, 1971, p. 23. See also Gelb's reply in December 2 issue, p. 31.

6. Article by Charles Mohr in *The New York Times*, cited in *Pentagon Papers, IV.C.8*, p. 1.

7. Roger Hilsman, *To Move a Nation*, Doubleday & Company, Inc., New York, 1967, pp. 578–579.

8. Summers, *Vietnam As History*, p. 134.

9. George K. Tanham and Dennis J. Duncanson, "Some Dilemmas of Counterinsurgency," *Foreign Affairs*, October 1969.

10. Cf. Chester L. Cooper, *The Lost Crusade*, Dodd, Mead & Company, New York, 1970. However, Cooper gives only a pro forma explanation of his "crusade" thesis.

11. Philip Geyelin, *Lyndon B. Johnson and the World*, Frederick A. Praeger, Inc., New York, 1966.

12. Gelb, in *Foreign Policy*, Summer 1971.

13. Dennis Duncanson, *Government and Revolution in Vietnam*, Oxford University Press, New York and London, 1968, gives a perceptive, largely eyewitness account of this failure on pp. 274–283.

14. Stanley Hoffmann, *Gulliver's Troubles, Or The Setting of American Foreign Policy*, McGraw-Hill, New York, 1968, p. 269.

15. Pfeffer, *No More Vietnams?* Harper and Row, New York, 1968, pp. 121–128.

16. Richard J. Barnet attempts to do just that, primarily with respect to how we got progressively more enmeshed in Vietnam. He argues that "The roots of the Vietnam failure lie more in the structure and organization of the national security bureaucracy" than in the roles of the President and his chief advisers. To him, Vietnam "illustrates the crucial role of bureaucratic momentum." The vast foreign policy bureaucracy really sets the pace and escalates commitments with "a kind of Parkinson inevitability. . . . The dynamism of the myriad bureaucratic empires dealing in national security assures not only the escalation of U.S. commitments but their progressive militarization as well," etc. For his freeswinging hypothesis plus rebuttals

by Wohlstetter, Schlesinger, Cooper, and others, see *No More Vietnams?* pp. 50–114.

17. *The Washington Post,* January 23, 1971, p. C-11.
18. Hoffmann, *Gulliver's Troubles,* p. 269.
19. Pfeffer, *No More Vietnams?* p. 11.

3
THE FLAWED NATURE
OF OUR CHOSEN INSTRUMENT

If any generalization can be made about the war in South Vietnam it is that the U.S. effort, both military and political, prospered to the extent that the government of Vietnam was strong, coherent, and active. The corollary, of course, is that none of our efforts had any chance of success in the periods during which the government was weak, divided, and thus ineffective.[1]

Though these prefatory words to General Westmoreland's final report may smack to some of apologia, they suggest how Vietnam's recurrent coups and other political problems "were as important and in some cases more important than the unfolding of the tactical situation on the ground."[2] In the last analysis, the U.S. effort in Vietnam failed largely because it could not sufficiently revamp or adequately substitute for a South Vietnamese leadership, administration, and armed forces inadequate to the task. Nor is it to excuse our own errors to point out that, despite all the help provided, the regimes we backed proved incapable of coping with the threat they faced. In retrospect, this was perhaps the greatest single constraint on the ability of the United States to achieve its aims. As George Ball put it in his well-known 1965 memorandum on "Cutting Our Losses in South Vietnam," "Hanoi has a government and a purpose and a discipline. The 'government' in Saigon is a travesty. In a very real sense, South Vietnam is a country with an army and no government."[3]

Though historical analogies are always imperfect, *Stilwell and the American Experience in China 1911–1945* recounts the similar frustrations we confronted at an earlier point in time.[4] Presumed U.S. responsibility for the "loss" of China also occasioned vicious controversy. But one cannot read Barbara Tuchman's book without realizing that a key reason for "the waste of an immense American effort" was the nonviability of the inept and faction-ridden regime of Chiang Kai-shek. Like Diem and his successors, Chiang was far more concerned over his position vis-à-vis other Chinese factions than he was intent on defeating the Japanese. Much as later in Vietnam, there was no dearth of official U.S. reporting of mounting deterioration and dissidence.[5] Again as in Vietnam, "China's misgovernment was not so much a case of absolute as of ineffective rule."[6] Tuchman concludes that Stilwell's mission

> failed in its ultimate purpose because the goal was unachievable. The impulse was not Chinese. . . . China was a problem for which there was no American solution. The American effort to sustain the status quo could not supply an outworn government with strength and stability or popular support. It could not hold up a husk nor long delay the cyclical passing of the mandate of heaven. In the end China went her own way as if the Americans had never come.[7]

The same held true of Vietnam, even though the American input was far greater and the immensity of the obstacles far less. The Saigon government too could not long survive U. S. disengagement. In the China case, of course, a war-weary America balked at bailing out Chiang via massive military intervention. In Vietnam we made proportionally a far more massive effort before disengaging from the war. But neither in China nor in Vietnam did U.S. leaders (Stilwell being a major exception) make sufficient effort to come to grips with the inadequacies of the regimes we backed instead of trying to go around them in some way. Allan Goodman contends that "The failure to understand the capabilities and limitations of our ally in Vietnam is probably the single most important explanation of what went wrong with U.S. policy there."[8]

These wartime problems go far deeper than the weaknesses or corruption of local leaders, important as these may be. They seem largely endemic in traditional preindustrial societies struggling to enter the modern age. True, they can be solved. Both the Peking and Hanoi regimes appear to have done so, if at a staggering human price. The British also solved them in Malaya, though under much more favorable circumstances than the U.S. faced in Vietnam. Moreover, in Vietnam the U.S. was plagued from the outset of its ill-starred entanglement by a factionalism which a knowledgeable firsthand observer has called "the most constant characteristic of Vietnamese society."[9]

Lack of much effectively functioning administrative machinery was also a major handicap. A truncated new nation created by compromise at the 1954 Geneva Conference, South Vietnam would have faced a host of problems even if no VC challenge had arisen. Its feeble institutions mostly were left over from the French colonial regime, but without the French administrators who had managed them. After a hopeful start in 1954–1957, the new and untried government of Ngo Dinh Diem proved increasingly incapable of governing effectively, much less of simultaneously meeting a growing insurgent challenge. The tangled story of the Diem regime's failure is well known.[10] It probably only lasted as long as it did because it was "one of the largest recipients of U.S. economic and military assistance in the world."[11]

If the fledgling GVN under Diem gradually came to take the mounting insurgency seriously, it did so even more slowly than the Americans. Despite U.S. urging, it failed to gear up politically, militarily, economically, or administratively to meet the needs it increasingly recognized. Duncanson vividly describes the weakness and inadequacy of the Diem regime's early halting efforts. [12] The feeble administrative structure outside the cities was allowed to erode further. The GVN launched a plethora of programs, but built no adequate administrative machinery to carry them out. It made all too little effort to compete with the Viet Cong in the vital countryside, until the belated Strategic Hamlet Program of 1962–1963. And this too failed largely for administrative reasons; all too much of it remained on paper.

The *Pentagon Papers* convey an overwhelming impression of growing American frustration and eventual disillusionment with Diem. Though eager for U.S. aid, he proved basically resistant to advice on how to use it from either his own Vietnamese advisers or U.S. and British advisers on the scene. While the U.S. eventually acquiesced in the fall of Diem, its trials did not end there. The generals who succeeded him—at least till June 1965—were certainly no more competent. Nor can one ignore the destabilizing impact of the Diem regime's demise and the recurrent coups of 1963–1965. The resulting turmoil further undermined South Vietnam's ability to combat the VC, and to a considerable extent forced the U.S. to choose between intervening and largely Americanizing the war or seeing the GVN collapse. Not until the end of the Buddhist affair in central Vietnam, in May 1966, did even relative GVN stability return.

Some of the most telling practical Vietnam critiques have been written by what one of its chief exponents calls the "administrative" school of counterinsurgency: mostly Britons with long field experience in Malaya as well as Vietnam. One of them argues that "the decisive factor" which brought about Diem's demise was "his ignorance [of] how to administer the ordinary machinery of government over which he presided. . . ."[13] In retrospect, it is hard to fault their conclusion that, despite all the massive help which the U.S. provided, the lack of a sufficiently viable, functioning government was a crucial handicap.

U.S. FAILURE TO MOVE THE GVN

Nor, throughout our long involvement in Vietnam, do we Americans seem to have made an adequate effort to remedy this crucial flaw. Thus to what extent was GVN failure a U.S. failure too? The ambiguous record of twenty years of U.S. dealings with the Saigon regime as its protector, banker, supplier, adviser, and finally wartime partner is by now well known. But even in hindsight it is difficult to evaluate how much our failure to move the GVN was owing to the intractable nature of the problem, and how much to the way we went about it. Nor is it at all clear that what aid and advice the GVN did accept from us was wisely given in the first place; this issue is addressed in Chapter 4 below. Some of the successes and failures of the unprecedented U.S. field advisory effort are discussed in Chapter 7.

In analyzing such questions, three separable periods must be considered. The first of these was 1954–1964, ten years in which we tried to build up a GVN and an ARVN that could stand on their own feet. Second was the 1965–1968 period of direct U.S. intervention and escalation, in which we largely pushed the South Vietnamese to one side and tried to win the war for them. Last was the period of U.S. disengagement beginning with the partial halt of bombing in the North, during which we again placed great emphasis on "Vietnamization." The first period ended in clear failure, the second was more mixed, and the third resulted in 1975 in final GVN collapse after the U.S. turned its back on its ally and Congress sharply reduced U.S. aid. William Colby considers this latter signal to have been "the root cause" of Saigon's fall.[14]

U.S. officials tried harder than is often realized to get Diem and his successors to deal more effectively with the threat they faced. This effort began with Diem's accession to power in 1954, and involved a series of advisory efforts, not just by the official U.S. mission, but the Michigan State University Group in 1956–1961 and a talented British Advisory Mission under Sir Robert Thompson and Dennis Duncanson during 1961–1965.

Some U.S. officials tried harder than others. Ambassador Durbrow (1957–1961) pressed Diem so hard on corruption, reform, and other issues that he was almost declared *persona non grata*. By late 1960, when his repeated efforts proved mostly unavailing, Durbrow began urging pressure on Diem and warning that alternative leadership might be needed.[15] In early 1961, the new Kennedy Administration tried to tie reforms to increased aid under a Counter-Insurgency Plan worked out by U.S. agencies during 1960. But the U.S. got almost nowhere, though it held up the new aid for some months in an effort to get Diem to act.[16] So in May 1961, the new Kennedy Administration decided to stop pressuring Diem and instead try to "coax him into reforming by winning his confidence."[17] In effect, we decided to "sink or swim with Ngo Dinh Diem," believing that no viable alternative existed. Despite his continued obduracy and declining grip, we redoubled our assistance. This, and Durbrow's replacement by Ambassador Frederick Nolting in 1961 to carry out the new policy, convinced Diem and Nhu that the U.S. had no other option, which cost us heavily in 1961–1963.

When the crisis deepened, Kennedy sent the Taylor-Rostow Mission to Vietnam in October 1961. It made many recommendations for greater U.S. aid, which Washington again decided to "make contingent on Diem's acceptance of a list of reforms; further Diem was to be informed that if he accepted the program the U.S. would expect to 'share in decision-making . . . rather than advise only.'"[18] General Taylor proposed that, along with increased U.S. aid, there should be a "shift in the American relation to the Vietnamese effort from advice to limited partnership," but a shift to be brought about via persuasion rather than pressure.[19] Even so the President decided to ask for *quid pro quos*, on the recommendation of Rusk and McNamara. Greater U.S. support was to be conditioned on GVN "undertakings" to (a) put the GVN "on a wartime footing to mobilize its entire resources"; (b) establish "appropriate governmental wartime agencies with adequate authority to perform their functions effectively"; and (c) overhaul "the military establishment and command structure so as to create an effective military organization for the prosecution of the war."[20] Here was the culmination of all the reform recommendations that the U.S. had been making for the previous two years.

But the result was even then predicted by U.S. Ambassador to India J. K. Galbraith, whom Kennedy had asked to stop off in Vietnam. He quickly wired back that, as indispensable as these changes were to GVN success in coping with the insurgency, there was scarcely any chance of getting them in fact:

We have just proposed to help Diem in various ways in return for a promise of administrative and political reforms. Since the administrative (and possible political) ineffectuality are the strategic factors for success, the ability to get reforms is decisive. With them the new aid and gadgetry will be useful. Without them the helicopters, planes and advisors won't make appreciable difference.

In my completely considered view . . . Diem will not reform either administratively or politically in any effective way. This is because he cannot. It is politically naive to expect it. He senses that he cannot let power go because he would be thrown out. He may disguise this even from himself with the statement that he lacks effective subordinates but the circumstance remains unchanged.[21]

Galbraith was prescient. He clearly favored getting rid of Diem, and found even military leadership a preferable alternative (we were not to get around to acquiescing in this until late 1963). He correctly predicted that Diem would not do what the U.S. thought was necessary. Indeed, "it did not take long for Washington to back away from any hard demands on Diem."[22] Thus ended another futile episode in the U.S. attempt to get the GVN to gear up for a conflict which, we concluded at the time, only the GVN itself could win.[23]

Only in late 1963, after Nolting had in turn been replaced by Henry Cabot Lodge, did the growing deterioration of the situation lead the U.S. to decide finally "to coerce Diem into a compliance with U.S. wishes." "Thus, the Kennedy Administration . . . had made a far-reaching decision. . . . It had chosen to take the difficult and risky path of positive pressures against an ally to obtain from him compliance with our policies."[24] But in October 1963, while McNamara and Taylor were in Saigon, they and Lodge vetoed the draft of a tough presidential letter to Diem that in effect laid down an ultimatum—either the Diem regime must change its repressive policies, or the U.S. might have to consider pulling out, or at least disassociating itself from Diem."[25] Instead, they proposed a series of lesser measures to "coerce" Diem, including "a selective suspension of economic aid."[26] Lodge did withhold such aid, and saw signs that it was bringing Diem around. Before this effort reached fruition, however, it helped trigger the army coup brewing against Diem, which led to his death.

The U.S. hoped that the generals who succeeded Diem would be able to strengthen the GVN and make it more united and effective. What happened instead was six changes of government up to June 1965, which only hastened the deterioration:

In 1964 the U.S. tried to make GVN strong, effective, and stable, and it failed. When the U.S. offered more aid, GVN accepted it without improving; they promised to mobilize, but failed to speed up the slow buildup of their forces. When the U.S. offered a firmer commitment to encourage them, including possible later bombing of North Vietnam, the GVN tried to pressure us to do it sooner. When the U.S. endorsed Khanh, he overplayed his hand, provoked mob violence, and had to back down to a weaker position than before. When Taylor lectured them and threatened them, the ruling generals of GVN defied him, and allied themselves with the street rioters. After several changes of government in Vietnam, the U.S. could set no higher goal than GVN stability. During this period, the USG was already starting to think about doing the job ourselves if our Vietnamese ally did not perform.

. . . the generals proved to be less than perfectly united. They found they had to bow to the power of student and Buddhist street mobs, and they lacked the will and the ability to compel the civil government to perform. Yet, the U.S. saw no alternative but to back them—to put up with Vietnamese hypersensitivity, their easy compliance combined with nonperformance, and their occasional defiance. Moreover, MACV was even less ready to pressure the generals than was the Embassy and the Embassy less willing than was Washington.[27]

Throughout 1964 various Washington civilian officials raised ways of pushing the GVN harder, such as seeking a greater U.S. role in GVN machinery and tying U.S. aid to GVN commitments. But the U.S. Mission in Saigon generally adopted a go-slow response.[28] Junta chief General Duong Van Minh himself proposed a "brain trust" of high level U.S. advisers, but this was stalled when Khanh ousted Minh.[29] When McNamara urged manpower mobilization, Khanh signed a decree, but it was never implemented.[30] In May 1964 Deputy Assistant Secretary of State William Sullivan urged integrating Americans into the GVN civil and military structure at all levels instead of having them operate as advisors, but this was soon watered down.[31] At the June 1964 Honolulu Conference Lodge and Westmoreland opposed "a more formal joint USG/GVN organization at the top" or "'encadrement' which would move U.S. personnel directly into decisionmaking roles."[32] In general, what the Mission did propose in 1964 met with GVN agreement in principle but little if any response in practice.

Though increasingly frustrated by chaos in the GVN, the Americans feared that pressure tactics might only backfire and hasten its collapse. Their concern was heightened by reports of infiltration from the North. The tone of policy assessments in 1964–1965 is one of growing fear that a feeble GVN and ARVN were increasingly unable to defend themselves and that the U.S. would have to find some other means of checking Hanoi.[33] The JCS solution was to recommend "strong military actions."[34] But once more, at Ambassador Taylor's urging, the U.S. (as in 1961) sought to use any direct U.S. actions as bargaining leverage for GVN reforms.[35] Taylor was warmly supported by President Johnson, who "made it clear that he considered that pulling the South Vietnamese together was basic to anything else the United States might do." The President asked Taylor whether we could not tell them "we just can't go on," unless they did pull together.[36] Taylor was instructed to impress on the GVN that U.S. actions against North Vietnam could not be taken until certain GVN steps to increase its effectiveness occurred. Taylor carefully explained this to new civilian Premier Tran Van Huong in December 1964, requesting "nine specific GVN actions." The *Pentagon Papers* comment that "this was the last time the USG tried to set GVN performance preconditions for U.S. force use and deployments. Its effect, if any, was the opposite of that intended."[37]

The exercise was short-circuited by a military move to take power back from Huong's civilian cabinet, thus directly flouting the U.S. position that the GVN should preserve unity. When Taylor sternly admonished Khanh and his generals, he was publicly repudiated by Khanh and almost declared *persona non grata*. The U.S. suspended joint talks and planning, which apparently made the generals back down.[38] But in January 1965 the generals did oust Huong, and the U.S., fearing collapse or neutralism in Saigon, let it happen.[39] Thus on yet another occasion, U.S. "insistence on an effective GVN along lines specified by the United States had been eroded."[40]

Duncanson, assessing U.S. failure to move the GVN during the decade before we intervened directly, includes as reasons the lack of a specific intergovernmental agreement tying U.S. aid to GVN performance, U.S. misperception of the reforms needed as political rather than administrative, and the lack of administrative knowhow on the part of U.S. advisers. But to him "the crux of the failure" was

> . . . want of coordination and want of direction in the application of aid and advice. . . . What the Vietnamese Government was most in need of after independence was minds able to grasp its structure and machinery as a working whole and to see the separate functions of its parts in relation to each other, not in laboratory isolation. Diem and Nhu were not of that calibre; the U.S. felt no duty to seek a way of making good the deficiency—felt rather a duty not to interfere, but to

treat "defense of freedom" as a problem separate from that of governing Vietnam.[41]

He concludes that ". . . aid and advice without any formal agreement to ensure consistent policy, coordination, and guidance, which ill-wishers might have condemned as 'colonialism,' tended to harden the defects of the Diem regime rather than to correct them, and to reinforce its defeats."[42]

In lieu of further pressures on a feeble, unresponsive, and now coup-ridden GVN, the U.S. felt compelled by the deteriorating situation to step in and take over the war. The first ROLLING THUNDER air strike against North Vietnam ushered in the new period of direct U.S. intervention. When the U.S. intervened, the nature of its concern over GVN effectiveness changed too:

> As the U.S. role increased and then predominated, the need for GVN effectiveness in the now and short run received less attention. The U.S. would take care of the war now—defeat the enemy main forces and destroy Hanoi's will to persist—then the GVN could and would reform and resuscitate itself.
>
> This view—a massive U.S. effort in the short run leading to and enabling a GVN effort in the long-run—set the tone and content of U.S.-GVN relations. In policy terms, it meant caution in the use of U.S. leverage. There seemed to be no compelling requirement to be tough with Saigon; it would only prematurely rock the boat. To press for efficiency would be likely, it was reasoned, to generate instability. Our objective became simple: if we could not expect more GVN efficiency, we could at least get a more stable and legitimate GVN.[43]

In this limited sense, U.S. policy toward the GVN may be said to have worked. There was a return to at least relative political stability after June 1965 under the Thieu/Ky regime, marred only by the abortive Buddhist troubles in I Corps in the spring of 1966. The U.S. was successful in promoting the 1966 election of a constituent assembly. It drafted a new constitution, which led in turn to the formal election of Thieu/Ky and a new National Assembly in September 1967. Also reasonably successful were the U.S.-sponsored economic stabilization measures (especially the June 1966 devaluation) rendered essential by the inflationary impact of a burgeoning U.S. military presence. Through its control of aid allocations, and by requiring joint planning and approval of GVN economic programs before it would provide indispensable aid and advisory support, the U.S. exerted considerable influence over their design. It was even possible in 1967 to get a new GVN pacification program belatedly under way (see Chapter 7).

Yet even in 1965–1967 many of the reformist measures that the U.S. got the GVN to undertake proved more promise than performance. Nor did the U.S. during this period ever use the full weight of the leverage provided by its massive aid to impel the GVN to better performance. Instead, the U.S. took over the main burden of prosecuting the war, relegating the Republic of Vietnam Armed Forces to a secondary role and devoting comparatively less policy emphasis to GVN or RVNAF improvement than during 1954–1964 (although the actual resources that went into this were greater than before).

We also, in our frustration, tended to push the GVN to one side. Perhaps typical was the thought expressed in Assistant Secretary NcNaughton's July 1965 memorandum to a special JCS study group tasked to study what was needed to win in Vietnam: "Is it necessary for us to make some assumption with respect to the nature of the Saigon government? . . . My own thought is that almost anything within the realm of likelihood can happen in the Saigon government, short of the formation of a government which goes neutral or asks us out, without appreciably affecting the conduct of the war."[44]

On the other hand, most experienced observers on the scene noted a marked improvement in overall GVN administrative performance beginning with Tet 1968. In part this was attributable to increased U.S. advisory influence and occasionally pressure. In part it was simply that the earlier efforts of 1965–1967 began to bear more fruit over time. But even greater influences on GVN behavior were the twin shocks of Hanoi's Tet and post-Tet offensives and the resultant clear beginning of U.S. deescalation.

Thus in a way Tet 1968 marked a watershed for the GVN as well as for the U.S. effort in Vietnam. GVN realization that a far greater effort on its part would be required to survive finally led to actual national manpower mobilization, extensive training programs for local officials, a major acceleration of pacification efforts, several economic reforms, and the like. After years of futile U.S. urging, the GVN in 1970 passed a radical land reform law, which was vigorously carried out. Though grave weaknesses still existed, most professional observers agreed that GVN leadership, performance, and administrative capabilities greatly improved from the 1963–1965 nadir. The U.S. also quietly laid down the law that further coups by generals were not to be tolerated. On the other hand, a major U.S. failure occurred when the 1971 national election campaign, expected to further legitimize the GVN as a government elected by a popular majority, ended up instead as a one-man referendum leading to an almost certainly inflated popular vote for Thieu.

As U.S. forces gradually withdrew, beginning in mid-1969, the so-called "Vietnamization" program also resulted in some distinct improvements in RVNAF capabilities. Despite accelerating U.S. withdrawal, the GVN managed during 1969–1971 to increase substantially its hold over the countryside and to keep the VC/NVA in check. Of course, this was also owing largely to Hanoi's reversion to protracted war tactics and the diversion of fighting to Cambodia and Laos, which relieved the pressure on South Vietnam. However, in 1972 the GVN, with U.S. help, managed to repulse the first major multi-front offensive which Hanoi was able to launch after the long hiatus caused by its staggering losses in the 1968 Tet offensives.

Of course, Saigon then failed the ultimate test of whether it could stand on its own feet after U.S. disengagement. The negotiated truce with Hanoi which Washington practically forced down Saigon's throat left Saigon laboring under severe handicaps. The "cease-fire in place" actually let Hanoi keep large forces in the south; indeed the intensity of combat was higher in 1973–1974 than during 1970–1971.[45] Nor did the action of the U.S. Congress in sharply cutting back promised American military assistance help Saigon's prospects. The Nixon Administration's promises of renewed U.S. air attacks if Hanoi violated the cease fire were emptied of content by Congressional opposition. These measures helped sap morale in South Vietnam. Thus we certainly contributed to the GVN's demise. But in the last analysis, it was Saigon's own continued weakness, plus some disastrous military mistakes by Thieu and his generals, which led to the precipitous 1975 collapse.[46]

Could the U.S. have done better at helping build a South Vietnam with better prospects for survival? We certainly invested enormous resources in the effort, but our influence was rarely commensurate with our investment. Many Americans were aware of the frequent corruption at all levels largely encouraged by the ridiculously low civil and military pay scales (which the author fruitlessly attempted to have raised in 1967–1968). But we were rarely able to do much about what had become a way of life. Worse yet was the pervasive incompetence of many GVN officials and officers at all levels, who owed their jobs all too frequently to favoritism, nepotism, and payoffs to their superiors. Duncanson, who was on the scene much of that time, finds that our mistake—and that of the GVN—lay in seeking solutions primarily in military and political rather than administrative terms:

the misjudgement of the U.S. was to decide that Diem's greatest needs were money and a big army, when what was really required was an efficient civil service; the failure of the *agroville* experiment was due in the main to administrative incompetence, only rectified to a very limited extent in the strategic hamlets; the colossal dishonesty rampant since Diem's death and the success of Vietcong symbiotic insurgency are a product of administrative inefficiency. Diem believed the problem could not be solved—he understood it imperfectly himself—and so, like the metaphorical grass of China, he bent before the east wind and tried to govern by manipulating factionalism and imitating the Communists, which compounded the disaster.[47]

THE ISSUE OF LEVERAGE

Aside from whether our advice was sound did we press it hard enough on the GVN, using fully the leverage which our massive backing provided? The *Pentagon Papers* are quite critical of U.S. reluctance to compel better GVN performance. They show how this issue was recurrently debated between Washington and Saigon from 1955 on.[48]

In fact the U.S. occasionally did try to employ various forms of leverage on the GVN, perhaps more often than generally realized, though with rather spotty results. We have already noted a number of instances in which the U.S. made a high level effort to tie its aid to GVN reforms of one kind or another—in 1961, late 1963, and late 1964. Washington also exercised considerable indirect leverage through its various aid programs, largely by funding those it favored and not funding those it opposed or by insisting on various changes before funding or material were provided. This bargaining process gave us considerable influence. It must also be granted that top U.S. leaders in the field on occasion discreetly pressured the GVN at various levels for removal of poor officers and officials or other measures, especially after 1966. The author can attest to instances in which both Bunker and Westmoreland used this technique. The author himself used it frequently in 1966–1968.

The planning exercise for phased withdrawal of U.S. forces from Vietnam which took place from July 1962 to March 1964 is also seen in the *Pentagon Papers* as in part an effort "to increase the pressure on the GVN to make the necessary reforms and to make RVNAF fight harder by making the extent and future of U.S. support a little more tenuous."[49] But it seems to have had no significant effects along these lines, being overtaken by the deterioration of the situation in late 1963 and 1964.[50]

At one point AID required a "joint sign-off" by its province advisers as well as GVN officials for the release of aid. This veto was agreed on in late 1963 and further extended in 1964.[51] It was highly favored by field advisers, but abandoned by the new USAID Mission director in June 1965. His decision was soon regretted, and the issue was reopened with the GVN, only to be dropped "when the State Department objected to the idea, insisting that it would undermine our efforts to make the Vietnamese more independent and effective."[52]

A modest USAID province advisers fund to increase U.S. leverage was set up in mid-1964.[53] In December 1964 MACV gave its advisers a similar fund, but dropped it after four months because Rural Development Minister Thang felt that it permitted bypassing his ministry.[54] However, such province and district pacification funds were revived on a far larger scale in 1967–1968, using counterpart piasters supplied by the GVN. Field advisers then made extensive use of these funds to help fund important local projects or programs for which inadequate GVN funds were available.

In several cases AID did cut off rural program funds to provinces as a means of pressure. In September 1965 it withdrew its people and support from Binh Tuy province on the grounds that the province chief was misusing AID funds. He was soon removed, but the incident received press attention, and Ambassador Lodge told USAID not to do it again. In June 1966 USAID briefly cut off shipments to Kontum Province to force proper accounting for AID supplies. Then in August 1967 the CORDS organization (see Chapter 7) successfully cut off aid to Bien Hoa province for eleven weeks for similar reasons. In contrast "MACV scrupulously avoided withholding MAP support from military units, regardless of circumstances."[55] Withdrawing such support was recommended as a last resort by the staff of the Military Assistance Command Vietnam (MACV) in April 1966, but rejected by General Westmoreland.[56]

Significantly, those concerned with pacification analyzed the leverage problem more systematically than any others, and sought to use leverage most consistently. The 1966 PROVN and "Roles and Missions" studies, CORDS' Project TAKEOFF of May 1967, and the 1968 Warner-Heymann study, all favoring greater use of leverage, were all pacification-oriented.[57] In late 1967 CORDS designed a program to force removal of the incompetent Go Cong province chief. It worked. A similar program was used in Kien Giang province. Then in early 1968 CORDS approved a standard procedure for use of leverage in such cases. CORDS systematically collected dossiers on incompetent or venal province and district chiefs and pressed the

GVN consistently for their removal. It didn't always work, but CORDS' batting average during 1967–1972 was respectable. Withdrawing support from numerous Police Field Force companies being misused or maldeployed also forced corrective action. The Hamlet Evaluation System and other periodic "report cards" prepared by CORDS advisors turned out to be valuable levers to get better GVN performance. Such measures, based on CORDS rapport with high GVN officials and the latter's confidence in CORDS reporting, had a marked effect on GVN pacification operations.

But even these examples hardly add up to consistent U.S. use of leverage as a policy tool over many years. It was certainly more talked about than practiced. The issue was frequently raised, with Washington usually pressing for greater use of leverage and the U.S. Mission (which had to do the dirty work) usually shying away from it.[58] McNamara in particular became an advocate of leverage-oriented mechanisms by 1965, "but [his] views did not prevail."[59]

In assessing the issue of leverage, one must bear in mind the dilemmas which the U.S. faced. Perhaps the most acute was the perennial question of stability vs. potentially destabilizing change. The more we Americans became entangled in Vietnam, the more concerned we were over the risks to our growing investment if the regime we were supporting should collapse. Constantly facing top U.S. policymakers was the dilemma of whether, if we pushed too hard, we would end up collapsing the very structure we were trying to shore up. The GVN was so weak, and the available alternative leadership so unprepossessing, that the alternative to Diem or Khanh or Quat was frequently seen as chaos. The destabilizing consequences when we did acquiesce in Diem's ouster made us doubly cautious, while a stable political environment became doubly important as our troop commitment grew.

After massive U.S. intervention staved off GVN defeat, these arguments against the use of leverage became less compelling. On the other hand, *the very massiveness of our intervention actually reduced our leverage.* So long as we were willing to use U.S. resources and manpower as a substitute for Vietnamese, their incentive for doing more was compromised. As Ambassador Taylor presciently foresaw when questioning the initial dispatch of U.S. Marines to Danang in February 1965, "once it becomes evident that we are willing to assume such new responsibilities, one may be sure that GVN will seek to unload other ground force tasks upon us."[60] Chester Cooper points out how Washington's ultimate sanction was U.S. withdrawal, yet "as the size of our forces and therefore the extent of our commitment increased, this sanction became less and less credible. In short, our leverage declined as our involvement deepened."[61] This hypothesis is also validated by the way that the start of U.S. disengagement, when President Johnson's 1968 suspension of bombing north of the 19th Parallel, right on top of the Tet shock, finally forced the GVN to mobilize fully and take many other steps. Further gradual U.S. disengagement after 1968 had similar impact in forcing the GVN to do more for itself.

Another constraint on use of leverage was that, no matter how deeply it became committed, the U.S. almost always saw itself as in an advisory and supporting role vis-à-vis a sovereign GVN. All U.S. agencies—civil and military—operated for the most part as if they were dealing not only with a sovereign but with an effective government, one that could carry out what it agreed should be done. We were deeply conscious of the dilemma created by our policy of shoring up a free government; to take over from the GVN—even in minor ways—would be inconsistent with the very purpose of our support. However generously we supported it, we always saw it as up to the GVN to choose. Even so, the GVN was still perceived as our puppet, which gave us the worst of both worlds.

We were also acutely sensitive to the nationalistic and often xenophobic tendencies of the GVN. Diem was particularly insistent that neither Vietnamese sovereignty nor his personal authority be compromised, lest any diminution of his power play into the hands of his domestic opponents—non-Communist as well as Communist. This lay behind his 1961 rejection of "the limited partnership" proposed by the U.S.[62] As will be seen in Chapter 6, concern over Vietnamese sensitivities also was a major reason why the U.S. did not propose a combined military command.

General Taylor reflects the dominant view of those senior officers operationally involved:

In retrospect I have often asked myself whether, during this period, my colleagues and I were too reluctant to intervene in Vietnamese internal affairs in order to stabilize the political situation. Personally, I avoided excessive interventionist zeal for two reasons. From my Korean experience I knew how sensitive Asian allies were to the charge of being American puppets, and how favorably they responded to treatment as respected coequals. Next, I was thoroughly aware of the limits of our knowledge of the true character of most of the Vietnamese with whom we worked. We were particularly ignorant of the complex relationships which linked individuals and groups within the heterogeneous society. However, such considerations did not deter us from expressing candid views to appropriate Vietnamese officials regarding the performance of duty of military and civilian officers within our range of observation. I had certainly done so in the case of the generals who overthrew the High National Council. After all, the parties to an alliance have pooled their resources in a common cause and have yielded to each other some of their own independence of action. Each has a right and a duty to urge actions on the other conducive to the success of the partnership. So I felt completely justified in pressing for such things as greater use of American advisers, unimpeded access to Vietnamese governmental data, and joint U.S./Vietnamese supervision of activities in the provinces.[63]

Such real life dilemmas, which persisted long after the U.S. became an active partner in the war, greatly inhibited the use of leverage on the GVN. It is also essential to remember how little there *was* to lever, especially before 1966 or so. GVN administration frequently proved too feeble to carry out effectively many of the measures we were pressing on it, even when it agreed to them. Moreover, the myth that Diem and Nhu, Ky, Thieu, and their colleagues were mere U.S. puppets eager to do our bidding has a hollow ring to anyone who had to deal with them face to face.

But a form of institutional constraint also seems to have been at work. The notable reluctance of U.S. bureaucracies—civil and military—to press their views on the bureaucracies of U.S. aid recipients is almost a fixed feature of U.S. relations with other countries. However much policy may call for helping those who help themselves or tying aid to performance, such policies tend to become eroded in execution by the U.S. agencies concerned. This certainly occurred frequently in Vietnam. Another serious constraint was the lack of any combined GVN/U.S. machinery through which the U.S. could exercise consistent influence (see Chapter 6).

Debate over how hard the U.S. should have pressed its Vietnamese ally will long continue. But the long record of our failures to move the GVN in directions which in retrospect would clearly have been desirable suggests that we would have had little to lose and much to gain by using more vigorously the power over the GVN that our contributions gave us. We became their prisoners rather than they ours—the classic trap into which great powers have so often fallen in their relationships with weak allies. The GVN used its weakness as leverage on us far more effectively than we used our strength to lever it.

Perhaps most grievous was our failure to insist on replacement at all levels of officials and commanders whom we knew to be incompetent. We stuck too long with Saigon regimes we realized were incapable, seeing little alternative to backing them. But in the event alternatives did emerge. Looking back, for example, wouldn't it have been better to allow Diem to fall in 1960, when the situation had not yet deteriorated so badly as it had by 1963?

Nor did the U.S. ever exert conscious, systematic leverage via the U.S. advisory network on the crucial issue of securing better GVN and RVNAF middle-level leadership. Though U.S. advisers were generally able to identify weak or incapable leaders, little consistent effort was made—except by CORDS in 1967–1972—to press for weeding out the incompetent or corrupt and promoting the competent. The U.S. advisory effort "never deviated . . . from the belief that the conscious and continuing use of leverage at many levels would undercut Vietnamese sovereignty and stultify the development of Vietnamese leadership."[64] On the latter count, however, it had more the opposite result. Similar reasoning led to the repeated rejection of leverage-oriented proposals for integrating U.S. and GVN forces or for various forms of joint command (see Chapter 6).

We also gave the GVN and RVNAF massive aid without tying it sufficiently to internal reforms and required performance standards to optimize its effective use. Using the leverage provided by our aid was usually rejected as too risky, even though when we did use it it usually proved its value. Instead by 1965 we intervened and did things largely for the Vietnamese, spending U.S. money and U.S. lives to make up for their deficiencies. While our record since 1966 looks rather better than that before, and though the GVN came to look quite different from its predecessors, our will and ability to influence it optimally remained to the end a question mark.

It could be argued—as indeed it was at various times—that full use of all available instruments of influence would have been tantamount to a U.S. "takeover" of the GVN, with all the unfortunate colonialist overtones and difficulties of subsequent disengagement that this implied. But such potential costs seem modest in retrospect compared to those which the U.S. actually did incur when impending GVN collapse led instead to our taking over the lion's share of the shooting war. To the extent that U.S. efforts to compel better South Vietnamese performance produced a more capable and self-reliant GVN and RVNAF, the need for such massive U.S. intervention would presumably have been correspondingly reduced. The at least partial success of the Nixon Administration's "Vietnamization" program during 1969–1973 is suggestive along these lines, though its feasibility rested largely on the extent to which prior U.S. intervention had stabilized the situation and bought time for the GVN and RVNAF to rebuild. Thus, in the event, the real-life alternative to greater U.S. efforts to move the GVN turned out to be an even greater U.S. "takeover" of the war than might otherwise have occurred.

NOTES

1. Admiral U.S.G. Sharp and General W.C. Westmoreland, *Report on the War in Vietnam* (as of 30 June 1968), Section II: Report on Operations in South Vietnam January 1964–June 1968, U. S. Government Printing Office, Washington, DC, 1969, p. 71.

2. Ibid., p. 71.

3. *United States—Vietnam Relations, 1945–1967: Study Proposal by the Department of Defense*, 12 volumes, U.S. Government Printing Office, Washington D.C., 1971 (Hereafter referred to as the *Pentagon Papers*), IV.C.7(a), p. 8.

4. Barbara Tuchman, *Stilwell and the American Experience in China, 1911–45*, The Macmillan Company, New York, 1970.

5. Ibid., pp. 455–457, and p. 366.

6. Ibid., p. 460.

7. Ibid., p. 531.

8. Allan E. Goodman, "The Dynamics of The United States–South Vietnamese Alliance: What Went Wrong" in *Vietnam As History*, p. 89.

9. Dennis Duncanson, *Government and Revolution in Vietnam*, Oxford University Press, New York and London, 1968, p. 376.

10. Perhaps the best accounts of Diem's failures are in Duncanson, *Government and Revolution*, Robert Shaplen, *The Lost Revolution*, Harper & Row, New York, 1955, and Bernard Fall, *The Two Viet-Nams*, Frederick A. Praeger, Inc., New York, (2nd rev. ed.), 1967.

11. *Pentagon Papers*, IV.A.4, p. 11. Opinions differ sharply on the Diem regime however. William Colby, who worked with Diem and Nhu for years, considers the "American-sponsored" overthrow of Diem "the worst mistake of the Vietnam War." *Honorable Men: My Life in the CIA*, Simon and Schuster, New York, 1978, p. 203.

12. Duncanson, *Government and Revolution*, pp. 252–262, and Chapters 6 and 7.

13. Ibid., p. 21.

14. Colby, *Honorable Men*, p. 287.

15. *Pentagon Papers*, IV.A.5, Tab. 4, pp. 57, 62–65.

16. Ibid., IV.B.1, p. 1; see also pp. 13–18.

17. Ibid., pp. i and iii.

18. Ibid., IV.B.1, p. v.

19. Ibid., pp. 102–103; see also pp. 115–116.

20. Ibid., p. 131, repeated in NSAM 111 of 11/22/61 (ibid., p. 133).

21. Ibid., pp. 139–146 (quotation is from pp. 143–144).

22. Ibid., pp. 146–147.

23. Ibid., p. 135.

24. Ibid., IV.B.5, pp. v, viii, 30–36 (quotation from p. 36).

25. Ibid., IV.B.4, p. 19.

26. Ibid., IV.B.5, pp. v and vi.

27. Ibid., IV.C.9(a), p. i.

28. Ibid., pp. 1–9, 17.

29. Ibid., pp. 7, 17–18.

30. Ibid., pp. 12 and 17.

31. Ibid., pp. 21–23.

32. Ibid., pp. 25–26.

33. See Ambassador Taylor's November 27, 1964, appreciation of GVN weakness which caused U.S. efforts to assist SVN to have little impact and created "a losing game in SVN" (*Pentagon Papers*, VI.C.2(c), pp. 42–44).

34. For example, JCS proposals of 10/27/64 cited in *Pentagon Papers*, IV.C.2(c), pp. 2–3; see also pp. 32–35.

35. Taylor's proposals, ibid., pp. 45–47.

36. Ibid., pp. 54–55.

37. Ibid., p. 68 and IV.C.9(a), p. 54.

38. Ibid., IV.C.2(c), pp. 67–71.

39. Ibid., pp. 71–72 and 75.

40. Ibid., p. 80.

41. Duncanson, *Government and Revolution*, p. 281, pp. 276–280.

42. Ibid., p. 282.

43. *Pentagon Papers*, IV.C.9(b), p. i.

44. Ibid., IV.C.6(a), p. 3.

45. Thomas C. Thayer, *War Without Fronts*, Westview Press, Boulder, CO, forthcoming, Ch. 2, p. 35.

46. See S.T. Hosmer et al., *The Fall of South Vietnam*, Crane Russak, New York, 1980, pp. 157–188.

47. Duncanson, *Government and Revolution*, p. 377.

48. See especially, *Pentagon Papers*, IV.B.3, pp. 63–66, 92–99,; IV.C.9(a), pp. 111-v and 17–25; and IV.C.9(b), pp. ii-iv, 23–26, 56–58.

49. Ibid., IV.B.4, pp. 111 and 23–24.

50. Ibid., IV.B.4, discusses the abortive phased-withdrawal exercise.

51. Ibid., IV.C.9(a), pp. 4 and 29.

52. Ibid., IV.C.9(b), p. 7. See also quotation from IV.B.3, p. 64.

53. Ibid., IV.C.9(a), p. 29.

54. Ibid., IV.C.9(b), pp. iii and 7.

55. Ibid., IV.B.3, p. 64; IV.C.9(c), pp. 111 [quote], 23, and 60.

56. Ibid., IV.C.9(b), pp. 26–27.

57. Ibid., IV.B.3, pp. 94–99.

58. Ibid., p. 92; IV.C.9(b), p. iii.

59. Ibid., IV. B. 3, pp. 65–66; quotation on p. 94.

60. Ibid., IV.C.4, p. 2.

61. Cf. Chester L. Cooper, *Lost Crusade*, Dodd, Mead & Company, New York, 1970, p. 426.

62. *Pentagon Papers*, IV.B.2, pp. 19–20.

63. Maxwell D. Taylor, *Swords and Plowshares*, W.W. Norton & Company, Inc., New York, 1972, pp. 355–356.

64. *Pentagon Papers*, IV.B.3, p. ix.

4
INSTITUTIONAL CONSTRAINTS ON U.S. PERFORMANCE

In any assessment of why the U.S. found it so difficult to cope with the special circumstances of Vietnam, the role of institutional constraints looms large. Why we fought the war the way we did is largely explicable in these terms. This is nowhere more evident than in our approach to its military aspects, both before and after 1965.

The great weight of the U.S. and GVN military in the post-1954 Vietnam picture in itself tended to dictate a predominantly military response. The institutional background of U.S. and GVN military leaders helped shape the nature of that response. "Mirror-imaging" was a natural concomitant of U.S. military aid. We organized, equipped, and trained the RVNAF to fight American style, the only way we knew how. All too little attention was paid to the French experience in the First Indochina War, or the successful British experience in Malaya. Even our own experience in "pacifying" the Philippines after 1898 seemed to have disappeared from the Army's institutional memory.

Then, when the U.S. in effect took over the war, we further "Americanized" it—on an even grander scale—by playing out our military repertoire. Instead of adapting our response to the enemy's way of fighting, we fought him our way—at horrendous expense—because we lacked the institutional incentive and much existing capability to do otherwise. The enormously costly "search and destroy" or attrition strategy was also an outgrowth of these factors. It was a natural response of American commanders deploying forces hugely superior in mobility and firepower against an elusive enemy who could not be brought to decisive battle in classic military style.

OVERMILITARIZATION OF THE WAR

What has been termed the "overmilitarization" of the war can be traced partly to such institutional factors as the dominant role of the

41

military in the U.S. aid and advisory structure and, over time, in the GVN. Military men are naturally going to give primary emphasis to the military aspect of any conflict. "It is in the nature of the military bureaucracy as of any bureaucracy that it tends to offer solutions to problems in its own terms. . . ."[1] Or as Arthur Schlesinger put it, "The Joint Chiefs of Staff, of course, by definition argue for military solutions . . . that is their business, and no one should be surprised that generals behave like generals."[2]

When, moreover, the military controlled the vast bulk of the resources going into the war effort, it is hardly surprising that military considerations became predominant. The simple fact that most of the war effort was financed by relatively unfungible U.S. defense appropriations reinforced this predominance, though Secretary McNamara and the author were ingenious in finding ways in which DOD funds could do double duty by also supporting pacification and anti-inflation measures. Moreover, the military field was about the only major area where the U.S. thought it could get results commensurate with its investment, because we were providing so much that Diem and his generals wanted. Thus military aid proved the line of least resistance, which contributed to the overmilitarization of the GVN/U.S. counterinsurgency response.

This overmilitarization was not a late bloomer, but dated almost from the outset of U.S. involvement. From 1950 on, the bulk of our aid to the French and then the GVN was military assistance, administered first by a Military Aid Advisory Group (MAAG) and later MACV. Vietnam became one of our largest military aid clients well before 1961. "In the years 1955 though 1960, more than $2 billion in aid flowed into Vietnam, and more than 80 percent of that assistance went toward providing security for the Government of Vietnam."[3] That the MAAG in Vietnam was the only one commanded by a lieutenant general is also significant.

The first U.S.-approved force ceiling for ARVN in November 1954 was only 88,000. But General Lawton Collins recommended that even this force be given a divisional structure, because our greatest concern was a North Vietnamese army attack across the Demilitarized Zone, as had occurred in Korea in 1950. Soon MAAG recommended a 150,000-man force structure, to be reorganized "according to American concepts" into four field divisions, six light divisions, and thirteen territorial regiments.[4] In 1959 ARVN was again reorganized into seven standard divisions under three corps headquarters and a GHQ.[5] Though there also was much high policy discussion of the need to strengthen GVN paramilitary and civil programs (see Chapter 8), it is important to look at the figures rather than the phrases.

Military aid far exceeded economic assistance during 1960–1964 as well, and much of the latter was designed primarily to support the GVN military budget. By 1960 growing insurgency in the rural areas had led to renewed U.S. focus on counter efforts, but in the 1961 Kennedy commitments and after these were even further militarized. One of the new President's first actions was to authorize aid for a 20,000-man increase in ARVN, from 150,000 to 170,000. Then in August 1961, after Diem had requested a further increase to 270,000, the U.S. accepted 200,000—including two more divisions.[6] In March 1964 the U.S. approved a further 50,000-man increase, mostly paramilitary.[7] Yet another modest increase of 20,000—including a tenth ARVN division—was approved in spring 1965. But actual RVNAF strength keep running so far below authorized strength that in June 1965 General Westmoreland finally had to impose a moratorium on further ARVN buildup, because combat losses and desertions made it difficult even to maintain the strength of existing units.[8] At this time the regular forces stood at about 262,000; the Regional Forces (formerly Civil Guard) at 108,000; and the Popular Forces (formerly Self Defense Corps) at 149,000 (the latter partly on paper), for a total of 519,000.[9]

Then, as the GVN and ARVN buckled, we "Americanized" the war by intervening with massive U.S. forces, and repeating much of the same conventional wisdom on a grander scale. By mid-1967 the U.S. had almost half a million troops in-country, while RVNAF as a whole had risen only to slightly over 600,000. True, these developments were responsive to a situation which had so deteriorated that U.S. military intervention seemed the only viable alternative to defeat. Our intervention also was partly precipitated by Hanoi's infiltration of regular units into South Vietnam and by the VC/NVA shift to Mao's "third phase" of overt, semiconventional warfare. In the ensuing years Hanoi and Washington proceeded to escalate and counterescalate their conventional force buildups, both focusing increasingly on the so called "main force" war. By 1969, U.S. troop strength in South Vietnam had risen to a peak of almost 550,000 plus many thousands more offshore or in adjacent areas, while RVNAF strength had reached over a million men.

The overwhelmingly military nature of our Vietnam response comes out even more clearly in comparisons of total manpower and financial allocations. The program budgets prepared by the systems analysts in the Office in the Secretary of Defense (OSD/SA) show that most of the GVN budget went for conventional military purposes, as did the vast bulk of U.S. war costs. For example, in FY 1968 the U.S. spent almost $14 billion for bombing and offensive operations, but only $850 million for pacification and socioeconomic programs.[10]

As military considerations became ever more predominant, the GVN and U.S. military largely took over the reins of power in Vietnam. After Diem's death, the ARVN generals ran the GVN and were able to give themselves full rein.[11] On the U.S. side, MACV overshadowed the civilian agencies, just as the military effort dwarfed the civil effort. Civilian officials in Saigon played little role in military decisionmaking, despite recognition that political and military factors were wholly intertwined in this type of conflict. One observer notes:

> Where the military bureaucracy is more likely to impose limits on the civilian desire for flexibility is in the conduct of military operations. The analytical review of military development, procurement, and organizational policies and practices simply has not been extended to military operations. Perhaps in the nature of things it cannot be extended. But in its absence the political authorities find it more difficult, as perhaps they should, to assert control over specific military operations— the choice, for example, between search-and-destroy and clear-and-hold—in order to avoid deepening political commitments.[12]

MIRROR-IMAGING AND CONVENTIONAL RESPONSE, 1954–1964

Aside from overmilitarization of the U.S./GVN response, the institutional background of the GVN and U.S. military shaped the very nature of that response. During the decade before direct U.S. intervention, all too little military attention had been paid to the special circumstances of Vietnam. Overinfluenced by the Korean War (and largely neglecting both French experience in Indochina and British experience in Malaya), the U.S. put the bulk of its military aid and advice into building a conventional ARVN ill-suited to the challenges it faced.[13] The French trained ARVN officers, equally conventional-minded, were eager to go the same route.

That this occurred almost in spite of high-level policy directives to the contrary is a tribute to the vigor of the institutional pressures involved. The initial policy direction given the MAAG when the U.S. took over the military aid role from the French clearly emphasized *internal security* as the principal mission.[14] But under a series of MAAG chiefs (O'Daniel, Williams, McGarr) of conventional bent and experience MAAG concentrated instead on preparing ARVN for a conventional delaying action against what it regarded as the most serious threat: a Korea-style NVA attack across the DMZ.[15] Though high U.S. policy directives kept reemphasizing the internal security mission, it almost inevitably took a back seat after 1955.

Analyzing what little was accomplished during 1954–1959, the *Pentagon Papers* eloquently conclude:

> U.S. efforts . . . failed to produce an effective Vietnamese counterinsurgent force due to contemporary perceptions of and reactions to the threat, to exaggerated estimates of the value and relevance of American military standards in responding to that threat, to lack of effective bargaining techniques vis-a-vis the Government of Vietnam, and to fragmentation and other inadequacies in the American system of determining and administering the overall program of assistance to Vietnam.
>
> . . . A strong desire to correct French mistakes generated considerable bureaucratic momentum; preoccupation with the perceived inadequacies of French practices led to underestimation of the problems the French had to overcome . . . in developing an effective Vietnamese army, and to overcorrection of French mistakes by the creation of a conventional military force. That Vietnamese army came to be organized in divisions— as the U.S. had so often and so unsuccessfully urged the French to do.
>
> . . . although it was consistently estimated that the DRV had the capability to overrun South Vietnam, it was just as consistently estimated that the DRV neither needed nor intended to do so. Nonetheless, U.S. doctrine regarding estimates of capability as opposed to estimates of intention with its characteristic emphasis on Order of Battle data (so small a part of the real intelligence problem in counterinsurgency) led to fixation upon the more massive, but less likely, threat of overt invasion.
>
> . . . Given the state of U.S. strategic thinking in the 1950's, the nature of SEATO, the withdrawal of the FEC, the pressures exerted by Diem, and the background of the U.S. MAAG, rooted in the recent Korean experience, it was virtually certain to lead to a conventional military establishment designed to counter a conventional threat. It did. In fact, given the strength of these influences and the lack of U.S. familiarity with effective counterinsurgent techniques, it is questionable whether assignment of a single mission related exclusively to internal security would have made any difference in the type of military establishment that resulted.[16]

Nor were high U.S. officers unaware of "allegations that the United States is overtraining the Vietnamese Army for a Korea-type war with little or nothing being done to meet the terrorist problem in Vietnam," as is evident from a fascinating memorandum written by General Lyman Lemnitzer (then Chairman of the JCS) in October 1961. Apparently concerned that the forthcoming Thompson Mission might "try to sell the Malayan concept of police control," he decried analogizing from the Malayan experience and came down heavily in favor of the U.S. military approach.[17]

Sir Robert Thompson regards "the creation of a large conventional army inside South Vietnam as the basic cause of the failure to defeat communist insurgency there."[18] In his classic *Defeating Communist Insurgency,* he describes the many political and economic as well as military costs entailed. Among other things, "The conventional organization of the army led naturally to operations of a conventional type." A "further side effect" was that conventional weapons "not suitable for anti-guerrilla operations" were nonetheless used.[19] Most observers agree that the MAP-sponsored ARVN performed poorly indeed against the insurgents in 1960–1964, though this was owing to much else besides organization, training, and equipment ill-adapted to the tasks.

These tendencies were reinforced by a bureaucratic characteristic typical of U.S. military aid programs—designing U.S.-supported allied forces more in the U.S. image than tailoring them for unique local conditions.[20]

> The result of the U.S. efforts was more a reflection of the U.S. military establishment than of the type of threat or terrain. With regard to the overall effectiveness of U.S. aid, it seems to have had, unfortunately, all the depth the term "mirror image" implies.[21]

Proposals that greater MAP resources be devoted to building up the Civil Guard, police, or other local security forces were often rejected in the 1950s on such grounds as that this was civilian agency business and not a proper function of the military aid program.[22]

Mirror-imaging extended to our advisory effort too. As General "Vinegar Joe" Stilwell had found in reflecting on American World War II experience in China, our advisers "knew how to deal only in the American way and when this failed to bring results they became confused and lost patience."[23] The *Pentagon Papers* make a similar assessment of the MAAG reaction to the Strategic Hamlet Program of 1962–1963:

The U.S. military advisors mistrusted arguments which stressed the Vietnamese struggle as essentially political rather than military. They were quite willing to concede that the struggle was multi-dimensional but they feared instinctively any line of reasoning which might appear to argue that military considerations were relatively unimportant in Vietnam. So too, they were wary of schemes which might lead ARVN to perpetuate its defensive tactical stance. Both dangers were present in the strategic hamlet program . . . Their creed, developed through years of experience and training (or vicarious experience) was to "close with and destroy the enemy." One could expect them, then, to be more than willing to turnover the job of static defense to the CDC [sic] and CG at the earliest opportunity, to keep a weather eye out for opportunities to engage major VC formations in decisive battle, and to chafe under the painfully slow evolutionary process which was implicit even in their own 1961 geographically phased plan.[24]

Yet U.S. and GVN neglect of the paramilitary forces, which continued up to 1967, seems in hindsight one of the great operational mistakes of the conflict. Diem had created a small Civil Guard (CG) in 1955, and in 1956 organized a village militia called the Self Defense Corps (SDC). The MAAG early regarded them as the primary internal security forces, and wanted them to relieve ARVN of the static security role to which it was then largely committed, so it might concentrate on external defense. But this never happened.[25] Among other things, the CG and SDC became a victim of "U.S. interagency competition." Police experts in the Michigan State University Advisory Group recommended that the Civil Guard be converted to a lightly armed, village-based rural constabulary under civilian control to combat subversion. But Diem wanted a strong, well-armed, militarized CG under the province chiefs, and MAAG bought his view. At MAAG urging, it was put under the Defense Ministry in 1960, and support and advice passed under MAAG control.[26]

In hindsight this may have been a mistake, because the MAAG as well as the ARVN staff tended to focus on the regular forces to the neglect of the territorials. True, for 1963–1964 MACV did call for a substantial increase in the CG/SDC, while regular forces were to grow only slightly.[27] But the latter continued to get the vast bulk of the resources, and the CG/SDC were not upgraded into the force that U.S. plans called for.[28] No MAP aid was allocated to them before FY 1962, and then only 3.7 percent of it, followed by 4 percent in FY 1963, 12.6 percent in FY 1964, 7.8 percent in FY 1965 and 9.8 percent in FY 1966. Indeed less than 20 percent of the total expenditures on RVNAF during FYs 1958–1965, from both U.S. and GVN resources, went to the territorial forces.[29] Similarly, until 1964 almost no U.S. advisers were assigned to province, district, or directly to RF/PF units; even by 1966 less than one-third of U.S. field advisers were so assigned.[30]

The weaknesses of conventional military thinking in counterinsurgency situations are also apparent in the early MAAG pressure during 1959–1962 for a single chain of command that would put under ARVN the territorial forces which were then under the province chiefs.[31] MAAG kept arguing for unity of effort, and finally got it in 1964, after Diem's demise. But pacification-type security forces continued to be sadly neglected in favor of the regulars. MAAG and then MACV did relatively little during 1955–1966 to upgrade and strengthen the territorials. Not until 1967, when the new pacification program led to emphasis on rapid expansion and upgrading of the RF/PF, and when these forces were put back under province control and province was taken out from under division control, did the territorials finally come into their own (See Chapter 7).

THE MILITARY PLAY OUT THEIR INSTITUTIONAL REPERTOIRES

What we did in Vietnam cannot be fully understood unless it is seen as a function of our playing out our military repertoire—doing what we were most capable and experienced at doing. Such institutional constraints as the very way our general purpose forces were trained, equipped, and structured largely dictated our response. The fact that U.S. military doctrine, tactics, equipment, and organization were designed primarily for NATO or Korean War-type contingencies—intensive conventional conflict in a relatively sophisticated military environment—made it difficult to do anything else.

The U.S. army's force structure, its choice of equipment, its logistic support, its whole style of warfare evolved after World War II with combat against sophisticated Soviet forces primarily in mind. So too did that of the U.S. Air Force. Since these ground and air forces were primarily designed for coping with such an enemy, it is unsurprising that they proved expensively ill-suited to meet the VC/NVA in Vietnam. Basically, Vietnam was a "small unit war," whereas the U.S. forces and their Vietnamese "mirror images" were designed for large scale combined arms tactics and operations.[32]

Yet was it so foolish that U.S. plans and force postures were primarily aimed at forcing a conventional pause on the NATO central front and secondarily at defeating another North Korean thrust? Since nobody contemplated so massive a U.S. commitment in Southeast Asia as eventuated, they didn't prepare for it. But even if they had, the higher priority given to NATO and Korean contingencies would have limited what special preparations could be made. "General purpose" forces do mean multipurpose, after all: forces designed to meet a variety of contingencies rather than tailored to suit one. But as it turned out, ours weren't very "general purpose" after all. Nor did the prevailing Pentagon concept that conventional forces designed to meet the worst-case contingency—high intensity nonnuclear conflict—would also be suitable for lesser contingencies prove to be as valid as expected.

On the other hand, the Kennedy/Johnson buildup of nonnuclear general purpose forces did facilitate the kind of U.S. military intervention undertaken in Vietnam. Capabilities naturally shape strategy and tactics, as well as vice versa. As a DOD official said in the Sixties, "If McNamara hadn't increased our conventional capability all along the line, we probably wouldn't have gone into Vietnam because we couldn't."[33]

That from the very outset of U.S. military involvement in Vietnam we focused first the RVNAF and then our own forces primarily upon the enemy "main force" threat is also largely attributable to institutional preferences. Armies like to fight other armies. It is what they are trained and equipped to do. The object of warfare in U.S. military doctrine is to defeat the enemy's forces as the means of imposing our will upon his. Hence MACV and the Joint General Staff (JGS) tended to focus all the more on the "big unit" war to the neglect of other facets of the conflict. We have seen how as early as 1955 MAAG was helping design ARVN chiefly against an NVA conventional threat. In the author's judgement this focus actually continued throughout the Vietnam War, though this is the subject of some debate. Col. Harry Summers Jr., argues that the U.S. Army focussed much too heavily on the guerrillas instead, at the expense of enough effort to defeat the enemy "main forces." Prof. Russell Weigby has more wisely taken the opposite view.[34]

However, it must be granted that the gradual superimposing of a quasiconventional war on rural insurgency through enemy creation of VC "main force" units and then increasing NVA unit infiltration after 1964 required a conventional response. By then a "big unit" shield became increasingly necessary behind which pacification could proceed. But this tended to become an end in itself, drawing the attention of MACV and the JGS further away from support of pacification as an essential corollary to going after the main-force units.

Soon after U.S. troop intervention it became accepted in MACV and in the Pentagon that U.S. forces were not to be used, except incidentally, in the clear and secure (pacification) role. This would be left to the Vietnamese.[35] Indeed, it would help free them for this purpose.[36] Implicit in this concept was the low U.S. opinion of the estate to which RVNAF had fallen at this time, and an institutional reluctance to employ highly mobile U.S. units with their great firepower in a more static role. This trend culminated in the GVN decision, announced at the October 1966 Manila Conference, to allocate over half of ARVN regular infantry battalions to support of RD.[37]

But the problems in relying on conventional ARVN forces to support pacification were clearly recognized. A December 1966 State Department analysis pointed out that, while our strategy called for fighting two interdependent wars—a conventional war and a counterinsurgency-cum-pacification war—in fact U.S. combat forces

> remain essentially oriented toward conventional warfare . . . ARVN meanwhile is also fighting essentially conventional war whether in sparsely settled areas or in populated ones such as the Mekong delta. Its commitment to pacification is negligible, and it continues to regard its mission essentially in conventional military terms. . . .
>
> The claims of top U.S. and GVN military officials notwithstanding, the waging of a conventional war has overriding priority, perhaps as much as 9 to 1, according to the personal judgements of some U.S. advisors. . . .[38]

State went on to predict that the shift of ARVN divisions to the pacification support role would not work very well, largely because of the same weaknesses which had undermined ARVN's conventional effectiveness.[39] This proved to be the case. In the new pacification program which began in 1967 primary reliance was finally placed on improvement and expansion of territorial forces for the "clear and hold" role of pacification support.

Another facet of our playing out our institutional repertoires was our introduction to Indochina of what some have called "the American style of war." As we have seen, we first organized and trained the Vietnamese to fight our way with our equipment. Then, as they buckled, we brought in massive U.S. forces and practiced war American style on a much grander scale. We sought to minimize U.S. casualties by massive use of sophisticated firepower, and further trained and equipped the RVNAF to do the same. Brigadier W.F.K. Thompson, military correspondent of the *London Daily Telegraph*, remarks: "The national style of the Americans springs from their being the leading technological country, and their natural reaction to any problem is to look for a technological answer. We saw it in Korea with their firepower." He also commented on it in Vietnam.[40]

Take our extensive use of technology and machines to extend the destructive reach of men. Great reliance on firepower to pave the way for infantry or tanks and minimize casualties had been successful in World War II and Korea. Therefore why not in Vietnam? Didn't our Army use tanks in Vietnam partly because it had them and was experienced in their use? Didn't its extensive use of artillery of all calibers spring at least in part from its availability and because American military doctrine was to use it lavishly, even though observable targets in Vietnam were far sparser than they would presumably have been in a European conflict? Didn't the Air Force use expensive high-performance jets to perform missions that other types of aircraft could have performed less expensively partly because these jets were what we had in our inventory? Understandably, it made little sense to air planners to develop too much of a separately tailored air capability for Vietnam when this would probably have had to be at the expense of buying aircraft also capable of coping with the Soviet threat.

We imported into a small, underdeveloped country all the enormous array of sophisticated technological means that the world's most advanced industrial nation thought might be useful, and used them to oppose an army that walked, that used mortars as its chief form of artillery, that used almost no armor until 1972, and that was nearly totally lacking in air support. Yet at the least, many of our military techniques were not very cost-effective, and in some respects proved to be seriously counterproductive in terms of "winning hearts and minds."

The extent to which our R&D effort was technologically oriented was also in the American style of war. Its chief focus, even in a low-intensity insurgency conflict, was on better machines or new technology. Much of this was highly useful (see Chapter 7), but would it not have been better to have devoted a more significant portion of our research to the nature of the conflict and the enemy, his patterns of operation, and better counterinsurgency techniques? Altogether, this type of research received only a tiny fraction of the total R&D effort attributable to Vietnam.

Even when the U.S. disengaged, we still put the great bulk of our aid into conventional regular Vietnamese forces. We also further remade RVNAF in our image—training and equipping it to continue practicing the very style of warfare that proved so costly and destructive in our own hands. Ironically, however, the attrition which it and other factors cumulatively imposed on our opponents, especially on the Southern Viet Cong, at long last led Hanoi to fall back on largely similar conventional warfare in its 1972 and 1975 offensives. In its last phase, the conflict became a more conventional one on the part of both sides. Ironically, the war ended as the American military had thought it would begin, with a massive North Vietnamese regular army assault using tanks, artillery and even air power. And in the end the RVNAF, stretched thin, badly led, and without adequate fire support, proved unable to cope with this assault.[41]

THE AIR WAR AGAINST THE NORTH

Though the air campaign against North Vietnam beginning in 1965 was the outgrowth of many factors, it also reflects the way in which an institution will tend to play out its preferred institutional repertoire. Fascinated with using airpower carefully and selectively to signal Hanoi to desist from war in the South, our civilian leaders seem not to have taken adequately into account the institutional pressures thus released. The fact that flexible U.S. airpower was readily available and could be used for counterpressures against North Vietnam— especially for quick retaliation—almost inevitably led to its use. The air forces also pressed to do what they knew best: to mount massive bombing campaigns both in the South and against the North. And the way in which these campaigns were conducted strongly reflected U.S. military doctrine about how airpower should be employed. Indeed, the conflict between doctrine and civilian preoccupations over its political impact helped foster some of the sharpest inhouse debates of the Vietnam war.

Early planning of air operations against the North focused primarily on the political objectives to be achieved through such pressures. The chief advocates were the U.S. military. By February 1964 the JCS were beginning to advocate bombing the North.[42] They based their case largely on the unlikelihood of arresting the deteriorating situation in the South in any other way. But the *Pentagon Papers* indicate how quickly the JCS and CINCPAC began shifting the weight of their argument to the military effectiveness of what could be achieved with air power, and how consistently they advocated a "massive bombing campaign."[43] Following the first reprisal strikes in early 1965, "gradual [top level] acceptance . . . of the need for a militarily more significant, sustained bombing program" led to a shift of focus from reprisal toward interdiction of North Vietnamese lines of communication.[44]

In contrast to the ground attrition strategy (see below), the air interdiction campaign soon became a controversial issue. Aside from sharp debate over whether it was achieving its political objectives vis-à-vis Hanoi, military and civilian officials also recurrently clashed over how militarily effective air interdiction was in limiting Hanoi's intervention in the South (the *Pentagon Papers* hardly mention the much larger air effort in the South and along the Ho Chi Minh Trail, which was apparently not seriously questioned). CINCPAC, the JCS, and MACV consistently made the case that bombing the North was exacting a worthwhile price, and that the chief problem was civilian reluctance to unleash a sufficient air effort. They fought the gradualism imposed by civilian decisionmakers for essentially political reasons, and blamed it for preventing the optimum weight and timing of attack. Most senior officers also favored mining North Vietnam's ports and hitting the "lucrative" targets in the Hanoi/Haiphong area as most consistent with the doctrine of strategic bombing, while the civilians tended to favor less politically risky strikes at infiltration routes to put a "ceiling" on what Hanoi could send south.[45]

The one strategic target system finally singled out for full-scale attack was POL. As early as November 1965 the JCS advocated such attacks as "more damaging to the DRV capability to more war-supporting resources . . . than an attack against any other single target system."[46] After intense debate lasting over six months, and revolving as much around political issues as estimates of military results, attacks were authorized on seven of the nine POL targets in June 1966. All targets were hit and North Vietnam's storage capacity was sharply curtailed. But the campaign failed to produce any significant decrease in Hanoi's ability to support the war in the South. It was "the last major escalation of the air war recommended by Secretary McNamara."[47]

A powerful case against the air campaign was made in the Jason Summer Study report by a panel of civilian scientists in September 1955. This report concluded that the bombing "had had no measurable direct effect on Hanoi's ability to mount and support military operations in the South at the current level."[48] In November McNamara recommended stabilizing the campaign against the North, and pressed instead for the anti-infiltration barrier proposed in the Jason study.[49]

His systems analysts estimated that the cost of the air campaign was over $250 million a month in late 1966, but with "no significant impact on the war in South Vietnam. . . ."[50] Some 148,000 sorties were flown in 1966, compared with 55,000 in the ten months of bombing in 1965.[51]

Intense debate continued during 1967. CINCPAC, arguing that the chief reason for failure in 1966 had been that much of the military plan had not been approved, favored a major escalation.[52] In May McNamara proposed instead de-escalating the air campaign and concentrating on the infiltration "funnel" south of the 20th Parallel.[53] The JCS countered with their previous proposals to mine North Vietnamese ports, especially Haiphong. In July a compromise decision was made to do neither, but to continue more of the same.[54] However, the approved target list was cautiously expanded in late 1967. Meanwhile, another study by the Jason Group, several CIA analyses, and an OSD/SA study all cast serious doubt on the air campaign's effectiveness in deterring or even impeding Hanoi from prosecuting the war in the South.[55] All the damage done certainly made the war more costly to North Vietnam, as pointed out by COMUSMACV and CINCPAC, but these losses were largely made up by increased Soviet and Chinese aid.[56]

Hanoi's ability to mount the 1968 Tet offensive was seen by the civilian critics as final proof that attacking the North by air was not worth the cost. This led to yet another civil-military confrontation, in which all the old arguments were rehearsed. The impact of the civilian critiques is apparent in President Johnson's decision of March 30, 1968, to suspend bombing north of the 20th Parallel.

However, this study is not directed at analyzing the merits of the air war against the North. Much of the evidence as to its impact is unavailable in any case until we hear (if ever) from the North Vietnamese. Moreover, the U.S. bombing campaign in response to Hanoi's 1972 offensive, which used "smart" ordnance and was conducted under fewer constraints than previous bombing of the North, seemed to prove militarily more effective. The 1972 mining at long last of North Vietnamese harbors, especially Haiphong, also had considerable effect. Finally, the so-called "Christmas" 1972 bombing campaign with B-52's against the Hanoi area is credited with finally bringing Hanoi to sign the terms negotiated between Kissinger and Le Duc Tho.

The intent here is rather to bring out some of the institutional reasons why we conducted the air campaign as we did. The extensive coverage of the 1964–1968 policy debates in the *Pentagon Papers* suggest a consistent underlying doctrinal conviction among its military advocates that a major air effort could not help but have significant results. While the air campaign was never carried out the way its advocates wished, it nonetheless represented a very high level of effort against a country so small and poorly developed as North Vietnam. But here too may have been the chief flaw in the strategy. Such a society and economy, and the kind of war it conducted, were simply not as vulnerable to air attack as our previous military experience tended to suggest. Instead of taking this fully into account, however, our air forces played out their institutional repertoires. They did what their doctrine called for, what they were trained and equipped to do, rather than tailor their response to the atypical situation they confronted. While this does not come through explicitly in the *Pentagon Papers*, it is powerfully implied in the way airmen argued their case.

Wasn't still another factor at play? Didn't we also mount a major bombing campaign because we had in existence a major capability to do so? It was a classic case of how having such a capability drove us to use it—even though it was soon recognized as less than optimum. Moreover, is it surprising that the JCS and DOD wanted to use all major components of our existing general-purpose capability rather than expand the ground force effort even more? The Army also was happy to have the Air Force and Navy share the budgetary and resource burden, while the latter two were eager to play a self-justifying role in "our only war" instead of leaving it all to the Army and Marines. Assorted military constituencies, once involved in Vietnam, had to prove: for instance, the utility not only of airpower (the Air Force) but of carrier-based air power (the Navy).[57]

Was something analogous to Parkinson's law at work? Did the need to tend to expand to the limits of the capability to fulfill it? Gar Alperovitz elevates this to what he calls "Parknamara's law," as it applied to Vietnam: "The more you increase the options and guns available, the more someone will find reason to use them; the more you use the options, the more your response becomes inflexibly military; the more you become inflexibly military, the more you lose your options."[58]

In the Besson Board report on Vietnam logistics there is a revealing statement that "the extraordinary increase in expenditures of air munitions over any previous experience stemmed from the employment of modern high performance aircraft capable of delivering large quantities of munitions at high sortie rates."[59] Since one of the key problems we confronted in Vietnam was that of finding and fixing a highly elusive enemy, there is great room for doubt as to how many lucrative targets were available. This suggests that our immense air ordnance expenditure was at least as much a function of its availability as of need. What commander isn't going to use all the air support he has?

No doubt the same could be said of artillery ammunition outlays, which also were immense. This tendency was further reinforced by organizational incentives. In the absence of sufficient hard intelligence on the results of their activities, artillery and air unit commanders tended to be evaluated largely on the ammunition expenditures or sortie rates of their units. One analyst has pointed out that the growing use of herbicides up though 1969 was also governed partly by "the availability of agents and delivery systems. . . ."[60]

THE STRATEGY OF ATTRITION

While no single term suffices to encompass the mixed strategies we employed in South Vietnam, it became mostly a ground-air attrition campaign on the military side. General Westmoreland himself quite honestly termed it as such, for example telling President Johnson on April 27, 1967 that "in the final analysis we are fighting a war of attrition in Southeast Asia."[61] The very nature of the conflict deprived the GVN/U.S. side of such classic military options as bringing the main enemy forces to a decisive battle. Similarly the limited war constraints under which the U.S. chose to operate, largely in order to limit the risk of Chinese intervention, long prevented operations outside of South Vietnam to cut enemy supply routes, or seize key territorial objectives like his chief logistic base areas. To the contrary, the very elusiveness of the enemy, his ability to hide among the population or in remote jungle and mountain areas, the difficulty of bringing him into battle when he desired to evade, his ability to retreat to sanctuary, and a host of other factors led us into trying to grind down enemy strength over time by all means available, while clamping down on his lines of communication. As it evolved during 1965–1966,

> General Westmoreland's strategy based upon exploitation of our inherent superior mobility and firepower was designed to simultaneously attrite [sic] the enemy and retain the initiative by disrupting VC/NVA operations before they completely materialized. This led to seeking engagement with enemy main force units well out into the border regions, where they literally could be held at distance before jumping off in operations. Related to this was the notion that the important thing was to fight—

to engage the enemy and create casualties. It mattered little that you accepted combat in regions with certain advantages for the enemy— the prime objective was to engage and to kill him.[62]

In short, this war of attrition seemed a natural role for an immensely superior conventional allied force, rich in mobility and firepower. We thought we had ample resources to fight a war of attrition against such an impoverished foe.[63]

This was also easier institutionally than trying to beat the enemy at his own game. "Search-and-destroy" was far more in accord with the doctrinal offensive-mindedness of the U.S. military than "clear-and-hold" or enclave strategies. "Probably the single most disturbing factor in the enclave approach was the implicit failure to try and seize the initiative from the enemy."[64] Hence "the preferred military doctrine dictated the strategy and the strategy determined the policy."[65]

The military strategy of attrition as pursued in Vietnam deserves far more thorough analysis than it has received to date. That facet directed against the opponent's base areas, logistic support, and LOCs did achieve considerable impact, though not enough—at least up to Hanoi's 1972 escalation—to force the enemy to give in temporarily. The naval "blockade" of the South Vietnamese coastline was perhaps its most successful aspect, forcing Hanoi to switch from a primarily seaborne LOC to the Ho Chi Minh trail and Cambodia. The enemy's main force units were also ground down over time. This, plus MACV's preemptive tactics of attempting to spoil the enemy's preparations before he could attack, largely frustrated the Communists' repeated attempts, except during Tet 1968 and in spring 1972, to launch multifront offensives. Moreover, it did over time provide a "shield" behind which a serious pacification effort could finally get under way.

Finally, it contributed to the gradual drying up of the southern VC "main forces," which were not able to replace their losses as easily as were the NVA. Hanoi found it increasingly necessary to replace VC losses by putting NVA fillers into VC main force units, and finally felt compelled to rely predominantly on its own regular forces, heavily reinforced by almost all that remained in the North, for its largely conventional 1972 and 1975 offensives. The final 1975 offensive was conducted almost entirely by NVA regulars. Thus it seems fair to conclude that the massive US/ARVN effort, and the pacification program which it shielded, did succeed over time in reducing at least the Southern VC threat to the point where Vietnam became mainly an "NVA war."

However, North Vietnams' ability to replace its own losses, and to dictate the tempo of combat, prevented the attrition strategy from grinding down the NVA forces to the point where they were no longer a major threat, not even after the 1970 Cambodian coup permitted incursions into many sanctuaries. More often than not, we were unable to find and fix the enemy and make him fight on our terms. Indeed, the chief military flaw in the attrition strategy was the enemy's ability to control his own losses, both by evading contact and by replacing his losses via VC recruitment and further infiltration from North Vietnam. He actually increased his main force strength right up through Tet 1968.[66]

By November 1966, when the military request for an increase to 570,000-odd U.S. troops was pending, Secretary McNamara was telling the President that, despite our buildup and the large number of enemy we were killing, he saw no reasonable way to bring the war to an end soon because the other side apparently was able to replace its losses. He therefore opposed continuing in 1967 to increase friendly forces as rapidly as possible and to use them primarily in "search-and-destroy" operations against enemy main force units. While he favored continuation of search-and-destroy, he wanted to "build friendly forces only to that level required to neutralize the large enemy units and prevent them from interfering with the pacification program."[67] McNamara won his case, and the new troop ceiling was held at 470,000 (to be achieved by June 1968).[68] Even MACV later granted that net enemy strength had actually increased by 42,000 in 1966.[69]

But not until 1967–1968 were the limitations of the attrition strategy—in the air as well as on the ground—fully analyzed, in response to renewed military requests for yet more U.S. troops. In spring 1967 MACV, CINCPAC, and JCS proposed a major increase of up to 210,000 in U.S. troop levels for FY 1968 to counter increased NVA infiltration, retain the strategic initiative, and shorten the war by accelerating the attrition of VC/NVA forces.[70] This precipitated a major debate, which foreshadowed the later and better known one after Tet 1968.

Here McNamara's systems analysis office played a major role in questioning whether MACV's attrition strategy could succeed in light of continuing NVA infiltration. It brought out for the first time how the enemy had considerable control over his losses, almost regardless of what U.S. force levels were. Nor would added U.S. forces help much in pacification.[71] Based on a study of small-unit engagements in 1966, OSD/SA concluded in May 1967 that "the size of the force we deploy has little effect on the rate of attrition of enemy forces."[72] It also pointed out that the military had made no comparable analysis to justify their requested increases. It is surprising that this critique of the attrition strategy was so little reflected in the flood of military and civilian memoranda cited in the *Pentagon Papers* on the spring 1967 force-level debate. Instead, the issue apparently turned on "political and economic considerations, especially the domestic U.S. political cost of having to call up the reserves."[73] In July 1967 agreement was finally reached on a new U.S. troop ceiling of 525,000 for FY 1968—a very modest increase compared to what had been requested.

By the time of the post-Tet 1968 debate over another major troop increase, others in Washington besides OSD/SA had begun to argue that the attrition strategy was not working and that the enemy could match each U.S. escalation. Again the issue was whether to keep the same strategy and simply increase our forces, as the military advocated, or to seek an alternative strategy. Again OSD/SA pointed out that the enemy's ability to control his losses within a wide range would permit him to continue fighting indefinitely even if his losses substantially increased.[74]

This time the Tet shock led most of the President's civilian advisors to conclude that we could not win the war the way we were fighting it. The outcome is well known. While President Johnson allowed a modest increase from 525,000 to 549,000, this became the peak of our commitment.[75] Significantly, however, the strategic debate over the attrition strategy was not resolved. No new strategic directive was issued to the field, and U.S. forces continued to pursue essentially an attrition strategy.[76]

As it turned out, the attrition strategy proved more successful in 1968 than in any year before or since, because the enemy had temporarily abandoned his previous hit and run strategy and attacked us rather than we him. In his three major attempts at multifront offensives—at Tet, in May, and again in August-September (together with his costly "siege" of Khesanh)—he incurred his peak losses in the Vietnam war. But this and other factors led him to revert in 1969 to a "protracted war" strategy, which again confronted the U.S. and GVN with the same old problem for the next four years, until Hanoi's spring 1972 offensive.

To the other flaws of the attrition strategy must be added its enormous costs—easily the bulk of all the billions the U.S. spent on the war. Beyond these are the adverse side effects of primary focus on the big-unit war: increased civilian casualties, economic damage, creation of refugees and the like. In their concentration on defeating the enemy in battle, the U.S. and GVN military gave wholly inadequate weight to the alienating impact of these side effects on the population whose control, if not support, was presumably the ultimate objective of the counterinsurgency effort. Throughout the *Pentagon Papers* one finds little indication that this factor was taken sufficiently into account in military planning. This suggests, moreover, that even success in attriting the enemy militarily could prove transitory if not irrelevant in a "people's war." As the French found in Algeria, "to win the military battle but to lose the political struggle" was to fail—a point made eloquently by Bernard Fall.[77]

The overall reliance on attrition helped spawn the quantitative measurement systems devised in an attempt to measure military "progress" in this strange war. If cutting the enemy down to size was the name of the game, then the "body count," comparative kill ratios, and weapons-captured to weapons-lost ratios were key indicators of progress—if valid, of course. Since it was even harder to assess the impact of indirect firepower such as air and artillery, the usual measurement of their effectiveness was one of output, not impact: how many sorties flown, how much ordnance dropped, how many rounds fired. Since so much destructive power was available, the pressure to use it up to capacity was strong. Again it was a case of capabilities dictating performance: We measured the measurable; how relevant it was is another matter. Henry Kissinger, discussing our "conceptual" failures in Vietnam, cites as one reason for them "the degree to which our heavy, bureaucratic, and modern government creates a sort of blindness in which bureaucracies run a competition with their own programs and measure success by the degree to which they fulfill their own norms, without being in a position to judge whether the norms made any sense to begin with. . . ."[78]

INTELLIGENCE INADEQUACIES

Though national intelligence estimates at the Washington level were generally realistic, what might be called tactical intelligence in the field was for long critically weak. General Taylor noted its many inadequacies as early as his visit in October 1961, and gave its improvement a high priority.[79] But all too little was done. Critical information gaps continued to cloud our perceptions as to what was really happening in Vietnam. To take one case, there was a notable lack of adequate intelligence on the full extent of VC activities in the countryside from 1958 through 1965. While the VC concentrated on guerrilla warfare in the rural areas, our focus was on the GVN in Saigon and on the conventional military balance. Even after 1965 these gaps persisted, though to a gradually diminishing extent.

Since the U.S. and GVN resources invested in intelligence were enormous in the aggregate, we must look elsewhere for the reasons behind its failures. Again, typical organizational behavior severely hampered achievement of optimum results. The kinds of intelligence most needed in Vietnam were simply alien to the standard institutional repertoires of most U.S. and GVN intelligence services involved. The U.S. and GVN military intelligence empires, which dwarfed their civilian counterparts, were focused in classic style mostly on military order of battle. Identifying and locating enemy main force units and movements (or targets) was the order of the day, to the neglect of such elements of a highly unconventional enemy establishment as local self-defense groups or the Viet Cong infrastructure. "Intelligence was oriented on the [enemy] combat units, so were the operations."[80] It was this mind-set which led MACV and the Pentagon to remove these "civilians" in 1967 from the *military* order of battle, as brought out in General Westmoreland's 1984–1985 libel suit against the Columbia Broadcasting System. Conspiracy and deception were not the reasons at all.

As a result, we tended to underestimate real enemy strength—a tendency reinforced by lack of much firm intelligence on VC recruiting in the countryside. Many military intelligence officers (with some notable exceptions) seemed to have closed minds to such other facets of the war. It was not their job, after all. All too little attention was paid to the operational code or tactical style of the enemy, to the fact that his tactics as well as his goals were as much political as military. We saw the enemy in our own image, one reason why we repeatedly thought we were doing so much better than we actually were. Nor was there ever an adequate effort to combine and rationalize the plethora of U.S. and GVN intelligence agencies, which overlapped and often got in each other's way. Institutional autonomy was more important than optimum results. This also contributed to the inadequacy of our intelligence despite all the enormous resources invested.

Nowhere was GVN/U.S. intelligence failure so marked (the Vietnamese were even worse than the Americans) as in meeting the crucial need to identify and neutralize the so-called Viet Cong Infrastructure (VCI), the politico-administrative apparatus which ran the insurgency. As early as 1957 the MSUG was suggesting greater activity along these lines, to be carried out by a national police force. Then, in 1961–1962, the British Advisory Mission urged that high priority be given to building up the police, especially a good Special

Branch, for this purpose. Among others, the author agitated this issue vigorously from the White House in 1966–1967. The PROVN and "Roles and Missions" studies both highlighted it. From an unexpected source, Assistant Secretary Enthoven urged McNamara prior to his July 1967 Vietnam trip to focus on how to get at the VCI.[81] As it turned out, Westmoreland had already agreed to the first major U.S. advisory effort designed to get the GVN moving in this key area. It evolved into the GVN's *Phung Hoang* program, begun in 1968. This controversial program, criticized by many as poorly managed and ineffective, especially in rounding up key senior members of the VCI, was nevertheless later acknowledged by the Hanoi leadership to have had considerable impact.[82]

U.S. CIVILIAN AGENCIES ALSO PLAY OUT THEIR INSTITUTIONAL REPERTOIRES

On the civilian side we find the same tendency for the U.S. agencies involved to focus primarily on that with which they were most familiar. The civilian agencies may have been more perceptive of the political dimensions of the conflict, but they too were slow to adapt to the exigencies of insurgency conflict and then major war. Perhaps the civilian agencies were more imaginative than the military; they mounted a number of interesting experiments (See Chapter 7). But none were supported and funded on a large enough scale to make much of a dent. For the most part, just like the U.S. military, the U.S. civilian agencies unsurprisingly "did their thing."

State's concept of its role in Vietnam—and that of our Embassy in Saigon—remained quite conventional from the outset. As we saw in Chapter 3, they did not often deviate from the concept of normal diplomatic dealings with a sovereign allied government, even when that government was falling apart. Similarly, State always carefully confined itself to its traditional role of *primus inter pares* in relation to the other U.S. agencies involved in Vietnam. It made no effort to assert managerial primacy, to control our military effort on political grounds. The *Pentagon Papers* paint a picture of recurrent State Department concern over what the U.S. was doing in Vietnam, but near-abdication of any executive responsibility for the U.S. effort except when it bore on the limits to which our out-of-country operations were subject.

The State Department's approach to institution-building in Vietnam turned largely on the encouragement of democratic institutions on the American model. Elections would legitimize the government, while a tripartite form of government with executive, legislative and judicial checks and balances would prevent the growth of dictatorial power. However well meant, was this the right answer? Or was it a form of political mirror-imaging comparable to what we did in the military field? Duncanson comments that

> too much weight was given to the political side of government and what American officials liked to call "the realities of power," by extension from the US constitution, regarded as a norm of the human political condition which only the aberration of colonialism had temporarily obscured in Vietnam. Any abatement of the principles underlying American democracy—of the pyramid of balanced vested interests at various political levels—would be wrong, would provide material for Communist propaganda, and therefore would make the Communist hold over the people stronger. With concentration of American support on the leader as the rallying point for vested interests harnessed to a national endeavor went disregard for the impersonal institutions of the state and the underestimation of the value of the civil service. . . .[83]

AID's role in Vietnam, on the other hand, has probably received more criticism than it deserves. While institutionally no more capable of gearing itself to counterinsurgency than other U.S. agencies, AID at least put the bulk of its resources into an essential corollary effort:

> The fundamental task which fell on USAID during the decade of 1962–1971 was to offset the budgetary cost of the war and to control as well as possible, the inflation. Therefore some two-thirds of the economic assistance provided by AID (including Food For Peace) took the form of commercial import financing, that is supply of goods to the marketplace.[84]

The Commercial Import Program had also been used in the mid-Fifties to combat inflation, and was similar to budget support techniques used to shore up the economies of such other U.S. aid clients bearing heavy military burdens as South Korea and Taiwan.[85] It was restarted in 1963, and was at its largest during the years of major U.S. troop presence. Although wartime inflation became severe after 1964, and averaged 25 to 30 percent per year during 1965–1969, it never got out of control—quite an unusual fact in a country at war like Vietnam. In 1971 prices rose only 15 percent. By contrast, in the first year of the Korean War retail prices rose 750 percent, and by the time the war ended three years later had risen 2400 percent. Better Vietnam inflation control via sensible economic policies, backed by U.S. aid, owed much to the role played by a handful of able U.S. officials—chiefly Leroy Wehrle, Charles Cooper, Richard Cooper, Rutherford Poats, and James Grant—who enjoyed unusual access to receptive policymakers in Washington and Saigon.

But AID's other programs were for the most part less successful, especially before 1968. Its normal concept of how to work through the existing local government, and of providing funding and technical assistance mostly at the central government level, did not fit the situation in Vietnam. Though AID decided, as part of the 1961 emphasis on counterinsurgency, to shift its focus to rural programs, this occurred in fact on only a very modest scale. AID representatives were assigned to all provinces in 1962, and AID provided modest support to the Strategic Hamlet Program. In July 1962 the AID Mission (then called USOM) created a new Office of Rural Affairs under Rufus Phillips to manage this support. However, Philips and his able successor, George Tanham, were never adequately backed up.[86] Instead, AID kept pressing development and "nation-building" programs on a GVN whose machinery to execute them had largely atrophied. For example, Tanham points out that even by the summer of 1965 his office included only a few more than 100 people, about 1/250th of the total U.S. military and civilian presence in Vietnam.[87]

Moreover, most U.S. civilian agencies (CIA was a notable exception) were not equipped, staffed, or structured to deal with the exigencies of a situation like Vietnam. As Chester Cooper put it,

> By and large the non-defense elements of the government were neither psychologically nor organizationally able to come to grips with an insurgency that was quickly getting out of hand. None of the courses given at the Foreign Service Institute, and none to the experiences of AID specialists and Foreign Service Officers elsewhere, seemed relevant to what was going on in Vietnam.[88]

Duncanson too is critical of the inexperience of U.S. civilian advisers.[89] The strongest criticism comes from General Taylor, who found the slowness of U.S. civilian agencies to move on political, economic, and information programs unfortunately lending color to later charges that the U.S. "tended to neglect the political and social aspects of the situation and fatuously sought an impossible victory."[90] The peacetime funding and personnel procedures of most civilian agencies also proved ill-suited to wartime contingencies. For example, AID estimated in 1966 that it took around eighteen months for supplies ordered through AID machinery to reach Vietnam.

NOTES

1. Richard M. Pfeffer, *No More Vietnams?*, Harper and Row, New York, 1968, p. 105.

2. Arthur M. Schlesinger, Jr., *The Bitter Heritage: Vietnam and American Democracy, 1941–1966*, Houghton Mifflin Company, Boston, 1967, p. 39.

3. *United States–Vietnam Relations, 1945–1967: Study Proposal by the Department of Defense*, 12 volumes, U. S. Government Printing Office, Washington, D.C., 1971 (hereafter referred to as the *Pentagon Papers*), IV-A, Summary, p. 1.1. More than 75 percent of the economic aid the U.S. provided in 1955–1961 went into the GVN military budget (IV.A.5, p. 39).

4. Ibid., IV.A.4, pp. 18–19.

5. Ibid., p. 21.

6. Ibid., IV.B.1, p. 63.

7. NSAM 288 cited in *Pentagon Papers*, IV.B.3, p. 42.

8. Ibid., p. 58.

9. Ibid., p. 108.

10. Alain C. Enthoven and K. Wayne Smith, *How Much is Enough?* Harper & Row, New York, 1971, p. 294.

11. See Sir Robert Thompson, *No Exit From Vietnam*, David McKay Company, Inc., New York, 1969, pp. 122–124 on the side effects of ARVN predominance.

12. Pfeffer, *No More Vietnams?*, p. 105.

13. Bernard Fall, *The Two Viet-Nams*, Frederick A. Praeger, Inc., New York, (2nd rev. ed.), 1967, p. 325; Thompson, *Defeating Communist Insurgency*, p. 58.

14. *Pentagon Papers*, IV.A.4, pp. 1–12 (also Chapter VIII, p. 129). See also reported comments of General Lemnitzer, then Chairman, Joint Chiefs of Staff, cited in *China in Crisis*, Vol. II, University of Chicago Press, Chicago, IL, 1968, p. 273.

15. *Pentagon Papers*, IV.B.3, p. 5.

16. Ibid., IV.A.4, pp. 21–41.

17. *The Pentagon Papers: The Defense Department History of United States Decisionmaking on Vietnam*, "Senator Gravel Edition," 4 volumes, Beacon Press, Boston, 1971, Vol. II, p. 650.

18. Pfeffer, *No More Vietnams?*, p. 166.

19. Thompson, *Defeating Communist Insurgency*, pp. 60 and 62.

20. For perceptive comments on this phenomenon of "mirror-imaging," see A. A. Jordan, *Foreign Aid and the Defense of Southeast Asia*, Frederick A. Praeger, Inc., New York, 1962.

21. *Pentagon Papers*, IV.A.4, p. 4.1; see pp. 24–31 for details on extent of mirror-imaging.

22. In 1960 training and equipping the Civil Guard became a MAP function. In 1961 the Self Defense Corps also was given military status and received MAP support. They got a very small share, however. See William

A. Nighswonger, *Rural Pacification in Vietnam*, Frederick A. Praeger, Inc., New York, 1966, p. 44.

23. Barbara Tuchman, *Stilwell and the American Experience in China, 1911–45*, The Macmillan Company, New York, 1970, p. 512, citing Stilwell's *History of the CBI Theater.*

24. *Pentagon Papers*, IV.B.2, p. 18.

25. Ibid., IV.A.4, pp. 20–21. See also John D. Montgomery, *The Politics of Foreign Aid*, Frederick A. Praeger, Inc., New York, 1962, pp. 64–70.

26. *Pentagon Papers*, IV.A.4, pp. 4.1, 21–23. Also IV.A.5, Tab. 4, p. 27, and IV.B.3, p. 7. See also Jordan, Foreign Aid, pp. 138–139.

27. *Pentagon Papers*, IV.B.4, p. 8.

28. Ibid., IV.B.3, p. 34.

29. See Tables in ibid., pp. 127–128.

30. Ibid., p. 126.

31. Ibid., IV.B.3, pp. 9–10.

32. See General Bruce Palmer, *The 25-Year War: Americas Military Role in Vietnam*, University Press of Kentucky, Lexington, KY, 1984, pp. 155–158. Russell Weigley, in his perceptive "Reflections on 'Lessons' from Vietnam" (in *Vietnam as History*, pp. 115–124) points out how the U.S. Army has persistently, over generations, refused to contemplate seriously the prospect of any kind of war except conventional warfare in the "European Style" (p. 46).

33. Stewart Alsop, *The Center*, Harper & Row, New York, 1968, p. 149.

34. Harry Summers, Jr., *On Strategy: A Critical Analysis of the Vietnam War*, Presidio Press, Novato, CA, 1982, p. 86. Also see the opposing views of Summers on pp. 109–114 and Prof. Russell Weigley on pp. 114–124 of *Vietnam as History*. In reviewing Summers' book in *Survival*, March/April 1985, pp. 94–95, the author wholly agrees with Weigley.

35. See, for example, JSCM 811–65 of 11/10/65, cited in *Pentagon Papers*, IV.C.6(a), p. 17, or DOD Memorandum on February 1965 Honolulu Conference Decisions on p. 32.

36. Ibid., pp. 34–35.

37. Ibid., pp. 55–61.

38. *Pentagon Papers*, IV.C.6(b), pp. 14–15.

39. Ibid., pp. 16–18.

40. "Lessons from the Vietnam War," Report of a Seminar held at the Royal United Services Institute, London, February 12, 1970 (hereafter called the RUSI Seminar Report), pp. 7–8.

41. Stephen Hosmer et al., *The Fall of South Vietnam*, pp. 335–38, 73–74, 83–91.

42. See JCSM 136–64 of 2/18/64, in *Pentagon Papers*, IV.C.1, pp. 37–39; also JCSM 174–64 of 3/2/64.

43. See, for example, *Pentagon Papers*, IV.C.2(a), pp. 20–21; IV.C.2(b), pp. ii, 25; IV.C.2(c), pp. 2, 9, 32–35.

44. Ibid., IV.C.3, pp. v–vi, 69–71, 74–80.

45. Ibid., IV.C.7(a) and IV.C.7(b).

46. Ibid., IV.C.7(a), p. 85.

47. Ibid., pp. 138, 140–145.

48. Ibid., pp. 149–155; OSD/SA analyses of air-war effectiveness reached similar conclusions, cited on p. 172.

49. Ibid., pp. 163–167.

50. Ibid., p. 175.

51. Ibid., p. 177.

52. Ibid., pp. 179–180.

53. Ibid., IV.C.7.(b), pp. 49–52.

54. Ibid., p. 80.

55. Ibid., pp. 112, 115–131.

56. Ibid., pp. 132–134.

57. James C. Thomson, "How Could Vietnam Happen?" *Atlantic*, April 1968.

58. Gar Alperovitz, *Who We Are*, Little, Brown & Company, Boston, 1969, p. 252.

59. *Logistic Support in the Vietnam Era*, Joint Logistics Review Board, Department of Defense, Vol. 3, June 1970, pp. 2–3.

60. *The Control of Chemical and Biological Weapons*, Carnegie Endowment for Peace, New York, 1971, p. 48.

61. *Pentagon Papers*, IV.C.6(b), p. 82. See also C.W. Corddry's article in *The Baltimore Sun*, July 1, 1972, p. 5.

62. *Pentagon Papers*, IV.C.6(a), p. 127.

63. Thompson, in criticizing allied strategy, sees its flaws as partly a product of American "wealth." "When the solution to a problem failed, no one questioned whether the solution itself was right or wrong. It was assumed that the resources had been inadequate. More of the same from bombing the North to fertilizers, was the constant remedy." *No Exit from Vietnam*, p. 127.

64. *Pentagon Papers*, IV.C.4, pp. 116–117.

65. Townsend Hoopes, *The Limits of Intervention*, David McKay Company, Inc., New York, 1969, p. 62. See also Thompson, *No Exit from Vietnam*, pp. 129–131 and 134–136.

66. See Enthoven and Smith, *How Much is Enough?*, pp. 295–299.

67. DPM of 11/17/76 cited in *Pentagon Papers*, IV.C.6(a), pp. 105–119. (The attrition analysis inputs to this DPM were provided by OSD/SA.)

68. Ibid., p. 103.

69. Ibid., IV.C.6(b), p. 28.

70. Ibid., pp. 61–77, 82–83.

71. Ibid., pp. 105, 107–109.

72. Ibid., p. 114. See also OSD/SA memorandum on pp. 117–118.

73. This debate is covered in the *Pentagon Papers*, IV.C.6(b); see especially p. 215.

74. Enthoven and Smith, *How Much is Enough?* pp. 298–299.

75. *Pentagon Papers*, IV.C.6(c), especially pp. 28–29, 35–36, 58–59ff.

76. Herbert Schandler, *The Unmaking of a President: Lyndon Johnson and Vietnam*, Princeton University Press, Princeton, NJ, 1977 is devoted to the post-Tet debates and resultant decisions.

77. Fall, *The Two Vietnams*, p. 349.

78. Pfeffer, *No More Vietnams?*, p. 11.

79. Maxwell D. Taylor, *Swords and Plowshares*, W.W. Norton & Company, Inc., New York, 1972, pp. 236–238 and 239.

80. RUSI Seminar Report, p. 2.

81. *Pentagon Papers*, IV.C.6(b), pp. 194–195.

82. Stanley Karnow, *Vietnam: A History*, The Viking Press, New York, 1983, pp. 601–602.

83. Dennis Duncanson, *Government and Revolution in Vietnam*, Oxford University Press, New York and London, 1968, pp. 278–279.

84. *Annual Report to the Ambassador from the Director of USAID Vietnam 1971*, USAID Saigon, Jamuary 1, 1972.

85. John D. Montgomery, *The Politics of Foreign Aid: American Experience in Southeast Asia*, Frederick A. Praeger, Inc., New York, 1962, pp. 85–92.

86. For the 1962–1965 efforts of a number of enlightened officials to reorient the effort of the USAID Mission, see G. K. Tanham, *War Without Guns*, Frederick A. Praeger, Inc., New York, 1966.

87. Ibid., p. ix.

88. Cf. Chester Cooper, *Lost Crusade*, Dodd, Mead & Company, New York, 1970, p. 225.

89. Duncanson, *Government and Revolution*, pp. 275–276.

90. Taylor, *Swords and Plowshares*, p. 249.

5
INSTITUTIONAL OBSTACLES
TO THE LEARNING PROCESS

If it is largely understandable, for reasons given earlier, why our early responses were so ill-suited to the atypical problems we confronted in Vietnam, this still leaves the question of why so little changed over the years. As late as 1969, a knowledgeable participant, Brian Jenkins dubbed it "the unchangeable war." True, both the U.S. and the GVN somewhat modified their early approaches because of changing circumstances; key examples of adaptive responses will be discussed in Chapter 7. But in over twenty-two years of Vietnam involvement in one form or another since we began aiding the French in 1950, our response was still overwhelmingly military and conventional, our ability to influence the GVN still limited, our conflict management still fragmented. Why didn't we learn faster?

Again it seems that institutional factors play a significant role. Brian Jenkins, for example, has cited numerous reasons for our unchanging military response, most of them revolving around typical organizational behavior or built-in institutional constraints: the belief that proposed changes might not work; the conviction that present strategy *is* working; the assurance that more was available and therefore change unnecessary; the belief that organizational changes were impossible in the midst of war; the view that the Vietnam war was an aberration and had no application to the future; the rejection of new doctrines as exotic and of marginal importance; incentives to continue what one was already doing; institutional loyalty that rejected external pressure for change even in the face of private doubts; the twelve-month tour; and the lack of a single commander to impose his will on the system. Whatever the relative weight one attaches to these factors, they all have relevance and reinforce the case that numerous institutional factors long inhibited U.S. military adaptation to the unusual circumstances of Vietnam.

Again, however, many of them are understandable. As already noted, it would be too easy to attribute such problems entirely to inadequate leadership. Though U.S. field commanders bear the brunt of criticism over U.S. military performance in Vietnam, many of these problems were either the province of Washington or were well-nigh incapable of solution except over time. This is because the underlying causes of these weaknesses are to be found largely in the "system" itself—the nature and behavior patterns of the organizations that waged the war. Ellsberg, drawing on his Vietnam experience, remarks that we do not know enough about the "learning properties of our bureaucracy."[1] Those bureaucratic properties of organizations—insensitivities, blindnesses, and distorted incentives—which slow up the learning process need to be more fully analyzed.

INSTITUTIONAL INERTIA

A hallmark of bureaucracy is reluctance to change accepted ways of doing things. This form of institutional constraint—the bureaucratic inertia so typical of organizational behavior—is strongly evident in our Vietnam experience. Bureaucrats prefer to deal with the familiar. They find it more comfortable and convenient to continue following tested routines, whereas to change may be to admit prior error—a cardinal bureaucratic sin. So, whether private or public, civilian or military, organizations typically like to keep operating the way they are operating, and to shift only slowly in response to changing situations. And the more hierarchical and disciplined they are—military organizations are almost archetypes—the greater the built-in institutional obstacles to change except slowly and incrementally over time. Even a cursory review of the fate of many military innovations and innovators would illustrate the point. Dr. Vannevar Bush, head of the World War II Office of Scientific Research and Development, has described some of the obstacles to technological innovation in the military services even during wartime. To him, military organization "suffers from a disease that permeates all governmental . . . organizations—a daft belief that if one does nothing one will not make mistakes, and the drab system of seniority and promotions will proceed on its way."[2]

Moreover, once large organizations become committed to a course of action, the ponderous wheels set in motion, vast sums allocated, and personnel selected and trained, it is difficult to alter course. Instead, programs tend to acquire a built-in momentum of their own. And if obstacles are encountered, the natural tendency is to do more of the same—to pour on more coal—rather than to rethink the problem and try to adjust response patterns. This "more of the same"—though perhaps with a few cosmetic changes—seems to be a typical bureaucratic response. Stanley Hoffmann describes how, given the nature of bureaucracy, it must painfully build an internal consensus and how, once reached, this "tends to be very difficult to reverse. Therefore, there is a built-in momentum or inertia." In particular, once a military operation is launched, "a certain logic of military operation" almost naturally takes over, one which "it takes a determined and unlikely combined overall effort of the other agencies, including sometimes the Pentagon, to reverse."[3]

This sort of institutional inertia is amply illustrated in the Vietnam case. Once we set a course and invested heavily in it, the machine proved very difficult to turn around. "More of the same" powerfully reinforced the escalatory trend in Vietnam until 1969, as several analysts have noted. James Thomson, for example, points to the "self-enlarging nature" of our military investment:

Once air strikes and particularly ground forces were introduced, our investment itself had transformed the original stakes. More air power was needed to protect the ground forces: and then more ground forces to protect the ground forces. And needless to say, the military mind develops its own momentum in the absence of clear guidelines from the civilians.[4]

While the sheer institutional and physical difficulty of shifting strategy (or de-escalating) should not be underestimated, President Johnson finally did begin the shift toward de-escalation in 1968 by suspending the bombing of the North. President Nixon carried it much further. During 1968–1971 the GVN/U.S. authorities in Saigon also at least modestly increased the weight of effort devoted to pacification and somewhat reduced the emphasis on search-and-destroy operations. The massive use of firepower was sharply cut back, and the attrition strategy modified. Yet one cannot escape the feeling that this change was forced mostly by U.S. disillusionment with the war and the gradual withdrawal of U.S. forces, together with the enemy's heavy 1968 losses and his consequent reversion to a protracted war strategy for four years. Nor can the diversionary effects of the incursions into Cambodia and Laos be left out of the equation. Nonetheless, until the bitter end bureaucratic inertia and other institutional constraints still laid a heavy hand on GVN/U.S. conduct of the war.

LACK OF INSTITUTIONAL MEMORY

Another organizational phenomenon with seriously adverse impact on U.S. ability to learn and adapt in Vietnam was the shocking lack of institutional memory. "We have devised a unique sort of bureaucratic machine which . . . tends to ensure that our operations in Vietnam will always be vigorous, will never grow tired, but also will never grow wiser."[5] Or, to cite John Vanhn, "We don't have twelve years' experience in Vietnam. We have one year's experience twelve times over."

To a great extent this was the largely unforeseen product of the twelve-month tour for U.S. military personnel. This followed the peacetime precedent of thirteen-month overseas tours designed to minimize inequity where dependents had to stay home. As early as October 1961 OSD apparently tried to extend the normal adviser duty from twenty-four to thirty months with dependents and from twelve to eighteen months without. But the Army successfully opposed this on grounds of equity.[6] The one year tour remained the norm, especially after dependents were no longer permitted in Vietnam, and became sacred after 1965. It also seemed highly desirable for political and morale reasons once draftees began to be sent to Vietnam.

But yet another factor was the desire of the armed services to rotate as many personnel as possible though Vietnam for training purposes. After all, it was "our only war." While the one-year tour facilitated rotating a large number of career officers though command slots, these slots were so much in demand that most combat commands were limited to six months.

The costs were horrendous, and far more than financial. Almost as soon as people learned their jobs, they were rotated out. This was a particularly serious handicap in intelligence work and in the advisory system. Of course, some stayed longer or returned for second or third tours (especially after 1969). But they were the exception rather than the rule.[7] Those who objected to this discounting of experience found Washington agencies adamant on grounds of equity and morale as well as of the presumed need for training as many people as possible by running them though Vietnam.

Further contributing to lack of institutional memory was the tendency to neglect such lessons as were available from the successful British counterinsurgency response in Malaya or French failures in the First Indochina War. Many tried to point out these lessons (see Chapters 1 and 3), but they lay outside U.S. institutional experience and so had little impact. Conditions in Malaya were considered so different as to make that experience almost irrelevant, which led to the ignoring of tested U.K. techniques.[8] As for the French, what could we learn from them since they had done so poorly? An American army historian who visited the French military attache in Saigon in 1963 was told that he was the only American who had done so. Such factors "misled American advisers into disregarding French experience, either political or military . . . even military lessons learnt from the *Corps Expeditionnaire* were not applicable to American or American-taught operations. This injudicious attitude was passed on from generation to generation of American advisers over the years, with considerable cost in dollars and in lives."[9] At least Lansdale and his disciples sought to apply in Vietnam what they had learned in backing Magsaysay's successful quashing of the Huk rebellion, but they too were largely ignored.

SKEWED INCENTIVE PATTERNS

A key reason why the great institutional participants placed such a low premium on adapting their responses to the atypical needs of Vietnam was that there were incentives to do the reverse. We didn't want to restructure or reequip our combat forces to optimize their capabilities for Vietnam because we regarded Vietnam as a temporary diversion from their more normal mission. To revamp a significant fraction of our general purpose forces for Vietnam hardly seems to have been considered, because it would have been so distorting to the preferred force structure, tactics, and doctrine.

On the contrary, there was greater incentive to use in Vietnam the weapons, organizational structures, tactics, and techniques which were institutionally preferred for other reasons, rather than adapt them to Vietnam. For example, the Navy and Air Force preferred to use expensive F-4 Phantom jets in Vietnam rather than propellor-driven A-1Es because this way they got more Phantoms for their inventory. The rationale was to have "general purpose" forces, even if the general purposes served were hardly those most relevant in Vietnam. The same was true of U.S. civilian agencies, which showed little inclination to adapt their regular structures, programs, or personnel policies to the atypical needs of Vietnam.

In particular, the peacetime military and civil personnel systems proved quite inflexible in terms of providing the right kind of career people, putting them in the right jobs, or retaining them for optimum tours of duty in Vietnam. In World War II men had been sent overseas for the duration; in Vietnam even careerists—not just draftees—served minimal tours. It was largely business as usual. No agency did much to design personnel policies which would have optimized performance in Vietnam. There was little organized effort to select people for key jobs on the basis of prior experience or adaptability.

Preferred career incentive patterns posed another institutional obstacle to adaptation. The best way to get ahead in U.S. military or civilian agencies is to stay in the "mainstream." The most desirable military slots for the purpose are those those in command of U.S. units. In Vietnam, therefore, the best officers naturally tended to gravitate toward these slots, toward which the military personnel system also pushed them. This system operated to the detriment of the advisory effort, which after 1965 tended to get less highly qualified men and to lose them as soon as they became experienced. It was even less desirable to be a military adviser in pacification than to be a tactical unit adviser. This was just not the way to get ahead. Fortunately, many qualified military men nonetheless volunteered for pacification work.

Many civilian bureaucrats too were reluctant to serve in a wartime theater like Vietnam, not for want of courage but because they saw such atypical duty as doing little to advance their careers. Some capable Foreign Service officers, for example, were reluctant to serve in CORDS, and the State Department began cutting back on its representation as soon as it felt it decently could. The same problems were reflected on the Vietnamese side, where able officers and civil officials hesitated to disrupt their normal career patterns to serve in "sideshow" programs like pacification.

Pressures for conformity, always strong in large hierarchical institutions, also militated against adaptiveness. An officer or official who wanted to do things differently often found that this was frowned upon rather than encouraged. Nor did funding or personnel procedures make experimentation easy. Though our Vietnam experience is replete with able men and promising experiments, all too few of the latter were followed up consistently, lasted long enough, or grew big enough to have significant impact (see Chapter 7).

INADEQUATE ANALYSIS OF PERFORMANCE

Yet a further reason why we were so slow to learn and adapt was the notable paucity of systematic analysis of performance—both in Washington and in the field. The irony is that such aggregative analysis proved well-nigh indispensable to understanding what was actually going on in so complex and multifaceted a conflict situation as Vietnam (a fact the U.S. media also never grasped). There is much to be said for the verdict of Enthoven and Smith as of end-1968:

> The problem was not too much analysis; it was too little. The President and his key advisors sought candid assessments of the war, but they would not pay the political costs in terms of friction with the military to get them. There was no systematic analysis in Vietnam of the allocation of resources to the different missions of the war and no systematic analysis of the effectiveness and costs of alternative military operations. Little operations analysis was being conducted in the field or in Washington. And even if all these analyses had been made, there was no good program budget or over-all organization in the Executive Branch of the government to put the findings to use on either the military or the civilian side.[10]

Their judgement seems a little harsh in some respects, particularly since some outstanding analytical work in fact was done by Enthoven's own Systems Analysis people in the Office of the Secretary of Defense. After 1966 it was extensively relied upon by the top decisionmakers in DOD, though largely ignored in the field. Indeed OSD/SA's *Southeast Asia Analysis Reports*, produced monthly or bimonthly from 1967 to 1973, provided in the author's judgement by far the best running analytical account of the course of the war.[11]

Also interesting is the sharp contrast between the extensive 1966–1968 analysis of the effectiveness of the air war against North Vietnam and the relative lack of such analysis of the ground war in the South (or of its associated air effort, which was even larger than that against the North). Because of the political sensitivity of the air campaign against North Vietnam, including the risks of triggering Soviet or Chinese intervention, the debate over it from 1965 through 1968 was buttressed by numerous analytical studies by CINCPAC, the Air Staff, and the JCS on the military side, and OSD/SA, CIA, and the Jason Study Group on the civilian side. These analyses had considerable impact on the 1968 decision to suspend the air war in the North and to switch the effort to the Ho Chi Minh Trail complex.[12]

In the field of tactical operations analysis, much more was done on the air side by the 7th Air Force, CINCPAC, and the Air Staff than was ever attempted for the ground war. It resulted in many tactical and technical improvements. This was partly because the problems involved were more amenable to analysis, and also because of greater prior experience with such studies on the part of the air establishments involved.

Even on the ground side, the OSD/SA analyses of the difficulty of winning the war by attrition influenced the 1967 and 1968 decisions to stabilize the U.S. force levels in South Vietnam (See Chapter 4). On the other hand, MACV never developed much capability to analyze U.S. or ARVN military performance. In line with the attrition strategy, the focus was mostly on such factors as casualty ratios and weapons-captured-to-weapons-lost ratios. Even these were regarded mostly as progress indicators. Little systematic attempt (comparable to that of OSD/SA) was made to discern operationally meaningful patterns.

Perhaps the most systematic attempt by MACV to collect useful data and analyze trends was made by its pacification advisory component—CORDS. This was deemed essential because "Analyses of 'pacification' and popular support for the GVN were much tougher to make than analyses of the military side of the war. The numerically analyzable aspects of progress were even fewer and less significant than those used for military operations. . . ."[13] Moreover, pre-1967 pacification reports had proved highly subjective and misleading. Hence CORDS created a sizable Research and Analysis Division and developed an array of new measurement systems which, while far from foolproof, provided a detailed and vastly improved picture of quantitative trends in the countryside. Then, beginning in 1969, systematic poll-type surveys of rural attitudes added greatly to our understanding. Yet even the pacifiers could in hindsight have usefully done a good deal more analysis than they did.

A particularly crucial analytical weakness was the lack of adequate program budgeting to show where the main costs were being incurred in relation to performance. Even a crude program budget of U.S./GVN costs by OSD/SA demonstrated that "the overwhelming bulk . . . was going into offensive operations, with relatively little into population security, pacification, and related programs. . . ."[14] The author, who sought consistently to make this point and to encourage more such analysis, believes that greater attention to costs and cost/benefit ratios would have facilitated a more balanced, effective, and less costly effort than that actually employed.

Among the reasons for this comparative paucity of systematic analysis, institutional factors bulk large. Organizations are usually neither long on self-criticism nor very receptive to outside analysis of their performance. For example, the Chairman of the JCS at least twice formally complained to the Secretary of Defense about the Southeast Asia Analysis Reports of OSD/SA. Enthoven and Smith stress such considerations in assessing why more systematic analyses were not done by the U.S. establishment in Saigon:

First, the leaders in Vietnam were not studying "theoretical" questions of this kind. They were extremely busy with the enormous day-to-day operating problems posed by the massive American build-up, the ubiquity and effectiveness of the VC/NVA attacks, and the condition of the South Vietnamese allies. In the beginning, staving off defeat was such a clear purpose that there seemed to be no need for a searching evaluation of long-range objectives. Unfortunately, this pattern was to persist. Secondly, typically the environment of a military staff, especially one serving a field commander, is not conducive to a self-critical evaluation of alternative strategies. Rather, the whole spirit of such an operation stresses teamwork. An officer who articulates and defends a policy different from the official position can expect to suffer in his fitness reports and subsequent promotions. Third, military staff and field commanders had a one-year tour and usually more than one job within the year, so that there was little time to assimilate the lessons of the war. Fourth, the leaders had no alternative strategy and so no incentive to make calculations that would call into question the strategy of attrition. Alternatives suggested from outside the command, such as General Gavin's "enclave strategy," were received by many in Saigon (and in Washington) as threatening criticisms to be rebutted rather than given serious analytical consideration.

Why did the Joint Chiefs not perform such analyses and report such conclusions to the President and the Secretary of Defense? Largely because the JCS made virtually no independent analysis of the Vietnam war. They viewed their role as supporters of the commanders in Vietnam and the Pacific. They used the vast flow of data from Vietnam as input material for keeping themselves informed of daily events in the war so that they could better argue General Westmoreland's case to top civilian officials. They did not attempt to organize the data for systematic assessment of strategy. They did not even establish an analysis group until late 1967, and then denied it the leeway necessary to analyze basic questions. In short, the JCS had no desire to second-guess General Westmoreland. The President and Secretary of Defense always consulted the JCS before making decisions, but the advice was absolutely predictable: do what General Westmoreland and Admiral Sharp ask, and increase the size of the remaining forces in the United States.[15]

Moreover, the "can do" spirit of the JCS and their loyal disinclination to quarrel with their civilian masters also inhibited the learning process. General Bruce Palmer severely criticizes them for never telling the civilians that what we were doing wouldn't work. "Not once during the war did the JCS advise the commander-in-chief or the secretary of defense that the strategy being pursued would probably be unable to achieve its objectives."[16] Col. Summers describes Army Chief of Staff Harold Johnson's anguished regret in retrospect that he had not gone to President Johnson and resigned over LBJ's refusal to mobilize the reserves, which denied much hope of ultimate victory.[17]

In sum, in an atypical situation that cried out for innovation and adaptation, a series of institutional constraints militated against them. For the most part, as Herman Kahn has aptly put it, Vietnam reflected a "business as usual" approach. Bureaucratic inertia, lack of institutional memory and other factors powerfully inhibited the learning process. In true bureaucratic fashion, each U.S. and GVN agency preferred to do more of what it was already used to doing rather than change accepted patterns of organization or operation. All this contributed to the failure of the U.S. support and advisory effort, despite the huge investments made, to generate an adequate GVN and RVNAF response to the challenges faced. It also helps answer the question why the enormous direct U.S. contribution to the war—almost 550,000 troops at peak, thousands of aircraft, and many billions of dollars—had such limited impact for so long.

NOTES

1. Richard M. Pfeffer, *No More Vietnams?*, Harper and Row, New York, 1968, p. 211.

2. Vannevar Bush, *Pieces of Action*, William Morrow, New York, 1970, p. 28. See also Chapters 11 and 111.

3. Pfeffer, *No More Vietnams?*, p. 100.

4. James C. Thomson, "How Could Vietnam Happen?" *Atlantic*, April 1968, p. 209

5. Samuel Huntington in *No More Vietnams?* p. 111.

6. *United States–Vietnam Relations, 1945–1967: Study Proposal by the Department of Defense*, 12 Volumes, U. S. Government Printing Office, Washington D.C., 1971 (hereafter referred to as the *Pentagon Papers*), IV.B.3, p. 29.

7. In 1967–1968 the author persuaded the Secretary of the Army and Army Chief of Staff to approve moving dependents to nearby countries like Thailand or the Philippines for selected CORDS advisors who accepted twenty-four month tours.

8. See R.W. Komer, *The Malayan Emergency in Retrospect: Organization of a Successful Counterinsurgency Effort*, The Rand Corporation, R-957-ARPA, February 1972.

9. Dennis Duncanson, *Government and Revolution in Vietnam*, Oxford University Press, New York and London, 1968, p. 273.

10. Alain C. Enthoven and K. Wayne Smith, *How Much is Enough?* Harper and Row, New York, 1969, p. 307.

11. Thomas Thayer, *War Without Fronts*, Westview Press, Boulder, CO, forthcoming, summarizes the key analyses made by OSD/SA.

12. See the *Pentagon Papers*, IV.C.6(a) and (b).

13. Enthoven and Smith, *How Much is Enough?*, p. 300.

14. Ibid., p. 294.

15. Ibid., pp. 299–300.

16. Bruce Palmer, *The 25-Year War: Americans Military Role in Vietnam,* University Press of Kentucky, Lexington, KY, 1984, p. 46.

17. Harry Summers Jr., "Palmer, Karnow and Herrington: A Review of Recent Vietnam War Histories," *Parameters*, U.S. Army War College, Carlisle Barracks, PA, Spring 1985, p. 81.

6
LACK OF UNIFIED MANAGEMENT

The very way in which the U.S. and GVN "managed" their roles in the Vietnam conflict created another series of institutional constraints which seriously limited their ability to overcome the problems already discussed. In retrospect, the diffusion of authority and fragmentation of command characterizing both the U.S. and the GVN efforts (and the inter-relationship between them) do much to explain why it proved so hard for so long to translate Vietnam policy into practice or to convert our overwhelming superiority in manpower and resources into operational results. They placed serious institutional constraints on GVN/U.S. performance in Vietnam.

In the Malayan insurgency, the British soon grasped the need for highly integrated civil-military/U.K.-Malayan conflict management, which proved crucial to their success.[1] In contrast, the U.S. and GVN at no time during the entire 1955–1971 period went far enough toward pulling together all the disparate facets of their anti-VC/NVA effort under some kind of unified conflict management. At a seminar held at the Royal United Service Institution (RUSI) in February 1969 on "Lessons from the Vietnam War," a group of senior British officers and civilians concluded that this lack of unified command in the field was one of the major errors made.[2]

This also contrasted strongly with the enemy's approach. Townsend Hoopes, an experienced management consultant, comments on the disparity:

For the enemy the war remained fundamentally . . . a seamless web of political-military-psychological factors to be manipulated by a highly centralized command authority that never took its eye off the political goal of ultimate control in the South. For the United States, however, the war had become by October 1967 a complex of three separate, or only loosely related, struggles: there was the large-scale, conventional war . . . the confused "pacification" effort . . . and the curiously remote air war against North Vietnam . . .[3]

Sir Robert Thompson too sees "all through the period an unfortunate tendency to regard the war being three wars" and finds that it resulted from "lack of unified control."[4]

Who was responsible for conflict management of the Vietnam war? The bureaucratic fact is that below Presidential level everybody and nobody was responsible for coping with it in the round. With relatively few exceptions, neither the U.S. Government nor the GVN set up any specialized planning or operating agencies to meet atypical needs. Nor was there much overall coordinating or supervisory machinery for pulling together disparate programs within the U.S. Government and GVN or between these two allies. Instead both governments were organized conventionally, with little room for large-scale activities that cut across traditional agency lines.

The way in which both governments ran the war in largely separate bureaucratic compartments, with each government and each agency within it largely "doing its own thing," had a significant adverse impact on its effective prosecution. Such diffusion of responsibility diluted managerial focus and limited the degree of adaptability needed to meet the special circumstances found in Vietnam. It encouraged instead what Stanley Hoffman describes as "parochialism . . . the inevitable concomitant of fragmentation" and "lack of imagination (or, more accurately, resistance to political creativity) in foreign policy."[5] And lack of adequate machinery for follow-through meant that even many policies that were adopted were never actually carried out in the intended way.

Lack of any overall management structure contributed to the overmilitarization of the war by facilitating the predominance of the U.S. and GVN military in its conduct. This in turn led to the tail wagging the dog, with everything else required to conform. Moreover, "The complete lack of balance and of coordination between military operations and civil programmes" also contributed to "the many harmful side effects of the war—refugees, inflation, nepotism, draft dodging, black markets and corruption."[6]

Though the U.S. military at any rate were quite responsive to civilian leadership, that leadership not only lacked machinery for exerting civilian control but for various reasons exerted relatively little influence over how the military functioned in the field. It is a serious misnomer to think that Lyndon Johnson and Robert McNamara ran the war from Washington; they did recurrently impose limits on out-of-country operations such as bombing North Vietnam. But these operations were far smaller than those within South Vietnam.

If anything, the "problem was not overmanagement of the war from Washington, it was undermanagement." In supporting this verdict, Enthoven and Smith point to "a deep resistance to trying to run the war from Washington."[7] This was certainly true of the JCS. Except for setting political limits on out-of-country operations and determining the level of manpower and resource allocations, Washington left the conduct of the war mostly to Saigon. And there the U.S. Ambassador, though the titular head, in practice left the military side of the war almost entirely to COMUSMACV.

By the same token counterinsurgency (or pacification) fell between stools. It was everybody's business and nobody's. The absence of a single major agency or directing machinery charged with it contributed greatly to the prolonged failure to press it on a large scale. McNamara himself, in his pessimistic October 1966 trip report to the President, noted that "a part of the problem undoubtedly lies in bad management on the American as well as the GVN side. Here split responsibility— or 'no responsibility'—has resulted in too little hard pressure on the GVN to do its job and no really solid or realistic planning with respect to the whole effort."[8]

Lack of unified management also diluted control over the oft-noted proliferation of overlapping GVN and U.S. programs—to the point where they competed excessively for scarce resources and even got in each other's way. One consequence of GVN and U.S. attempts to deal with the unusual requirements of insurgency war through the existing bureaucratic structure was a plethora of programs conducted by different agencies, each jealously guarding its own prerogatives and insistent on its own procedures. Add to U.S.-sponsored programs those created by the GVN, and the list is long indeed. Ambassador Taylor notes that by early 1965 "about sixty programs" were being conducted under the aegis of the U.S. Mission.[9] Starting in 1967 some of these were gradually pulled closer together according to central pacification plans agreed upon by the U.S. and GVN, but their field execution was still highly diffused. For example, a province chief did not control the budgets of the provincial technical services. These were developed and administered exclusively by the ministries in Saigon.

Another consequence of GVN/U.S. utilization of essentially peace-time management structures was the use of mostly peacetime planning, programming, financial, resource allocation, and distribution procedures, which changed only slowly under pressure. The extent to which these procedures inhibited flexible and timely adaptation to counterinsurgency needs has been frequently remarked upon and deserves fuller examination than is feasible here. As might be expected—since they were not designed to cope with wartime exigencies—the civilian agencies were far more hidebound than the military. Most AID procedures, designed for conventional assistance programs, were particularly cumbersome and slow moving.

However, even U.S. military logistic support—generally one of the brighter aspects of U.S. performance in Vietnam—was constrained to an extent by the high-level U.S. decisions to deal with Vietnam essentially via the existing U.S. military establishment (only gradually expanded) and via largely peacetime procedures. The Besson Board report, in drawing logistic lessons for Vietnam experience, cautiously alludes to this problem in many instances.[10]

Last but not least, lack of combined U.S./GVN management machinery seriously inhibited U.S. ability to secure better performance from the South Vietnamese. It deprived the U.S. of an institutional framework for exerting influence toward the solution of problems which it recognized as critical from the outset. Though South Vietnam's leadership and administrative weaknesses undermined its ability to cope with the VC threat—indeed led in time to a felt need for direct U.S. intervention—the U.S. did little even after its intervention to create machinery for overcoming these weaknesses. Instead, the U.S. ended up largely taking over the war from the GVN. By doing so we tended to undermine South Vietnamese initiative and self reliance, which took its toll when South Vietnam was on its own again.

As will be seen, many such suggestions were made for improving U.S. and interallied conflict management. Secretary McNamara, more than any other key official, kept raising these issues. He proposed a DOD-led task force in 1961, proconsular power for the Ambassador in 1964, combined command in 1965, and unifying the U.S. civil-military pacification support effort in 1966. He apparently didn't push very hard, however, probably because of the difficulty of overcoming the many service and non-DOD interests eager to preserve the status quo.

U.S. CONFLICT MANAGEMENT— WHO RAN THE STORE IN WASHINGTON?

By and large, the U.S. ran its share of the war with an essentially peacetime management structure. Cooper notes how, even after the war escalated, no Vietnam "high command" emerged to coordinate all aspects of Washington war management. "Nor, even in the Pentagon, was there a single focal point—a 'Mr. Vietnam.'"[11] Few major changes were made in Washington to unify conflict management, even after the direct U.S. force commitment grew to proportions exceeding that in the Korean War. Instead, we mostly made do with what structure existed at the time. This is not to say that top officials neglected the war. On the contrary, the President and his top advisers probably spent even more time on it than would have been necessary if the supporting structure had been better organized.[12] The President himself spent a great deal of time following the war in detail, as did necessarily his White House national security staff, particularly his Special Assistant for National Security Affairs. The same was true of the Secretaries of State and Defense, and the Chairman of the Joint Chiefs of Staff.

Nor was there any lack of field visits, meetings, conferences, study groups, and staff inputs. President Kennedy sent several fact-finding missons to Vietnam in 1961 alone. The periodic trips of the Secretary of Defense were another important device for management review and proposing decisions. They linked together Washington and the field. But such informal liaison and occasional ad hoc committees were the order of the day. The war management process was basically one of ad hoc interaction between the key agencies, with little formal machinery created—especially for systematic planning, programming, and follow-through. Below the top there was very little structure for pulling together the many interlocking strands of counterinsurgency/quasi-conventional war.

If the *Pentagon Papers* are any guide, Washington-level management issues were only infrequently addressed in the welter of high-level discussions on programs and force levels during 1955–1965. One interesting early attempt was in April 1961, apparently at the instigation of General Lansdale. Walt Rostow advised the new president that "gearing up" our Vietnam response needed "the appointment of a fulltime first-rate backstop man in Washington. McNamara, as well as your staff, believes this to be essential."[13] When Kennedy asked Deputy Secretary of Defense Gilpatric for a Vietnam action program, the latter set up a high-level interagency task force sparked by Lansdale to provide it. Gilpatric's report called for not only a substantially increased U.S. aid and advisory effort but creation of an ongoing Presidential Task Force to provide "overall direction, interagency coordination and support" for the proposed programs. Gilpatric was to head it, and Lansdale was to go to Vietnam as expediter and coordinator.[14] But this most unusual proposal never had much chance. Bureaucratic politics promptly intervened. State objected successfully to such roles for Gilpatric and Lansdale. Having an ambassador report to a task force chaired by the Deputy Secretary of Defense with Lansdale as his executive apparently was too much for the Department of State to swallow.[15]

Instead, a middle-level career diplomat, Sterling Cottrell, took over leadership of what was "downgraded to a conventional interagency working group."[16] When Cottrell left in 1963, only an action officer-level Vietnam Working Group was continued. In 1964 a slightly higher-level interagency Vietnam Coordinating Committee under William Sullivan (later Leonard Unger) was again formed. While given direct access to the Secretary of State, in practice it served mainly as a vehicle for middle-level exchange of ideas.

In any case, the laboring oar on Vietnam remained mostly with Defense. As Arthur Schlesinger comments, the very composition of the October 1961 Taylor-Rostow Mission (the absence of a comparable senior State official) apparently connoted "a conscious decision by the Secretary of State to turn the Vietnam problem over to the Secretary of Defense."[17] The State Department retained its titular coordinating role as *primus inter pares* among the great national security bureaucracies, but this existed more in theory than in practice— at least on Vietnam. General Taylor complains that State, which should have assumed a supervisory and coordinating role in Washington, did not. Later Taylor, by then a presidential consultant, engineered a new interdepartmental committee system in early 1966, designed to strengthen the State Department role. But as he sadly notes, it did not rise to the challenge, playing no role on Vietnam.[18]

Nonetheless, some steps were taken to strengthen Washington management as U.S. intervention grew. An informal "war cabinet" gradually developed in late 1965 or so, at what became known as the "Tuesday Lunch" in the White House family dining room. Originally it consisted only of the President, Rusk, McNamara, McGeorge Bundy (later Rostow), and Bill Moyers (later George Christian). The author too sat in frequently during 1966–1967. Later the Tuesday Lunch was expanded to include CIA Director Helms, the Chairman of the JCS, and others.[19] It provided an invaluable forum for intimate top-level discussions but had no full-time machinery to support it.

At least one senior military man—General Harold K. Johnson (Army Chief of Staff) believed that

> close integration of the political, economic, information, security, and military branches of government is essential to ensure a concentration of effort against an insurgency. One must constantly keep foremost in

mind that military action is only a part of counterinsurgency and that a well integrated "team" can often compound a military success or minimize a failure.[20]

General Johnson commissioned the massive PROVN study by an Army staff team, which in March 1966 decried the lack of unified Washington backup for Vietnam and prescribed a Special Assistant to the President for Vietnam Affairs to "coordinate" on the President's behalf the five separate and often competing agency efforts involved in Vietnam. Its greatest direct impact was on the author's own subsequent proposals for reorganizing pacification management.

However, growing concern over the neglect of the paramilitary and civil dimensions of the Vietnam conflict, and the by then apparent inability of the agencies concerned to pull it together and provide it wartime impetus, did lead eventually to perhaps the only major U.S. organizational innovations of the Vietnam war. A group of senior officials convened at Warrenton in January 1966 to consider how to develop more of a pacification effort in Vietnam also pointed to the need for better Washington backup arrangements.[21] This theme was picked up at the February 1966 Honolulu conference, where the U.S. side acknowledged that improvement of U.S. organization was essential. In order to balance our military effort by doing more to win what President Johnson termed "the other war," the new Deputy Ambassador to Saigon, William J. Porter, was told to pull together and direct all U.S. support efforts not under MACV—the beginning of a process which led to the unified pacification advisory effort of 1967 (See chapter 7). However, Porter regarded his new role "primarily as a coordinating effort," and genuine unified management was not to be achieved till mid-1967.[22]

After some interagency debate as to whether Washington backup for the "other war" should be in State or in the White House, the President resolved the issue by appointing the author in late March 1966 his White House Special Assistant to oversee it. What this "other war" encompassed was left deliberately vague, except that it clearly excluded what was by then called "McNamara's War." On the other hand, the new Assistant's charter charged him with "supervision," not just coordination—a unique grant of management authority to a White House staff officer.[23] The new Assistant, with a small but select staff, did manage to help pull together and impart some vigor to the "other war" effort.[24] But the post was in effect downgraded by the President after the author was transferred to Vietnam in mid-1967.

In late 1966, at the author's suggestion, President Johnson also set up a highly informal subcabinet group, chaired by Under Secretary of State Katzenbach, to think through the knotty problems of the war. Informally called the "non-group," it met fairly frequently—particularly after mid-1967—but did not seem to play much of a role. Fortunately, the Nixon Administration restructured the group, and formalized it as the Vietnam Special Studies Group of the NSC, chaired by the President's Assistant for National Security Affairs and supported by an interagency working group.

Another management change sparked by the author was the creation in early 1967 of a separate Vietnam Bureau in AID, headed by an Assistant Administrator, to deal full-time with Vietnam programs, which by then took up over one-fourth of the total AID budget. In DOD, however, the only pre-1969 organizational innovations were DDR&E's creation of a special deputy to pull together and expedite R&D for Southeast Asia, and the special arrangements made for the new "sensor" program. CIA also created a small analytical staff under George Carver in the Director's own office.

Aside from these modest efforts, however, there was little systematic attempt to bring together interagency and even intra-agency Washington management of the Vietnam war.[25] Instead, each of the agencies basically sought to cope with Vietnam requirements through its own peacetime management structure, without much effort even to design special procedures to meet wartime exigencies. Aside from those mentioned in the previous paragraph, not a single senior-level official above the rank of office director or colonel in any U.S. agency dealt full-time with Vietnam before 1969.

The Nixon Administration created more formal committees, but the situation did not basically change. The Under Secretary-level Vietnam Special Studies Group headed by Henry Kissinger met infrequently and apparently did not play a continuing policy or management role. The real work was done by a group of able analysts on Kissinger's own staff, who provided the White House with an important analytic capability which did not exist before. In mid-1969 DOD finally created a full-time Vietnam Task Force headed by a brigadier general and then a major general, with a small staff. It briefed the Secretary, but was layered under the Deputy Assistant Secretary of Defense for East Asia/Pacific Affairs. Under the Task Force was an intra-DOD Vietnamization task group with observers from other U.S. agencies. All these groups may have led to more systematic policy coordination, but they did not add up to unified Washington management in any sense.

WHO WAS IN CHARGE IN SAIGON?

Generally the same lack of unified U.S. conflict management characterized the situation in the field. Hilsman points out that

> From the beginning, the United States effort lacked both the "unified civilian political, and military system of command and control" and the subordination of civic, police, social, and military measures to an over-all counter guerrilla program that were the first principles of the strategic concept that had been worked out.[26]

In particular, the thorny issue of U.S. civil and military command relationships was never addressed head-on in Vietnam, despite full recognition that it existed.

When the MAAG in Vietnam was complemented in 1962 by a military assistance command (MACV), the question of giving its commander a directive "consistent with the desire of the President for unity of responsibility for all activities related to the counterinsurgency effort" was addressed, but the solution left him still essentially independent of the Ambassador.[27] MACV finally absorbed the MAAG in 1964, and later became a full-scale theater headquarters pulling together the U.S. military effort in South Vietnam. It did business directly with Washington, but also had to deal partly through CINCPAC and the satellite service component commands set up in World War II to control multifront Pacific operations. CINCPAC also had primary responsibility for out-of-country air operations. It is an open question whether this intervening bureaucratic layer was a net help or a hindrance when Vietnam was our only war. "Serious consideration had been given during 1964 to eliminating CINCPAC from the chain of command between Washington and Saigon."[28] But this never happened.

All of the civilian agencies dealt directly with their missions in Vietnam. Overcentralized management and unwieldy procedures requiring constant reference to Washington inhibited flexible responses, especially in AID programs.[29] Forrestal and Hilsman reported to President Kennedy, in an "Eyes Only" annex to their early 1962 trip report, that "the real trouble . . . is that the rather large U.S. effort in South Vietnam is managed by a multitude of independent U.S. agencies and people with little or no overall direction."[30]

But it remained to the end a conventional "country team" operation, with the Ambassador the acknowledged senior and usually able to veto or modify those policies or proposals of other agencies to which he objected. He kept abreast of developing problems and dealt with interagency disputes through weekly meetings of a Mission Council composed of the top U.S. officials in Vietnam (the Council was established by Ambassador Taylor). In general, however, no American ambassador ever imposed positive, consistent, unified control on U.S. agency operations in Vietnam. As Thompson remarks, "Americans are averse to the appointment of pro-consuls but that is what the situation demanded."[31]

During 1958–1961 Ambassador Durbrow was several times unable to overcome disagreements with the MAAG. His successor, Nolting, apparently sought greater authority to pull together the growing U.S. civilian and military effort, but was "rebuffed."[32] By late 1963, when Lodge took over as Ambassador, the U.S. Mission in Saigon was already one of our biggest, and the problems of pulling it together loomed even larger. It is regrettable that Lodge was no manager, as he understood the Vietnam problem better than most. By 1964 the President, increasingly concerned over the Saigon management problem, urged on Lodge "a top ranking officer who is wholly acceptable to you as chief of staff for country team operations. My own impression is that this should be either a newly appointed civilian of wide governmental experience and high standing, or General Westmoreland. . . ."[33] But Lodge resisted.

When Lodge left in mid-1964, the need for stronger and more unified management played a role in the President's selection of the Chairman of the JCS, Maxwell Taylor, to replace him. Reportedly on the advice of Sir Robert Thompson that a Malaya-style proconsul was needed, McNamara successfully urged that the nation's foremost soldier be put in unquestioned charge of the entire U.S. effort. That President Johnson agreed is clear from the unprecedented authority he gave Taylor in a special letter. Having reaffirmed the Ambassador's overall responsibility to oversee and coordinate all U.S. activities in-country, the President added: "I wish it clearly understood that this overall responsibility includes the whole U.S. military effort in South Vietnam and authorize the degree of command and control that you consider appropriate." To assist him, Taylor was also given a strong deputy, U. Alexis Johnson, in the newly created post of Deputy Ambassador.[34]

But they apparently became far too preoccupied with the chaotic succession of coups in Saigon to make much use of these unprecedented powers. In fact, General Taylor's comments in retrospect make clear that he saw little need for major changes in the U.S. organization in Vietnam. Rather, as a professional military man, he was more concerned over whether his new mandate "could be interpreted to conflict with the responsibility of . . . CINCPAC . . . and the Joint Chiefs of Staff for the conduct of military operations, and thus would . . . put General Westmoreland in the unhappy position of having two military masters."[35] So, rather than exploit his unique directive, he took pains to assure these military colleagues that he did not intend to disturb the existing arrangements.

When Lodge returned in August 1965, he was given a mandate similar to Taylor's but never used it either.[36] Lodge did bring out General Lansdale again, with a small but talented team designated the Mission Liaison Group, to work with the GVN on pacification and political action. But a combination of bureaucratic hassles undercut Lansdale's role, and he left in frustration in 1968.[37]

The need for stronger management kept being raised in Washington and was usually resisted by the Mission. For example, in March 1965, when Army Chief of Staff Johnson visited Saigon, putting U.S. civilian pacification support under MACV was considered but rejected by Ambassador Taylor and General Westmoreland.[38] The Army staff's PROVN study of March 1966 also recommended that the U.S. Ambassador be designated a "single manager" with operational control over the entire U.S. effort in Vietnam, and that he be provided a supraagency planning staff to help him.

In the event, divided responsibility in the U.S. Mission in Saigon persisted to the end, with only two significant exceptions. The *Pentagon Papers* aptly describe the problem:

> Skeptics have said that whenever things are going poorly "Americans reorganize." But the opponents of various reorganization schemes have been unable to defend the existing Mission Council system, which must definitely be rated one of Vietnam's casualties. Not since the beginning of the "country team" concept in the 1950s (Mission Council being another name for the same structure) had the concept been tested the way it was to be tested in Vietnam. The pressure of events, the tension, the unprecedented size of the agencies, and a host of other factors made the system shaky even under the strong manager Maxwell Taylor. Under the man who didn't want to manage, Lodge, it began to crumble. Each agency had its own ideas on what had to be done, its own communication channels with Washington, its own personnel and administrative structure—and starting in 1964–1965, each agency began to have its own field personnel operating under separate and parallel chains of command, This latter event was ultimately to prove the one which gave reorganization efforts such force, since it began to become clear to people in Washington and Saigon alike that the Americans in

the provinces were not always working on the same team, and that they were receiving conflicting or overlapping instructions from a variety of sources in Saigon and Washington.[39]

After many fits and starts, Washington did finally force a consolidation of all U.S. pacification support efforts in mid-1967 (see Chapter 7), which unified all U.S. field advisers—civil and military—under MACV.[40] Earlier, a small Joint U.S. Public Affairs Office (JUSPAO) had been created in 1965 to pull together U.S. civil/military psychological operations at the Saigon level (though MACV retained responsibility for tactical psyops). Interestingly, Barry Zorthian, the first civilian director of JUSPAO, is an outspoken critic of the lack of unified management structures:

> Some of the most astute observers in Vietnam insist that the greatest contribution made by the Viet Cong to the art of insurgency has been organization—and there is much to be said for the theory. Conversely, it might be argued with considerable validity that the greatest American weakness in Vietnam was organization. In effect, we sought to conduct our portion of the effort for many years through the mechanism of a bureaucratic structure designed for normal government operations in Washington. We worked closely with a military that, like the military in all underdeveloped countries, was intensely political—and told our own military to stay out of the political aspects, a restriction our own military accepted much too willingly. Similarly, our civilian agencies—State, AID and USIA—avoided the military aspect of the effort for too long. Only the CIA tried to bridge the gap but it was too inhibited by its very nature to serve the purpose. It was not until the late stages of the war that some of these artificial barriers began to break down—and, in truth, we must recognize that the essential erasing of agency distinctions was never complete, nor was command and responsibility in Vietnam ever truly unified under one chief.[41]

WEAKNESS OF GVN CONFLICT MANAGEMENT

The same attempt to cope with the unconventional via a conventional organized government structure typified the GVN as well. Basically, the GVN attempted to deal with a life-and-death struggle through a traditional array of French-style ministries only loosely pulled together at the top. Diem inherited a fledgling French-style army and civil administration, centralized in character. He and Nhu centralized it even further, and otherwise perverted it for their own political ends. Archaic civil service procedures, mostly inherited from the French, were another impediment to timely, flexible responses: The military war was run by the President himself dealing directly with corps and division commanders. The Joint General Staff did not have operational control over the latter. The civilian ministries dealt mostly with the Prime Minister.

Throughout U.S. reports and critiques from the late Fifties on run criticisms of this inadequate GVN organization and administration. But over seventeen years the U.S. made little sustained effort to press for changes that were repeatedly seen as essential—except in the regular military establishment and, belatedly, in pacification. As early as September 1960, a JCS-approved CINCPAC study called for encouraging the GVN "to adopt a national emergency organization to integrate civil and military resources under centralized direction for the conduct of counterinsurgency operations." A detailed draft plan was sent to the MAAG stressing the need to appoint a National Emergency Council and a Director of Operations for this purpose, and to formulate a National Counterinsurgency Plan.[42] The GVN complied on paper, but little happened.

Then the Rusk-McNamara Memorandum of November 11, 1961 recommending action on the Taylor Report, proposed that in return for more U.S. support the GVN be required to undertake "establishment of appropriate governmental wartime agencies with adequate authority to perform their functions effectively" and "overhaul of the military establishment and command structure so as to create an effective military organization for the prosecution of the war."[43] This was never done by Diem in any meaningful way. Galbraith saw such reforms as decisive, and in the event he was proved right.[44]

Like the U.S. the GVN attempted few organizational innovations in conflict management. True, from the Interministerial Committee om Strategic Hamlets created by Diem in February 1962 through Khanh's making Hoan his Vice Premier for Pacification and creating a shadow National Security Council in 1964, there were recurrent efforts to create a GVN supervisory machinery. But this existed more on paper than in practice.[45] At various times interagency provincial, regional, and central pacification committees were created or revived. But not until 1969 did a GVN Central Pacification and Development Council acquire shape and substance, and meet regularly under the personal aegis of the President amd Prime Minister. Equally important, it was given a full-time staff (57 by end-1971) under a competent Secretary General (Lt. Gen. Cao Hao Hon), which prepared plans and monitored performance. Another notable departure was the creation of a Ministry of Revolutionary Development (a much expanded version of Diem's old Civic Action Directorate) in late 1965 to spark a revived pacification effort. It is discussed in Chapter 7. But the overall weaknesses of GVN conflict management persisted to the end, as became amply evident in 1975.[46]

WHY SUCH FRAGMENTED CONFLICT MANAGEMENT?

Why did both the U.S.and the GVN settle for such conventional, diffuse, and fragmented management structures—in contrast to an enemy who practiced so high a degree of centralized control over all his activities? Here is one more example of perceptions outrunning performance. The truism that a complex politico-military insurgency conflict like that in Vietnam required a multifaceted response was early recognized. Thus it is surprising that, when we saw its need so clearly, and so many advocated at various times management changes to help generate better GVN and U.S. performance, we did so little to create the necessary machinery. Senior officials did recurrently focus on this problem. However, we didn't ever do enough about it.

In part, especially in the period before U.S. intervention, this was a consequence of the gradualism inherent in the U.S. approach to Vietnam. Not until late in the day did our Vietnam problems appear so overwhelming as to demand exceptional efforts to deal with them. But even then we remained reluctant to take the obvious managerial steps which some advocated. Cooper attributes this reluctance to a persistent belief that the war was likely to be over soon, once the U.S. intervened. In this case, "why wrench the system?"[47] However, long after we realized that this hope was an illusion, the same reluctance persisted. So we must search further for the reasons why.

In part, as the *Pentagon Papers* show, it is because we simply did not focus enough on how to best to translate policy into performance in Vietnam. The structuring of adequate conflict management was not given much priority among the many critical issues we confronted. Somehow neither the U.S. nor the GVN at various levels seemed to stress sufficiently the need for management reorganization to optimize the multifaceted response which their perceptions told them was essential to an effective counterinsurgency effort. As Thompson points out, the sheer wealth of available resources also lowered the premium on their optimum use. "In Vietnam resources were constantly substituted for efficiency and organization."[48]

The Americans at any rate were conscious from early on of the need to restructure the GVN to confront more effectively the challenges it faced. Why they failed for so long to have much impact was discussed in Chapter 3. Also at play was the reluctance of Vietnamese leadership groups at various times to risk redistributing power, notably in the case of Diem. Moreover, it must be granted that the GVN faced a dual task of governing and fighting, whereas the enemy could gear his whole organization in the South to defeating the GVN.

But again institutional constraints help provide at least partial explanations as to why neither the U.S. nor the GVN optimally structured itself for the task it faced. Bureaucratic inertia—sheer reluctance to change accepted ways of doing business except slowly and incrementally—appears to have been a major factor. The organizational politics involved in shifting the distribution of power also played a role, each proposal for change arousing the protective instincts of the various departments, agencies, and ministries concerned. These institutions had long since carved out their respective operational areas, and were generally careful not to violate the conventional dividing lines between their responsibilities.

Such a dividing line was especially noticeable between military and civilian agencies. By and large, the civilian agencies steered clear of the military's business and did not exert much influence on the conduct of military operations. In turn, the military long eschewed involvement in police and pacification matters, which they regarded as civilian business. When jurisdictional issues arose, as in the case of CIA use of U.S. Special Forces personnel, these were usually resolved by a return to the traditional relationships.

Reluctance to change the traditional relationship of civilian versus military leadership, even in a highly atypical conflict, was also a powerful institutional constraint. This is not a question of ultimate military responsiveness to civilian authority, which was rarely at issue in Vietnam, but rather one of relative spheres of responsibility. The British have a long tradition of subordinating the military to the local civil authorities in less than all-out conflict situations. In contrast, the U.S. military have had little such experience, and they have always been insistent on an independent role in wartime.

True, the president and secretary of defense made the final decisions on overall personnel ceilings and on the political constraints within which the military should operate outside South Vietnam (e.g., choosing eligible bombing targets in North Vietnam or deciding to suspend, and then to halt, bombing the North). However, they never infringed on the traditional military control over the conduct of the war inside South Vietnam. Nor did our ambassadors in Saigon. Many senior civilian officials in Saigon and Washington had distinct views on how to fight the war and often expressed their views, raised questions, requested studies, and the like. But by and large they left it to the military to decide how the war would be fought, even though they realized the political risks involved. The author at least cannot recall any major instances in which senior civilian officials (the President and White House staff, the State Department, the civilian leadership of DOD, or ambassadors in the field) directly intervened in the way the U.S. military ran its in-country war after 1965 (except in such admittedly civil/military fields as pacification). In commenting on McNamara's ambiguous role in the 1965 strategy debates (see Chapter 8), the *Pentagon Papers* state that "From the records, the Secretary comes out much more clearly for good management than he does for any particular strategy."[49]

Also at work was the institutional constraint inherent in the traditional relationship between Washington and its commanders in the field. It is part of the operational code of U.S. military institutions, in particular, to give great latitude to the field commander so long as he stays within the broad strategic or policy guidance given him. Traditionally, one either backs up one's field commander or changes him; hence, in the case of Vietnam, the JCS generally supported the field commander even when individual JCS members had reservations. Thus the military tended to present a united front to the civilian leadership.

In effect, the military was accorded "full autonomy" inside South Vietnam, without much supervision from Washington. "Westmoreland was the field commander and, in accordance with the traditional dictates of professional courtesy, Washington would not attempt to second-guess him."[50] During 1966–1968 at any rate, Washington did not issue COMUSMACV any new strategic guidance nor question the annual campaign plans which he submitted, despite the recommendations of General Taylor (who notes that COMUSMACV was thereby entitled to assume that his conduct of the war was wholly acceptable to Washington).[51] In late 1966 the author too pointed out the lack of any overall Washington directive to the field, and proposed a National Security Action Memorandum (NSAM). But the draft NSAM was pigeonholed because of agency efforts to insert too much special pleading.[52]

As to the lack of management structure in Washington for dealing with Vietnam, Hoopes sees the problem as arising largely from the decline of the NSC machinery under Kennedy and Johnson, and a parallel decline of long-range policy planning.[53] General Taylor similarly finds that the 1961 abolition of the NSC machinery led to a "lack of order" in addressing key security issues.[54] But the fact is that the Eisenhower era NSC Planning Board, NSC Staff, and Operations Coordination Board had never engaged in operational planning or follow-through. They were simply interagency coordinating bodies for broad policy papers or progress reports on their implementation. The author, who served in the NSC machinery under Eisenhower, Kennedy and Johnson, believes that they would have proved wholly unsuitable to the sort of conflict management under discussion here.

Chester Cooper, sharp critic of how Washington ran the war, focuses on President Johnson's "compulsive secrecy" and his preference for "tight personal control and loosely structured organizations."[55] The personal style of the presidents naturally affects the organizational machinery they prefer to utilize. But Washington's failure to organize better war management was the result of far deeper factors than this. Moreover, the record shows President Johnson and Secretary McNamara to have been far more sensitive to management problems than most other senior personalities involved. They themselves proposed several major initiatives, which usually were either rebuffed or frustrated by more conventional-minded key officials in Washington and Saigon. The author also found President Johnson most receptive to the various proposals he made on both Washington and Saigon management.

U.S. AND GVN FIGHT TWO SEPARATE WARS

Yet another major organizational constraint affecting the way the U.S. and GVN fought the war was the lack of any interallied conflict management. Despite America's massive contribution to the combined effort, its relationship to the GVN remained—from top to bottom—almost wholly advisory. While there were many proposals for and a few abortive experiments in combined machinery, the linkage between the U.S. and GVN remained informal and ad hoc from the outset. This was more understandable in the days of Diem, but even after direct U.S. intervention in 1965, we still fought what often seem in many respects—especially militarily—two separate wars.[56] Generals Westmoreland and Abrams both rightly favored what they termed the "one war" concept. However, this applied to integrating the various facets of the U.S. effort not to unification of allied war management, which neither advocated.

Instead of the U.S. being too conventional in this instance, it was—in light of its Korean and World War II experience—not conventional enough. The analogy to the Korean War comes quickly to mind. As the feeble South Korean (ROK) forces collapsed under the initial North Korean onslaught, a U.N. (really U.S.) Command was created and the ROK forces remained thereafter under this unified command. A variant was the incorporation of Korean contingents directly into U.S. units (the KATUSA concept). General Ridgway has pointed out how, as CINCUNC, he was also able to secure the relief of unsatisfactory ROK unit commanders as a recognized command function.

The frustrating experience of General Stilwell in wartime China is also relevant. When Stilwell was chosen to become Chief of Staff to Chiang in the latter's capacity as Supreme Commander China Theater, he told Secretary of War Stimson that the whole success of his mission would depend on whether Chiang would turn over any part of his army to American command.[57] Though Stilwell and the War Department kept pressing this issue, never more than a few Chinese divisions in Burma came under his command. Instead there ensued a frustrating struggle, in which Stilwell's pleas to let him use Lend-Lease as leverage to force the Chiang regime to perform were repeatedly denied by Washington. Not until mid-1944 did Roosevelt finally urge the Generalissimo to put Stilwell directly in command of all Chinese and U.S. forces.[58] What he got instead, after much Chinese evasion, was Chiang's insistence on Stilwell's recall.[59]

That the U.S. made no effort to develop full-scale machinery for combined U.S./GVN management before its direct intervention in 1965 is unsurprising. Our whole policy rationale was that this was the GVN's war. But various means of securing a greater U.S. role in GVN war management were recurrently considered even before 1965. When in 1961 Diem was thinking about forming a National Emergency Council patterned on our NSC, State asked Nolting whether Diem would consider including on it "a mature and hard-headed American . . . to participate in all decisions."[60] Both the Taylor Report of October 1961 and the subsequent Rusk-McNamara Memorandum to the President called for individual U.S. administrators and advisers to be inserted "into the governmental machinery of SVN in types and numbers to be agreed upon by the two Governments."[61]

President Kennedy accepted Taylor's concept that the United States should move beyond an advisory effort to a limited partnership with the GVN, in which "we would expect to share in the decisionmaking process in the political, economic, and military fields as they affect the security situation."[62] But Diem proved highly reluctant to risk looking like a U.S. puppet, and the U.S. backed away from enforcing that bargain.[63]

In the early Sixties Sir Robert Thompson fruitlessly proposed a Joint Operations Center on the Malayan model, to issue joint operational directives.[64] By early 1964, U.S. realization of how badly the situation had deteriorated, plus the demise of the xenophobic Diem, led Thompson to suggest that United States go even further and assume command. He recalls suggesting such a "proconsul" on the Malayan model to top Pentagon leaders shortly before Maxwell Taylor became Ambassador. But McNamara retreated in the face of opposition from U.S. officials in Saigon. In a memorandum to the President, which in March 1964 became NSAM 288, he stated:

U.S. Taking Over Command. It has been suggested that the U.S. move from its present advisory role to a role that would amount in practice to effective command. Again, the judgment of all senior people in Saigon, with which we concur, is that the possible military advantages of such action would be far out-weighed by its adverse psychological impact. It would cut across the whole basic picture of the Vietnamese winning their own war [*sic*] and lay us wide open to hostile propaganda both within South Vietnam and outside. Moreover, the present responsiveness of the GVN to our advice—although it has not yet reduced military reaction time—makes it less urgent [*sic*]. At the same time, MACV is steadily taking actions to bring U.S. and GVN operating staffs closer together at all levels, including joint operating rooms at key command levels.[65]

A more modest idea raised during the dark days of 1964–1965 was to infuse Americans directly into the GVN and RVNAF structure to jack up performance. As U.S. frustration over poor Vietnamese performance grew, civilian officials in Washington began urging this expedient, usually against field reluctance. In May 1964 State argued that, since the Khanh regime was failing to translate its "good" plans into effective action, the U.S. should abandon its passive advisory role. It suggested a Joint GVN/U.S. Pacification Operations Committee to spur implementation of these plans, interlarding key GVN ministries with U.S. officials, putting about ten American civil officials in each of seven lagging provinces, adding U.S. advisers to paramilitary units, and even putting some Americans down at district level.[66] Washington put on the agenda for the May 1964 Honolulu Conference such encadrement of U.S. civil and military personnel in the seven provinces; they were to be called "assistants" to GVN officials but would in fact "carry a major share of the burden of decision and action. . . ."[67] At highest-level request, the JCS also studied encadrement of U.S. teams with the Civil Guard (CG) and Self Defense Corps (SDC) along the lines of the earlier ill-fated White Star Teams in Laos. MACV poured cold water on this too.[68]

Washington kept pressing such expedients, especially in connection with the feeble pacification effort. They were raised again with Ambassador Taylor in early April 1965 and included in NSAM 328.[69] Soon thereafter Taylor was told that "the President has repeatedly emphasized his personal desire for a strong experiment in the encadrement of U.S. troops with the Vietnamese." Again MACV rejected the idea.[70] Washington also proposed integrating U.S. Army Civil Affairs teams experimentally into two province administrations, but Ambassador Taylor stepped on this as both destabilizing and duplicatory of what U.S. civilians were already doing.[71] In the end, all that took place was a modest increase in U.S. *advisers.*

It is more suprising that joint command as well as encadrement (which would have compelled some form of joint command) continued to get short shrift even after direct U.S. intervention in mid-1965, especially when it was the approaching collapse of ARVN forces that precipitated this fateful decision. Nighswonger cites a former MAAG chief as stating in 1965 that "he believed United States command in Vietnam was essential for victory."[72] Even General Westmoreland considered some form of U.S. command over ARVN units in his "Commander's Estimate" of March 1965, though he never actually proposed it.

Interestingly, combined command was also proposed by a Vietnamese, Prime Minister Quat, to Army Chief of Staff General Johnson during a Vietnam visit. General Johnson followed this up, when urging U.S. troop deployment in March 1965, by also recommending creation of a joint command. Ambassador Taylor found Quat's ideas of how to do this hazy but his purpose "very clear."

> He hopes by some joint command device to bring his maverick generals under the steadying influence of General Westmoreland. Taylor told him he sympathized with motive but had never hit upon a command arrangement which offered much hope of accomplishing this end. Although Quat's ideas are hard to disentangle, he seems to have in mind a mixed US/ARVN staff element reporting to General Westmoreland and a VN/C(ommand) Staff. He visualizes the staff element as a clearing house for joint studies which would pass recommendations on to the senior officers. By implication General Westmoreland would have the power of ultimate decision based upon an unofficial understanding which Quat hopes generals would accept. Quat concedes their acceptance far from certain.[73]

Westmoreland promptly opposed this, preferring informal cooperation and coordination.[74] He thought full command integration
should be deferred until some later time, when the GVN might be
better disposed. He suggested instead a limited joint staff under a
U.S. Brigadier General with a Vietnamese deputy, but Generals Thieu
and Minh opposed even this.[75] Nonetheless, in mid-May McNamara
authorized a formal combined command and staff. Since Ky and
Thieu had just publicly condemned any such idea in press interviews,
Taylor, Westmoreland, and CINCPAC again recommended against it
on essentially local "political" grounds. The *Pentagon Papers* ask,

> . . . why COMUSMACV (backed up without exception by the Ambassador
> and CINCPAC) uniformly opposed integrative measures designed to
> provide that which was and is almost an article of faith in the military
> profession—unity of command? U.S. troops in both World Wars and
> in Korea had fought under at least nominal command unity. There had
> been reservations for national integrity, to be sure, but the principle
> of unified command was both established and generally accepted. Why
> then did the U.S. military commander in Vietnam recommend against
> its adoption?
>
> The answer to this question is not to be found by an examination
> of military factors. The issue, rather, was a political one . . . The U.S.
> military leaders feared the exacerbations of US-SVN differences which
> they thought would accompany an overt Americanization of the war.
> They wished to increase U.S. influence in the conduct of the war but
> only as a result of persuasion and example. They tended to eschew
> the use of leverage. A unified command arrangement would have
> provided—assuming that a U.S. officer would have been the overall
> commander—an open and obvious means by which to exercise leverage.
> The U.S. leaders in Saigon rejected its adoption for this reason.
>
> The rejection of a unified military command is only one example
> of the tendency in 1965 to renounce leverage oriented mechanisms at
> the very time that the U.S. was committing major land forces to the
> war. It was as though the U.S. increased its determination to avoid
> arrangements which smacked of direct, open leverage at the same time
> that the inadequacy of earlier, indirect measures was made obvious by
> the deployment to South Vietnam of U.S. ground combat forces.[76]

McNamara returned to the attack on July 20, 1965 in a memorandum
to the President, calling this time for "a veto on major GVN commanders."[77] According to General Taylor, "many leading American
officials, including some senior military officers" favored from the
beginning of the U.S. troop buildup giving Westmoreland operational

control over ARVN forces on the Korean War model. But Westmoreland and Taylor were opposed, and their view prevailed.[78]

Despite the growing U.S. commitment and the continuing frustrations over how to get better Vietnamese performance, the combined command idea was rarely officially raised again. Even the PROVN study, which urged unified control of the U.S. effort in Washington and Saigon, played down this idea. When the author suggested it informally in 1966, McNamara reiterated Westmoreland's objections. The author again fruitlessly suggested it in his final report to the President in April 1967 "as a means of getting more out of RVNAF. . . ."[79] Under Secretary of State Katzenbach also raised it separately at the same time for the same reason, and repeated it in June.[80] He apparently struck no spark either.

Various forms of encadrement were occasionally suggested again, usually by Washington. For example, in July 1967 Washington pushed for a Korean War-type augmentation of U.S. squads with two or three ARVN soldiers. This was rejected by MACV as unsound, as was a proposal to put U.S. officers in command of ARVN units.[81]

In the aftermath of the Tet Offensive and the felt need to galvanize ARVN in lieu of sending 200,000 more troops, DOD included in its recommendations to the President a proposal that MACV be required to devise alternative arrangements short of joint command to give the U.S. "a greater role in ARVN employment."[82] But again it was not highlighted and apparently got lost in the shuffle. The only experiments in encadrement were a few carried out by subordinate U.S. commanders in the field, notably the U.S. Marine Combined Action Platoons of 1965–1971.

The late John Paul Vann, who served longer in Vietnam than any other senior U.S. official, also believed that an integrated GVN/U.S. command structure could have produced major gains in effectiveness. He saw continuing poor ARVN performance as stemming primarily from failure in leadership rather than failures in organization, training, or logistics, and argued that the only short-term way to rectify this crucial shortcoming was a joint command structure. In November 1967 he actually proposed a detailed scheme based on his field experience.

Why, if improving RVNAF performance was such a critical variable and RVNAF leadership so spotty, did neither the U.S. nor the GVN ever take more than a few minor steps in the direction of a unified command? The most frequent explanation is an essentially political one, such as that given by General Westmoreland:

I consistently resisted suggestions that a single, combined command could more efficiently prosecute the war. I believed that subordinating the Vietnamese forces to U.S. control would stifle the growth of leadership and acceptance of responsibility essential to the development of Vietnamese Armed Forces capable eventually of defending their country. Moreover, such a step would be counter to our basic objective of assisting Vietnam in a time of emergency and of leaving a strong, independent country at the time of our withdrawal. Subordination also might have given credence to the enemy's absurd claim that the United States was no more than a colonial power. I was also fully aware of the practical problems of forming and operating a headquarters with an international staff.[83]

Westmoreland further felt that MACV's close relationship with the JCS, his own intimate association with his Vietnamese opposite number, and the fact that the U.S. provided the bulk of RVNAF's equipment and logistic support plus much of its budget gave him so much informal influence over RVNAF as to provide most of the advantages of joint command without its disadvantages. Among the latter were the extent to which U.S. forces might be robbed of independence of action because of participation in a combined command, and the pressures which could be generated through such a command for even greater U.S. commitments. There was also consistent U.S. concern lest the intensely nationalistic Vietnamese leaders reject any proposals for U.S. command over their forces. Rightly or wrongly, we remained highly sensitive to Vietnamese sensibilities.

But an institutional characteristic doubtless was also operative here; the preference of any organization to operate as an autonomous homogeneous unit. Throughout U. S. participation in modern coalition warfare, this preference has been marked. Pershing in World War I insisted that U.S. forces should operate as soon as possible as a homogeneous field army instead of being brigaded with other allied formations. The same general practice was followed in World War II. Didn't American generals in Vietnam feel that to integrate RVNAF and U.S. forces on any scale would impair U.S. organizational integrity and effectiveness? Thompson similarly sees as one "great appeal" of the U.S. attrition strategy that "it did not involve the South Vietnamese [sic]. American military operations only required perfunctory co-ordination with corresponding South Vietnamese commands. In this way the war could be fought as an American war without the previous frustrations of co-operating with the Vietnamese."[84]

Whether some form of real combined command would have so materially improved RVNAF effectiveness as to have justified risking the disadvantages is legitimately debatable. COMUSMACV, his staff, and U.S. advisers at all levels unquestionably did exert great influence over RVNAF, especially on force structure, training, and tactics. There are also many examples of genuinely combined operations, though compared to the overall total they were the exception rather than the rule.

On the other hand, the evidence is overwhelming that RVNAF's often poor leadership and planning were critical weaknesses hampering its optimum employment, weaknesses that persisted over the years. Moreover, in the event the way the U.S. took over the war did help "stifle the growth of leadership and acceptance of responsibility" of the RVNAF officer corps. RVNAF always formed the bulk of the overall allied order of battle. Bringing these Vietnamese forces under vigorous U.S. leadership at least at theater level might have greatly improved their effectiveness. Above all, it would have given the U.S. a greater say in the assignment and removal of senior RVNAF commanders, whose often indifferent quality was one of RVNAF's gravest weaknesses. The author for one believes that the post-Diem GVN, led by generals, would have accepted overall U.S. command—especially in the dark days of 1965–1966. In informal soundings John Vann also found a suprising consensus among Vietnamese that a combined command under U.S. leadership would be desirable. In retrospect, General Bruce Palmer and others have come down in favor of it.[85]

A related issue was U.S. or combined command over the other allied forces, particularly the two plus South Korean divisions. COMUSMACV would have preferred to have them placed under his command, but Seoul was unwilling to do so for its own domestic political reasons.

LACK OF ADEQUATE OVERALL PLANS

Another consequence of the lack of either unified U.S. management or combined command was the corollary reduction of institutional incentive to develop comprehensive politico-military strategic plans for coping with the atypical Vietnam problem. In January 1963, in their report to President Kennedy after a long trip to Vietnam, Forrestal and Hilsman singled this out as "the most serious lack."[86] The continuing absence of much in the way of overall U.S. politico-military strategic planning in Washington or in the field is largely traceable to the sheer lack of any single locus of responsibility for preparing such plans.

It is not that this problem was neglected, but rather that most of the many plans which evolved were neither sufficiently comprehensive nor an adequate blueprint for operations. As early as 1954 the JCS had noted that U.S. aid to Vietnam should be based on an adequate overall strategic plan for its effective use. But little had been agreed upon (or even produced) by the time the U.S. decided, in late 1961, to increase aid under the "limited partnership" concept advocated by the Taylor-Rostow Mission.[87] In 1960 Washington and CINCPAC had begun stressing the need for a comprehensive national-level plan along lines which make considerable sense in retrospect.[88] By the end of the year, the U.S. country team in Saigon had produced a "C-I Plan for Vietnam" which called mainly for an integrated effort that would overcome the two "bilineal" RVNAF command chains via both province chiefs and military channels, and also for GVN machinery for coordinated national planning.[89]

MAAG produced a complementary and more substantive operations plan in September 1961. But the U.S. Mission had little success in getting Diem to buy it, least of all the idea of a unified chain of command through ARVN to both unit commanders and province chiefs. When MAAG Chief McGarr pressed General "Big" Minh, the ARVN chief of staff, on the need for an overall plan, the latter pessimistically cited his inability to get cooperation either from province chiefs or other GVN agencies on developing comprehensive plans.[90]

The next attempt at overall planning was the so-called "Delta Plan" prepared in November 1961 by Sir Robert Thompson's British Advisory Mission newly arrived in Saigon. This Mission was to give the GVN the best counterinsurgency-oriented advice, based on Malayan experience, that it received during 1961–1965.[91] In mid-February 1962, Diem approved the Delta Plan, which, though perverted in practice, was the progenitor of the Strategic Hamlet Program. Washington was impressed with Thompson's emphasis on clear-and-hold, improved administration, better and more unified police-type intelligence, and gradual "oil-spot" expansion of pacified areas. But the plan was less well received by the MAAG advisers and the JCS, who quite naturally feared deemphasis of military means or offensive operations against the VC[92] (see chapter 4 for General Lemnitzer's reservations).

What emerged as Diem's Strategic Hamlet Program was only loosely dovetailed to the RVNAF buildup being pursued by MACV. In any case it cannot be called a detailed plan so much as a statement of goals, which may be one reason for its failure. In 1962 MACV prepared a proposed GVN National Campaign Plan for offensive military operations and support of the Strategic Hamlet effort. In November of that year it was accepted by the GVN, and a short-lived GVN/ U.S. Joint Operations Center was created "to centralize control over current operations."[93] But MACV's stress remained on buildup and reorganization of the regular forces, as opposed to counterinsurgency-type activities. The Khanh regime developed an elaborate National Pacification Plan for 1964 (see Chapter 7), but it proved mostly a paper exercise.[94] A master plan for "Rural Reconstruction" in 1965 was not even approved by the RVNAF high command until after the first quarter of the year.[95] It too proved mostly a dead letter.

As U.S. ground troops were committed piecemeal during 1965, the *Pentagon Papers* show that there was no overall strategic plan agreed on between the U.S. authorities in Washington and those in Saigon for their employment, nor any agreed plan between the U.S. and GVN. Rather, these were emergency deployments used on what was called a "fire brigade" basis to avert collapse. Even thereafter, the absence of combined machinery resulted in a dearth of combined GVN/U.S. planning, except to a limited extent. Beginning in 1966 a series of annual Combined Campaign Plans (the AB series) were prepared. But these were more a set of broad goals and guidelines for all the allied forces than operational plans. Poor RVNAF security was often cited as a reason for avoiding detailed joint planning.

The most detailed U.S./GVN operational plans worked out systematically at regional, province, and lower levels were the annual and special pacification campaign plans developed for 1968 and after by CORDS and the GVN pacification authorities. They were originally prepared mostly by CORDS advisers and then reworked by the GVN, but gradually the GVN took over this function with U.S. help. Developed at province level on the basis of fiscal and operational guidelines laid down by Saigon, these plans became quite comprehensive and detailed during 1968–1972. The culmination of this planning effort was the comprehensive four-year Community Defense and Local Development Plan for 1972–1975, prepared by the GVN's own central pacification staff. Promulgated in early 1972, it set goals and guidelines for all significant pacification-related programs, and provided the framework within which detailed annual plans were prepared.

Granted that integrated plans and programs can turn out to be a curse as well as a blessing. If overdone, they can become a straight-jacket. In a situation like that in Vietnam, they could well have confirmed error rather than corrected it. They could also have inhibited flexibility. On balance, however, their relative absence seems in retrospect to have been a serious lack. Not only did this lack facilitate an overly militarized war effort, but it deprived the U.S. of an important form of leverage to move the GVN in desired directions.

NOTES

1. See R.W. Komer, *The Malayan Emergency in Retrospect: Organization of a Successful Counterinsurgency Effort*, The RAND Corporation, R-957-ARPA, February 1972, pp. vi, 15, and 25–31.

2. "Lessons from the Vietnam War," Report of a Seminar held at the Royal United Services Institute, London, February 12, 1970 (hereafter called the RUSI Seminar Report), p. 6.

3. Townsend Hoopes, *The Limits of Intervention*, David McKay Company, Inc., New York, 1969, pp. 61–62.

4. Sir Robert Thompson, *No Exit from Vietnam*, David McKay Company, Inc., New York, 1969, p. 149; and "Squaring the Error," *Foreign Affairs*, April 1968, p. 452.

5. Stanley Hoffmann, *Gulliver's Troubles, Or The Setting of American Foreign Policy*, McGraw-Hill, New York, 1968, p. 269.

6. Thompson, *No Exit from Vietnam*, p. 146.

7. Alain C. Enthoven and K. Wayne Smith, *How Much is Enough?*, Harper and Row, New York, 1971, p. 307.

8. *United States–Vietnam Relations, 1945–1967: Study Proposal by the Department of Defense*, 12 Volumes, U.S. Government Printing Office, Washington, D.C., 1971, (hereafter referred to as the *Pentagon Papers*), IV.C.6(a), p. 86.

9. Maxwell D. Taylor, *Swords and Plowshares*, W.W. Norton & Company, Inc., New York, 1972, p. 339.

10. Joint Logistics Review Board, *Logistics Support in the Vietnam Era.*

11. Cf. Chester Cooper, *Lost Crusade*, Dodd, Mead & Company, New York, 1970, p. 413.

12. Hoopes sees the problem as arising largely from the decline of the NSC machinery under Kennedy and then Johnson, and a parallel decline of longer-range policy planning (*Limits of Intervention*, pp. 2–6). The author, who served in the NSC machinery under them and also under Eisenhower, feels Hoopes overstates the case. The NSC staff was never an operating staff.

13. *Pentagon Papers*, IV.B.1, p. 23.

14. Ibid., pp. 19–31. See also IV.B.3, p. 18.

15. See ibid., discussion in VI.B.3, pp. 15–21.

16. Ibid., IV.B.1, p. 35.

17. Arthur M. Schlesinger, Jr., *A Thousand Days*, Houghton Mifflin Company, Boston, 1965, p. 545. Roger Hilsman agrees in *To Move a Nation*, Doubleday & Company, Inc., New York, 1967, p. 421.

18. Taylor, *Swords and Plowshares*, pp. 251 and 360–362.

19. See Henry F. Graff, *The Tuesday Cabinet*, Prentice-Hall, Englewood Cliffs, N.J., 1970.

20. Preface to Brigadier Richard L. Clutterbuck, *The Long Long War*, Frederick A. Praeger, Inc., New York., 1966, p. ix.

21. *Pentagon Papers*, IV.C.8, p. 27.

22. Ibid., IV.B.3, pp. 72–73.

23. NSAM 343, cited in *Pentagon Papers*, IV.C.8, p. 63.

24. *Pentagon Papers*, IV.C.8.

25. Cooper sees President Johnson's personal management style and compulsive secrecy as largely responsible for how Washington ran the war. *Lost Crusade*, pp. 413–417.

26. Hilsman, *To Move a Nation*, p. 442

27. Taylor, *Swords and Plowshares*, p. 250.

28. Cooper, *Lost Crusade*, p. 276.

29. In A.A. Jordan, *Foreign Aid and the Defense of Southeast Asia*, Frederick A. Praeger, Inc., New York, 1962, pp. 152–155.

30. Hilsman, *To Move a Nation*, p. 446.

31. Thompson, *No Exit from Vietnam*, p. 158.

32. Hilsman, *To Move a Nation*, p. 442.

33. *Pentagon Papers*, IV.C.8, p. 21; see also McNamara's December 1963 comments to the President on p. 59.

34. For Ambassador Johnson's description of how he and Taylor operated, see ibid., pp. 21–22.

35. Taylor, *Swords and Plowshares*, p. 316.

36. *Pentagon Papers*, IV.C.8, pp. 9, 12, 55.

37. Ibid., IV.C.1, p. 109.

38. Ibid., IV.C.8, pp. 8–9.

39. Ibid., pp. 20–21.

40. IV.C.8 of the *Pentagon Papers* describes the many problems Washington had during 1966–1967 in forcing this consolidation on a reluctant Lodge and Porter, not to mention the Saigon agencies and their Washington partners.

41. Barry Zorthian, "Where Do We Go From Here?", *Foreign Service Journal*, February 1970.

42. *Pentagon Papers*, IV.A.5, Tab. 4, pp. 60–62.

43. Ibid., IV.B.1, p. 131.

44. Ibid., p. 143.

45. William A. Nighswonger, *Rural Pacification in Vietnam*, Frederick A. Praeger, Inc., New York, 1966, pp. 191–192. Also *Pentagon Papers*, IV.B.2, p. 17.

46. See *The Fall of South Vietnam*, for statements by key participants on how these problems persisted.

47. Cooper, *Lost Crusade*, pp. 424–425.

48. Thompson, *No Exit from Vietnam*, p. 127.

49. *Pentagon Papers*, IV.C.5, p. 108.

50. Hoopes, *Limits of Intervention*, pp. 62–63; also p. 147.

51. Taylor, *Swords and Plowshares*, pp. 375 and 389.

52. *Pentagon Papers*, Gravel Edition, Vol. IV, pp. 392–400.

53. Hoopes, *Limits of Intervention*, pp. 2–6.

54. Taylor, *Swords and Plowshares*, p. 198.

55. Cooper, *Lost Crusade*, pp. 413–417.

56. Those Britons with Malayan experience find this particularly hard to understand. Sir Claude Fenner, Inspector General of Malayan Police 1963–1966, remarks how during his August 1968 survey trip to Vietnam (at the author's request) "it appeared to me that the war was being conducted by the U.S. and GVN in separate and almost watertight compartments. Coordination of the combined U.S./GVN effort would seem to be achieved by personal liaison on an ad hoc basis at all levels." RUSI Seminar Report, p. 5.

57. Barbara Tuchman, *Stilwell and the American Experience in China, 1911–45*, The Macmillan Company, New York, 1970, p. 243.

58. Ibid., pp. 468–471.

59. Ibid, pp. 495–504.

60. *Pentagon Papers*, IV.B.1, p. 116.

61. Ibid., pp. 96 and 130.

62. Ibid., p. 138.

63. Ibid., pp. 139 and 147.

64. Ibid., pp. 140–146.

65. *Pentagon Papers*, IV.B.3, pp. 41–42.

66. Ibid., IV.C.1, pp. 78–79.

67. Cable from the President to Ambassador Lodge, dated May 26, 1964, in ibid., pp. 76–78.

68. Ibid., IV.B.3, pp. 44–45.

69. Ibid., IV.C.1, pp. 111–113. General Taylor also notes how he opposed both encadrement and U.S. civil affairs teams in *Swords and Plowshares*, p. 343.

70. *Pentagon Papers*, IV.B.3, pp. 59–60; see also IV.C.4, p. 20, and IV.C.1, pp. 115–116.

71. Ibid., IV.C.1, pp. 116–118.

72. Nighswonger, *Rural Pacification*, p. 209.

73. *Pentagon Papers*, IV.C.9(a), pp. 68–69.

74. Ibid., IV.B.3, pp. 61–63; see also IV.C.9(a), pp. 69–70.

75. Ibid., IV.B.3, p. 62.

76. Ibid., pp. 63–64.

77. Ibid., IV.C.9(b), p. 3.

78. Taylor, *Swords and Plowshares*, p. 350.

79. *Pentagon Papers*, IV.B.3, p. 80.

80. Ibid., IV.C.6(b), pp. 78 and 187.

81. Ibid., IV.C.9(b), pp. 51–52.

82. Tab B. of Memorandum for the President from the Clifford Task Force, cited in ibid., IV.C.6(c), p. 56.

83. *Report on the War in Vietnam*, by CINCPAC and COMUSMACV, U.S. Government Printing Office, Washington, D.C., 1969, p. 104.

84. Thompson, *No Exit from Vietnam*, p. 135.

85. Gen. Bruce Palmer in *The 25-Year War*, University Press of Kentucky, Lexington, KY, 1984, p. 52 says that "In retrospect, I believe that the advantages of having U.S. commanders exercise operational control over other forces, especially South Vietnamese, would have far outweighed the drawbacks." See also Gen. Cao Van Vien, *The Final Collapse*, U.S. Army Center for Military History, Washington, DC, 1984, p. 162.

86. Hilsman, *To Move a Nation*, p. 464.

87. *Pentagon Papers*, IV.B.2, pp. i and 7.

88. Ibid., IV.A.5, Tab 4, pp. 60–62.

89. Ibid., IV.B.2, p. 7; also IV.A.5, Tab.4, pp. 80–81.

90. Ibid., IV.B.1, p. 111.

91. Ibid., IV.B.2, pp. 10–15.

92. Ibid., p. 18.

93. Ibid., IV.B.4, pp. 5–6.

94. Ibid., p. 38.

95. Ibid., IV.C.5, p. 51.

7
ATTEMPTS AT
ADAPTIVE RESPONSE

While U.S. performance in Vietnam is most notable for sheer conventionality and slowness to adapt, it would be misleading to ignore the many examples of adaptive change designed to meet felt needs. Naturally, most of these were the sort of relatively modest, evolutionary, or frequently technological changes that the institutions involved could fit into their existing repertoires without much de-stabilizing impact. There were far fewer major innovations involving real discontinuities and, as will be seen, these almost invariably required outside intervention to induce them. Moreover, far more was proposed, from both within and outside the "establishment," than was ever adopted—at least on a scale commensurate with the need.

On the military side, such innovation as occurred tended to be either technological or in the realm of modifying organization and tactics to utilize new technology. This often improved military per-formance, but it contributed to the overmilitarization of the war by reinforcing the tendency to seek only military solutions. It also enhanced the Americanization of the war, since only technically qualified U.S. personnel could handle many of the new devices and equipment introduced. These caveats call into question the ultimate relevance of many such technological innovations to the achievement of U.S. aims in Vietnam. Moreover, the use of advanced technology often had major side effects which proved counterproductive to the achievement of these aims.

We have seen in Chapter 6 how many proposals were advanced for adapting GVN or U.S. organization to the particular needs of the situation but how few were accepted—even over time. Yet in those instances where adaptive solutions tailored to specific problems were tried, they usually proved to be substantial improvements. In fact, they proved sufficiently so to suggest that much more could and should have been done—and would have resulted in much better

U.S./GVN performance. One example was the unique civil/military organization that the U.S. finally set up for pacification support, which sparked a similar GVN reorganization. Another example was the unprecedented expansion of the U.S. advisory effort to the GVN. Both are discussed below.

TECHNOLOGICAL INNOVATION

Unsurprisingly, such innovation as occurred was far more notable on the technological than on the tactical or organizational planes. In the best American tradition, we spent heavily on advanced technology for coping with an elusive enemy. Among the examples were the widespread tactical as well as logistic use of helicopters (including several new models), development of "gunships" (both planes and helicopters), a variety of new ordnance, small naval craft for riverine warfare and offshore blockade, extensive use of herbicides, "Rome plows" for jungle clearing, new sensors and detection devices, and the like. USAF use of B-52s, designed for strategic nuclear delivery, for conventional bombing of enemy base areas was a major adaptation of existing capabilities (though its real cost effectiveness has yet to be measured). So too was the effective use of precision-guided munitions in the 1972 bombing campaigns.

A push was given to technological innovation by several sensible organizational devices. As early as 1961 the Advanced Research Projects Agency of the Defense Department began a special program (Project AGILE) aimed at counterinsurgency research and development with special reference to Southeast Asia. It was quite productive of new ideas and insights, though few were fully exploited by the military services. in 1966 the Director of Research and Development in the Pentagon appointed a Deputy Director for Southeast Asia matters to work full-time on expediting relevant research and development. This dynamic deputy (Leonard Sullivan) and his staff did much to promote new equipment and devices.[1] So too did their counterpart in Saigon, a Science Advisor and staff set up by General Westmoreland in 1966 and reporting directly to him.

Perhaps the most striking single case of technological and managerial innovation was stimulated by the 1966 Jason Summer Study Group proposal for what came to be called the "McNamara line." Though its potential was hotly debated and it was overtaken by events before it could be fully installed, this concept for an electronic "barrier" system along South Vietnam's northern border (and perhaps extending into Laos) was designed to inhibit infiltration while reducing the need for costly and politically risky air operations against the North. Its most innovative feature was a variety of small sensors linked to central receiving stations which could direct the desired responses. In September 1966 Secretary McNamara established a Defense Communications Planning Group (DCPG) under Lieutenant General Alfred Starbird to develop and deploy the anti-infiltration systems called for in the McNamara line. Its second director, describing DCPG's "unique and unprecedented" management authority over all aspects of system implementation, testified that "by providing the requisite authority, responsibility, funds, and organizational arrangements to a centralized sole manager, we have been able to reduce the normal five- to seven-year defense development cycle by a factor of four."[2]

As noted, however, the use of new technology may well have been counterproductive in many respects. For example, Sir Robert Thompson believes that without the helicopter the "search-and-destroy" attrition strategy which he decries would not have been possible.[3] Extensive use of defoliants, though often of real military value, drew adverse psychological reactions from the civilian population—aside from causing possible ecological damage. Crop destruction agents, used far less extensively, probably did little to cut off enemy food supplies, while entailing even more adverse psychological repercussions in both Vietnam and the United States.

INSTITUTIONAL ADAPTATION

Though the U.S. approach to Vietnam was distinguished more by its conventionality than by its adaptiveness, there were some organizational modifications too. Force structure changes were required, for example, for full utilization of helicopter assets. Another large-scale example was the CIA's design and support of the company-sized Civilian Irregular Defense Groups (CIDG), using Army Special Forces advisers. This was a particularly cost-effective use of indigenous manpower (support of the CIDG was transferred from CIA to MACV in 1964). At its height the CIDG manned over 100 camps with 50,000 men, mostly along Vietnam's borders.

The only sustained experiment with encadrement in our entire Vietnam experience was the Combined Action Platoons (CAPs), each composed of twelve U.S. Marines and twenty-four Popular Force militiamen. They made a real contribution to hamlet security, unfortunately on a very small scale.[4] CAPs began to be created informally in mid-1965, and were made a formal program in November. But by 1967 there were only some 70 CAPs, and at peak only 114. The

Army's 353 Mobile Advisory Teams (MATs), which gave on-the-job training to the Regional and Popular Forces, were another innovative approach begun on a countrywide scale in 1967. The Army and Marines also made good use of selected long-range combat and reconnaissance patrols.

Also deserving of mention is the Navy's imaginative use of small craft on the Mekong Delta inland waterways. Indeed, the Army and Navy jointly developed a brigade-sized Mobile Riverine Force for operations in the Delta.[5] However, probably the Navy's greatest single contribution in the Vietnam war is one seldom even mentioned— the classic and traditional use of naval blockade to cut off North Vietnam's main waterborne logistic and reinforcement routes to the South, forcing greater development of the Ho Chi Minh Trail complex as the alternative.

Perhaps the most successful U.S. military adaptations to the special needs of Vietnam lay in the logistic field, usually an American strong suit. Though the so-called Besson Board report reviewing this experience is critical of the tight control over fiscal and manpower restrictions imposed by the Secretary of Defense "to minimize the effect on the national economy," the military showed considerable flexibility in adapting to these constraints.[6] Through a variety of expedients and specially tailored procedures too numerous and complex to mention here, the U.S. military logistic system sufficed to support not only the U.S., forces but most needs of the Vietnamese and allied forces, aside from providing major support to pacification and a variety of civil programs. As the Besson Board concluded, "Overall . . . logistic support provided the combat forces in Southeast Asia was adequate and responsive to the needs of the combat commanders." However, "the many critical problems associated with the rapid expansion of force levels and combat operations in this distant underdeveloped area led to a number of innefficient and costly actions."[7]

There also are some important cases of adaptive responses by U.S. civilian agencies, particularly by CIA. Suffice it to say that CIA proved far more imaginative and flexible than the military in encouraging and supporting various types of counterinsurgency-oriented paramilitary forces, notably the Civilian Irregular Defense Groups and the Revolutionary Development Cadre started in late 1965 (see below). The Census Grievance Cadre program was another case in point; most other CIA activities remain classified.[8]

AID experimented with rural programs on a small scale in the sixties. Perhaps its most successful effort was in helping to stimulate the rapid revival of agriculture output after 1967 through extensive use of new "miracle rice" varieties, fertilizer imports, improved agricultural credit, and the like. AID also played a major role in designing the GVN's revolutionary 1970 Land-to-the-Tiller program, and in developing unusually effective computerized procedures for rapid surveying and issuance of land titles under chaotic wartime conditions.[9] The civil-military CORDS organization (see below) also played a role in carrying out these programs, along with pressing village hamlet development programs and promoting revival of autonomous local administration. Indeed the cumulative impact of all these pacification oriented measures might be said to have added up to a GVN/U.S.-sponsored socio-economic revolution in the countryside of South Vietnam. Over time this could conceivably have had as much to do with the successful countering of Viet Cong insurgency as the restoration of sustained local security.

PACIFICATION 1967–1972:
AN EXAMPLE OF INSTITUTIONAL INNOVATION

Perhaps the chief example of large-scale institutional adaptation to the special needs of Vietnam, which contributed greatly to this rural socio-economic revolution, was the so-called "new model" pacification program, begun in 1967. It represented a major discontinuity with the more or less conventional way in which the GVN and U.S. had organized to cope with the war, and had considerable though belated impact on the way they fought it. Thus its brief history is instructive in any analysis of bureaucratic constraints on GVN/U.S. performance in Vietnam. It is also significant that the only part of the *Pentagon Papers* which focuses largely on organizational issues is the slim volume on *Re-emphasis on Pacification: 1965–1967.*[10]

The earlier history of GVN/U.S. pacification efforts helps to illustrate the point. It reflects the same contradiction that marked the overall GVN/U.S. approach to the Vietnam conflict: greater perception than generally realized of the need for some major pacification-type effort to help cope with rural-based insurgency, but delayed and inadequate execution in practice owing mostly to the bureaucratic obstacles to generating such an atypical effort through existing institutions (see Chapter 8). Both the Diem regime and U.S. experts quickly saw pacification-type programs as important to meeting the VC threat, even though the techniques Diem favored were often critically flawed. As early as 1954 Diem created Civic Action Teams totaling at different times 400–1,800 cadres. They did some good work in the provinces but were soon dissolved or absorbed into other GVN organizations.[11] Diem's agroville program begun in 1959, his Strategic Hamlet Program of 1962–1963, and his creation of a Civil Guard were other initiatives in this direction.

But whatever the perceived need, neither the GVN nor the U.S. invested much in such programs. Nor did they ever provide sustained local security for them. This stemmed from several causes, including the lack of funding sources and organizational backing for such atypical programs, the general deterioration of the increasingly repressive Diem administrative apparatus as it gradually lost control of the countryside, and the fact that Diem and his U.S. advisers turned increasingly to conventional military means to combat the growing insurgency. This trend was powerfully reinforced in 1964–1965, when the Viet Cong turned more to military pressures and insurgency was supplemented by NVA infiltration. It was also reinforced by the advent of government by the military after the fall of Diem, and by the increasing militarization of GVN local administration as civilian officials fled the countryside. A similar trend took place on the U.S. side, where the more the U.S. turned to military solutions the less its relative emphasis on politico-military pacification measures.

By this time, of course, thwarting the VC/NVA "main forces" had become indispensable to creating a climate in which pacification could get started again. After 1964 it was essential to fight both main-force and village wars. They had a symbiotic relationship, even though the balance of our military effort was tilted heavily against pacification and clear-and-hold. The political turmoil and frequent coups in 1963–1966 also contributed to the hiatus in major pacification efforts. Only after U.S. military intervention staved off GVN collapse and regained the initiative in the big-unit war, and a measure of political stability returned, did greater attention begin to be paid to reviving some form of pacification to complement the big-unit war.

This revival was mostly American-stimulated, though Vietnamese-executed. The most promising early pacification approaches after U.S. intervention were sponsored by that most flexible of U.S. agencies, the CIA. It played a major role in initiating the Revolutionary Development (RD) program. In August 1965 Prime Minister Ky established a Ministry of Rural Construction, which "absorbed functions and personnel from predecessor groups and other ministries for the announced purpose of providing centralized direction to the pacification effort."[12] Fortunately, it soon became headed by an unusually talented and energetic officer, Major General Nguyen Duc

Thang. A Central Rural Construction Council was also established to coordinate all the ministries, but it seldom functioned.

The new program was spearheaded by deployment of the first 59-man armed RD teams in black pajamas to selected hamlets. AID participated in the corollary New Life Development Program under the Thang Ministry. AID also actively supported the creation of a fledgling Police Field Force (PFF) as a start toward a rural constabulary. Both the RD teams and the PFF represented civilian efforts to generate paramilitary forces for the rural security mission. But these efforts suffered from two major weaknesses: insufficient scale in relation to the needs of the countryside, and lack of a territorial security environment within which they could thrive.

Another important institutional constraint on pacification was the lack, until very late, of any management structure for it. Neither in Vietnam nor in Washington—in neither the GVN nor the U.S. establishment—was there any agency charged with managing anything so atypical as a pacification program. However important, this aspect of counterinsurgency had no bureaucratic vested interest speaking for it. Not until this was created did pacification begin to acquire new shape and substance. For example, the *Hop Tac* scheme of 1964–1965 to pacify the area around Saigon failed largely because of GVN/U.S. differences which there was no unified management to resolve.

Whether the U.S. should in effect take over responsibility for rural administration and pacification was raised on occasion. In spring 1965 the JCS proposed that, if the U.S. intervened, MACV not only assume responsibility for much of AID's rural programs but assign U.S. military civil affairs teams "as in World War II" to run GVN provincial administrations. This was apparently the result of a Presidential suggestion that U.S. civil affairs teams be integrated into provincial governments on an experimental basis.[13] U.S. civilian agencies were strongly opposed, however, and Ambassador Taylor vetoed the idea.[14] President Johnson also occasionally queried whether U.S. officials shouldn't take over such direct administrative tasks. However, the revived pacification effort was designed from the outset as a GVN responsibility, with the Americans playing essentially a supporting role.[15]

Lodge had assigned General Lansdale, who came out with him in late 1965, to be chief adviser to the new RD program then beginning under General Thang. But in practice Thang looked more to MACV.[16] Lansdale was also hamstrung by more conventional-minded U.S. Mission officers, and his role atrophied amid growing bickering. Instead, the February 1966 Honolulu Conference, which laid stress on the "other war" in Vietnam, led to the designation of Deputy Ambassador Porter as field coordinator of U.S. support programs, and appointment of a new Special Assistant to the President to supervise Washington support to the "other war." Growing Washington dissatisfaction with the loose coordination of the still faltering GVN pacification effort next led to the creation in December 1966 of an Office of Civil Operations (OCO) in Saigon to pull together all pacification-type support by U.S. civilian agencies.

But these were half-measures affecting mostly the civilian tail and not the military dog. The U.S. and GVN military, concerned mostly with the "main force" war, regarded pacfication as primarily civilian business, to be handled by the vestiges of GVN civilian ministeries backed by AID and CIA. Yet by this time the military controlled most of the available in-country forces and resources. Without them, territorial security could not be expanded rapidly enough to exploit whatever successes were being achieved in pushing back the enemy's main forces.

The solution was to require the U.S. and ARVN military to take on most of the pacification job. On the U.S. side Washington decreed a series of management changes which in May 1967 finally pulled together all U.S. civil and military pacification support and placed it under the U.S. military, but with a civilian in charge. The managerial key to U.S. ability to stimulate at long last a major GVN pacification effort was *the creation of CORDS* under COMUSMACV.* It was a unique, hybrid civil-military structure which imposed unified single management on all the diffuse U.S. pacification support programs and provided a single channel of advice at each level to GVN counterparts.

It is significant that not until an organization was created to focus specifically on pacification as its primary mission and to integrate all relevant military and civilian agency efforts did a major sustained pacification effort begin to take shape. The bureaucratic price that had to be paid for creating this military elephant and civilian rabbit stew was to put CORDS under the military. *Paradoxically, this resulted in greater U.S. civilian influence over pacification than had ever existed before;* it also powerfully reinforced pacification's claim on U.S. and GVN military resources, which constituted the great bulk of the inputs after 1966.

---

*CORDS, an acronym for Civil Operations and Revolutionary Development Support, combined the names of its two predecessor organizations, OCO and RD Support Directorate of MACV.

How did so marked a departure as CORDS finally come about? The key stimulus was cumulative Washington frustration with the reluctance, even inability, of the fragmented U.S. Mission in Saigon to get a major pacification effort going.[17] But at every point there were bureaucratic obstacles to overcome. For example, all U.S. civilian agencies opposed putting their pacification support activities under the military. It took a presidential decision, plus the backing of Ellsworth Bunker, the strong new U.S. Ambassador in Saigon, to put it into effect. The U.S. military too were unenthusiastic about accepting a major added responsibility, but loyally acquiesced. In large measure, Washington finally insisted upon this experiment in unified field management precisely because it finally came to realize that if a major concerted pacification effort was ever to be successfully mounted, it would have to be free of the existing doctrine, techniques, and organizational practices of old-line agencies or programs.

How was CORDS different? First, it was a field expedient tailored to particular needs as perceived at the time. Second, it was a unique experiment in a unified civil/military field advisory and support organization, quite different from World War II civil affairs or military government. Soldiers served directly under civilians, and vice versa, at all levels. They even wrote each other's efficiency reports. Personnel were drawn from all the military services, and from State, AID, CIA, USIA, and the White House. But CORDS was fully integrated into the theater military structure. The Deputy for CORDS served directly under General Westmoreland and later General Abrams—perhaps the first American of ambassadorial rank to serve directly in the military chain of command as an operational deputy, not just a political adviser. To support him, a MACV general staff section was created under a civilian assistant chief of staff with a general officer deputy. Four regional deputies for CORDS served under the U.S. corps level commanders. The cutting edge was unified civil-military advisory teams in all 250 districts and 44 provinces.

A third notable feature of CORDS was its relatively flexible and pragmatic approach to the problem of pacification. Less constrained by prior practices than other agencies, since it had little precedent to go by, CORDS in effect wrote its field manual as it went along. One key achievement was its initial stress on generating sustained local security in the countryside as the indispensable prerequisite to effective pacification at that late date.[18] Since this would take para-military forces far larger than those previously available, and time was of the essence, the primary instrument chosen was the long neglected Regional and Popular Forces, which were upgraded and greatly expanded. Between 1966 and 1972 RF and PF grew by 73 percent.[19] Building on this force-in-being was greatly facilitated by the fact that pacification support was now under military auspices. The RF/PF were later supplemented by the GVN's Phung Hoang (Phoenix) program, designed to pull together and improve the efforts of a plethora of GVN agencies aimed at dismantling the Viet Cong infrastructure, and by the People's Self Defense Forces (PSDF) of part-time civilians created in 1968 after the Tet Offensive.

But the pacification effort comprised much more than just restoration of local security. Restoring autonomous local administration, rural economic revival, refugee care and resettlement, rural education programs, rebuilding of roads and waterways, massive health and medical efforts, and the like were supported by CORDS in concert with the AID Mission and the U.S. military. To utilize all available resources, the GVN and CORDS pushed multiple programs simultaneously—the various program assets were not readily fungible—under unified management and with a firm set of priorities.

Generating an adequate management structure on the GVN side was much more difficult, since what needed to be pulled together was not just a modest U.S. advisory and support effort but major administrative and operational programs. Nevertheless, CORDS efforts led, partly by example and partly by influence, to eventual reorganization and unification of the GVN pacification structure at all levels, culminating in the 1968 revival of a functioning ministerial-level Central Pacification Council, creation of a Deputy Prime Minister for Pacification in March 1969, and Thieu's own assumption of the chairmanship of the Central Council (and creation of a central staff) in July 1969. Thus, in just three years, GVN pacification management reached the status where its top policymaker on a regular basis was the president himself. CORDS efforts also led to the only sustained large-scale example of intimate combined U.S./GVN planning at every level, from national down to district, in the Vietnam war.

Compared to other major GVN/U.S. programs, the level of innovation in the pacification field was relatively high. Aside from CORDS itself and the related GVN organs, some of the many examples were: (a) a series of new measurement systems designed primarily for management purposes, of which the Hamlet Evaluation System is the most widely known; (b) the imaginative "Chieu Hoi" defector program, which began in 1963 but only hit its stride in 1966–1967; (c) the 59-man RD teams and the associated village self-development program; (d) the GVN National Training Center at Vung Tau; (e) a new Vietnam Training Center in Washington to train CORDS advisers;

(f) the GVN *Phung Hoang* program; (g) the CORDS Evaluation Branch of field evaluators reporting directly to top management; (h) the People's Self-Defense Forces; and (i) the CORDS Evaluation Branch procedure for assessing popular attitudes by systematically polling a sample of the rural population (using Vietnamese evaluators).

The shifting emphases of the "new model" pacification program after the creation of CORDS are also suggestive of its adaptiveness. In general, the initial emphasis was on buildup of territorial security forces and clarification of their role. Then, as the enemy's Tet and May 1968 offensives petered out, emphasis shifted to rapid if thin expansion of the area being pacified via two Accelerated Pacification Campaigns (APCs). In July 1969 Thieu shifted pacification priorities again, from expansion to consolidation. Instead of the APC emphasis on upgrading contested hamlets to a "C" rating, he ordered stress on upgrading "C" hamlets to "A" or "B" status. This, along with the 1969 Village Development Program and local elections, reflected a gradual shift from stress on the security aspects of pacification toward stress on its political and developmental aspects. This became even more marked in the GVN's 1970 Pacification and Development Plan. Then, in early 1971, the GVN decided that pacification had made such progress that the term itself had become outmoded. It was abandoned in favor of a 1971 Community Defense and Local Development Plan.[20]

The purpose here is not to laud pacification, even during 1969–1971, as an efficient, well-run program. On the contrary, its weaknesses and flaws were all too numerous; it was at best only a qualified success.[21] The point is rather that, in strong contrast to the sheer conventionality of most aspects of the GVN/U.S. response, it did eventually prove possible to set up and carry out a major GVN/U.S. wartime program specifically designed to meet many of the atypical problems of people's war in South Vietnam. Of all large scale U.S.-supported efforts mounted during the Vietnam conflict, it stands out as perhaps the one most precisely tailored to the need.

Pacification 1967–1972 also shows how it was possible via unified management and close U.S./GVN collaboration to overcome many of the institutional constraints which so hampered other aspects of our Vietnam effort. And in notable contrast to the big-unit war, it remained an essentially Vietnamese program, with the U.S. in only an advisory and supporting role. Lastly it proved far more cost-effective than most other parts of the allied war effort, entailing only a modest fraction of the costs of the Vietnam war.[22]

THE UNPRECEDENTED U.S. ADVISORY EFFORT

Though the substantive weaknesses of the U.S. advisory effort limited its positive impact, its gradual expansion to the point where it was supporting almost every aspect of the GVN war effort does represent another attempt at adaptive response. Compared with any previous U.S. advisory effort, that in Vietnam was unprecedented in extent and in the depth to which it went in the field. This is evident from comparison with the only three wartime U.S. advisory efforts of analogous size—in China during World War II, in Greece during the 1947–1949 civil war, and in Korea during 1950–1953.

By 1945 the U.S. military forces in China included, as one of their many components, over 8,000 men advising the Chinese forces.[23] Originally, they were under General Stilwell; when Stilwell was recalled, General A.C. Wedemeyer filled a dual role, after October 1944 both commanding the new China theater and serving as one of Chiang's two chiefs of staff (in effect as his senior military adviser in the fight against the Japanese).[24] Most major U.S. elements under Wedemeyer had advisory as well as other roles. At peak, in 1945, his Chinese Combat Command included 3,147 Americans in liaison/advisory teams with four Chinese Group Armies of some 500,000 men. Advisors often worked down to regimental level with about 36 divisions. A Chinese Training Center operated a General Staff School, Infantry Training Center, Field Artillery Training Center, Automotive School, and Ordnance Training Center, and later a Heavy Mortar Training Center and Signal School. A U.S. Service of Supply helped support the 36 divisions, and its commander also became in February 1945 the commander of the parallel Chinese Service of Supply for this purpose.[25] By mid-1945 about 650 Americans were working in various parts of the Chinese Service of Supply.[26] At that time a combined headquarters staff for the 36-division force was formed.[27] The end of the war cut short what was gradually becoming both a major U.S. advisory effort and quasicommand of a major fraction of the Chinese forces.

In the Greek civil war a Joint U.S. Military Advisory and Planning Group was set up under Lieutenant General Van Fleet in early 1948. By mid-1949 an army section of about 350 "advised the Greek Army from the General Staff down to division level." Smaller naval and air sections performed similar functions. Plans and operations remained a Greek responsibility, but in fact owed much to U.S. advice.[28]

In Korea the small Korean Military Advisory Group (KMAG) organized in 1948 was expanded to almost 500 by end-1949 to provide training and advice down to battalion level to the new Korean army, though it remained far too thinly spread to do so full time. KMAG also founded a school system.[29] When the 1950 invasion came, KMAG advisers often had to assume command. A strengthened KMAG then played a major role in rebuilding the ROK army. By September 1951 its strength had grown to 1,308[30] and it was advising ten ROK divisions, many still in process of formation. Still later, with almost 2,000 men, KMAG created a Field Training Command to train ROK forces. At one point in 1951 Washington suggested that U.S. officers be put in command of various ROK elements, but this was rejected by the field.[31] On the other hand, all ROK forces during the Korean War were under the overall command of the U.S. theater commander.

During 1955–1960 the U.S. advisory effort in Vietnam was handled by a more or less conventional MAAG of under 700.[32] Its advisory task was "concentrated in training centers and in Saigon. . . . It was essentially an attempt to give advice from the top."[33] However, MAAG was later authorized to provide advisers at regimental level.

In 1961 the MAAG began to assume the role of operational adviser. As part of the Kennedy commitments, the U.S. decided to increase its military advisory effort by establishing teams at province and battalion level.[34] Both Lansdale and MAAG chief McGarr favored using U.S. advisers in combat areas.[35] In January 1962 McNamara approved battalion advisory teams for ARVN infantry and artillery battalions, and three U.S. advisers for each province, plus advisers for CG and SDC training. By April 1962 adviser strength had risen to about 3,150 (including 805 Special Forces personel with CIA-supported programs), at which level it stabilized till mid-1964. Within this ceiling, the number of field advisers was increased from 1,351 in April 1961 to 2,028 by November 1963.[36] The bulk of the effort went into improving ARVN capabilities, but it was not enough to forestall the growing threat of an ARVN collapse.[37]

After the fall of Diem, the still deteriorating situation led in 1964 to another attempt to improve RVNAF performance by beefing up the field advisory effort. MACV, favoring a "gradualistic approach," created the first district teams of one captain and one NCO in thirteen key districts.[38] The AID Mission also expanded its small rural affairs staff. Then the JCS suggested adding 70 training advisers—mostly in mobile training teams—in each of fourteen critical provinces to train the paramilitary CG and SDC. MACV preferred using this further increment to put two-man operational adviser teams in every district rather than create a new training establishment.[39] JCS also studied the possibility of putting advisers down to company level in ARVN, but the field rejected this as likely to lead to greater U.S. casualties, requiring too much prior language training, and probably objectionable to ARVN.[40] Under prodding from Washington, MACV finally decided to request 900 more advisers for five-man teams in 45 districts of eight priority provinces, plus 68 other districts, and an increase in ARVN infantry and artillery advisory teams.[41] The naval and air advisory groups were also increased, for a net expansion of over one thousand. By end-1964 there were district advisory teams in half the then 239 districts in South Vietnam.

Though in 1965 the advisory effort "sank into relative obscurity" as the U.S. introduced its own forces, in fact its greatest expansion took place after the U.S. entered the war.[42] MACV made the commander of U.S. forces in each corps area the senior adviser to the ARVN corps commander, an added function which in most cases had to take second place to his handling of U.S. troops. As U.S. forces took over the brunt of the "main force" war, the concept developed that RVNAF should focus mostly on pacification support. Hence the chief issue with respect to U.S. advisory support during 1966–1968 became that of how best to organize and extend the advisory effort to the new pacification program which was emerging. The result was to add a whole new dimension to the U.S. advisory effort on a scale and to a depth never attempted before.

A related issue was how best to pull together the military pacification advisers and the various civilian advisory teams from AID, CIA, and USIA also operating in the field.[43] The growing number of civilian advisers at region and province level were placed under OCO in December 1966. Then, in May 1967, the entire pacification advisory effort—about 4,000 military and 830 civilian advisers—was integrated under CORDS. It is important to note that CORDS military advisers performed numerous nonmilitary functions, and vice versa. CORDS advisory staffs worked with each ministry involved in pacification matters, not just at the center but at every level down to district, and even hamlet.

CORDS also stimulated the most far-reaching attempt yet to improve the performance of the neglected paramilitary forces. In mid-1967 MACV requested 2,577 more military advisers, some 2,331 of them asked for by CORDS to beef up the RF/PF advisory effort in the field. The plan was to create 353 five-man Mobile Advisory Teams (MATs) to give on-the-job training to RF/PF units.[44] Ten Mobile Advisory Logistics Teams (MALTs) also were created in 1967 to jack up logistic support to the RF/PF from the provincial depot system. Later 400 military *Phung Hoang* advisers were gradually added to provide administrative help to the accounting system. Thus total U.S. military advisers had risen from only 335 actually assigned in 1954 to 10,254 by end-1967—including almost one thousand naval and air advisers. To these must be added another thousand civilian advisers under CORDS operational control.[45]

At probably the peak of the overall U.S. advisory effort, in 1969, it numbered over 16,000 Americans, including several hundred civilians in AID, CIA, and USIA besides those in CORDS. By mid-1969 army advisory strength alone had risen to over 13,500—of which CORDS had about 6,500. Of the latter, a striking 95 percent were in the field rather than Saigon—the great bulk at province or district and with the mobile advisory teams. This was the largest foreign advisory effort in U.S. history. During 1967–1970 it provided technical and operational advice to just about every GVN unit, governmental organ and training installation both at the national level and in the field.* In addition, several thousand Vietnamese military and civilian officials were sent to various training courses in the U.S. or other countries.

What did all this massive effort accomplish? Clearly in 1955–1965 it failed to help create Vietnamese forces capable of stemming the insurgency. After 1966 these forces tended to perform better on the average, though performance still varied widely, as became painfully evident in their response to Hanoi's 1972 offensive and in the 1975 collapse. But without U.S. advisory support it is highly questionable whether RVNAF would have performed even as well as it did during U.S. disengagement. Indeed, when in 1972 RVNAF underwent its first major quasi-independent test since 1964, though still heavily backed by U.S. airpower, MACV rediscovered that U.S. advisers still had a "critical role" to play. Reportedly, MACV decided to accelerate withdrawal of the two remaining U.S. infantry battalions in order to permit retaining more advisers.[46]

There is little question that the sixteen-year U.S. advisory effort improved RVNAF administration, training, and logistics. RVNAF ended up with all the appurtenances of a modern conventional military establishment—an extensive logistic and school system, a modern personnel system, command and staff organization, and the like. Technical proficiency was notably higher than in the Fifties. On the civil side, the same held true. U.S. advice and assistance are generally

---

*With U.S. disengagement overall army adviser strength declined to about 7,800 by end-1971, of whom fewer than 2,700 were in CORDS (the naval and air advisory efforts had grown significantly, however).

regarded as having significantly improved the average GVN administrative performance during 1966–1972. Perhaps even more important, the in-depth U.S. advisory network became, as General Abrams told the author, the "glue" that held the situation together in many respects at the critical local level. It provided a shadow channel of advice, communications, liaison, and support which was invaluable in knitting together various aspects of the GVN effort as well as coordinating GVN and allied efforts in the field.

After 1963 the growing advisory network in the countryside, together with unit advisers, also began giving both the U.S. and GVN a far better picture of what was actually going on than had been the case before. This advisory role as "eyes and ears" proved an important one. Even more important, the advisers came to be the source of an indispensable management tool: periodic reports on RVNAF and GVN performance. These were increasingly used by the GVN itself as more disinterested and accurate evaluations of the performance of its own subordinate echelons than the reporting from these echelons themselves. In effect, the U.S. advisory network provided the GVN with its best means of evaluating its own performance. Such "report cards" served as an important instrument of U.S. leverage as well.

Nowhere were these advisory roles developed more fully than in U.S. pacification support during 1967–1971. Without a comprehensive advisory network, the pacification upsurge that began in late 1968 could not have been achieved. The improvement was particularly visible in terms of RF/PF expansion and performance, which would not have been possible without roughly a tripling of the adviser input after 1966—including the Mobile Advisory Teams. At its peak strength, around the end of 1969, CORDS had about 6,500 military and 1,100 civilians assigned to it (by January 1972 this had dropped to 2,670 military and 730 civilians). But the important thing is that they were by then advising over 900,000 Vietnamese in every district and province of Vietnam—over 500,000 RF/PF, 50,000 RD cadre, 80,000 police, and on the order of 300,000 civil servants—on a wide variety of civil and military matters. Their cumulative impact was incalculable, yet their total cost only a tiny fraction of the total cost to the U.S. of the Vietnam war.

On the other hand, hindsight suggests that this long and eventually massive advisory effort was flawed in many respects. The *Pentagon Papers*, completed in the mood of pessimism following Tet 1968, raise some fundamental questions as to its basic utility, especially with respect to the "U.S. unstated assumption . . . that more advisers somehow equate to better performance" and the belief that "leverage" should be eschewed.[47] It is regrettable that the *Pentagon Papers* do not cover the years 1968–1971, because it was in this period that the U.S. advisory impact was greatest, especially in pacification.

In the author's view, fortified by field experience, the greatest weakness of the U.S. advisory effort was not that it was too large or omnipresent, but that it didn't go far enough. In retrospect, it was too technical-assistance oriented and not sufficiently performance oriented. We made an all-out effort to train, equip, and organize the GVN and RVNAF to *enable* them to perform better, but generally drew the line at measures aimed at *requiring* them to perform better. This was more than failure to use leverage. It was fundamental to our concept of how to advise—persuasion but not pressure.

Perhaps the greatest flaw was the failure to come to grips directly with the gross inadequacies of GVN and RVNAF leadership at all levels, as discussed earlier in Chapter 3. U.S. advisers early recognized that this was the critical problem, without a solution to which the massive structure the U.S. was subsidizing would not perform effectively. But we usually drew the line at direct intervention. Instead of pressing for removal of unsatisfactory commanders, and if necessary suspending aid as a lever to this end, MACV and U.S. civilian agencies confined themselves mostly to such indirect means as improved personnel selection procedures, schooling, and the like. These did not suffice; no matter how well trained, equipped, and organized the GVN and RVNAF became, poor leaders all too often remained its Achilles heel. Only CORDS developed systematic procedures for identifying poor province and district chiefs and other officials, and pressing consistently for their replacement. The author, who instituted this system, found top GVN officials reasonably responsive, and believes that the U.S. could and should have insisted more vigorously on removal of unsatisfactory officials and commanders. It might have made more of a difference than anything else.

Other major advisory flaws, inherent in the institutional background of U.S. advisers, were the conventional warfare emphasis and "mirror-imaging" discussed in Chapter 4. This helped create ARVN forces trained, equipped, and organized for American-style conventional warfare instead of for meeting the actual threat in Vietnam. Among other things, ARVN became highly dependent on extensive U.S. air and artillery support, which the advisory structure then served as the liaison channel to provide.

U.S. personnel systems proved remarkably resistant to devising procedures for optimizing advisor quality and experience. Before 1965, the overall quality of advisers was considerably higher than after U.S. intervention, when most of the best officers were assigned instead to U.S. units. Moreover, the one-year tour, and the services' interest in rotating as many careerists as possible through Vietnam, seriously lowered the experience level. The phasing out of a separate MAAG in early 1964 was probably another mistake, especially when growing U.S. troop commitments meant that MACV inevitably focused chiefly on its role as a U.S. theater headquarters—to the neglect of its advisory role.

Even so, the advisory effort still nets out as a relatively inexpensive and useful employment of U.S. resources compared to the rest of the costly U.S. involvement in Vietnam. At its peak strength of around 16,000, it was still barely 3 percent of the over 550,000 American civilians and soldiers serving there. Those critics who argue nonetheless that the U.S. overwhelmed the Vietnamese with "huge" numbers of advisers also ignore that these were advising a GVN military, para-military, and civil establishment of well over 1.5 million, an adviser-to-advised ratio of only one to a hundred or so. And a large number of advisers was essential to the adaptive extension of the U.S. advisory presence down to the battalion, province, and district level, where so much of the Vietnam war was really fought.

Lastly, it must be remembered that a sizable proportion of the 16,000 "advisers" were in fact housekeeping or administrative personnel for the advisory teams, which after all had to be maintained American style. So rather than question the excessive number of U.S. advisers in 1967–1970, one might equally well ask whether much earlier and more rapid expansion—plus greater stress on adviser quality and use of leverage—might not have achieved enough improvement in GVN/RVNAF performance to reduce the need for so massive a U.S. troop commitment as in the event occurred.

The ultimate proof of the value of the U.S. advisory effort was that when the "glue" it provided to the RVNAF was removed after 1972, RVNAF planning, command and control, and performance began to break down. However, in summarizing their interviews with Vietnamese officers and officials on the causes of the final 1975 collapse, RAND researchers note that

It was also the American role, in the view of the respondents, that dissuaded them from cleaning their own house, or at least effectively trying to do so while there still seemed to be time. The Americans, they said, misreading the war and the enemy, had saddled them with a military organization ill-suited to meet the enemy after the Paris

Agreement and impossible to maintain with declining aid. The South Vietnamese soldier had been "conditioned" by the U.S. presence to rely on vast air and artillery support in combat and had "forgotten how to walk." Furthermore, many respondents felt that ARVN . . . had been organized along the wrong pattern: It had far too big a "tail," and it lacked the mobile reserve divisions essential to counter a conventional North Vietnamese assault.[48]

NOTES

1. For his analysis of his job, see Leonard Sullivan, Jr., "R&D for Vietnam," *Science and Technology*, October 1968, p. 28.

2. Statement of Major General John R. Deane, Director, Defense Communications Planning Group, to Special Committee of Senate Armed Services Committee, November 13, 1970.

3. Sir Robert Thompson, *No Exit from Vietnam*, David McKay Company, Inc., New York, 1969, p. 136.

4. See F. J. West, Jr., *The Village*, Harper & Row, New York, 1972, for a lucid account of the role of a Combined Action Platoon during 1966–1967.

5. Bruce Palmer, *The 25-Year War*, University Press of Kentucky, Lexington, KY, 1984, pp. 60–61.

6. Joint Logistics Review Board, *Logistic Support in the Vietnam Era*, Vol. 2, pp. 26ff.

7. Ibid., p. 275.

8. See Blaufarb, *The Counterinsurgency Era*, pp. 106–107, 212, and 259–260.

9. Blaufarb calls Thieu's decision to throw his weight behind the Land To The Tiller law of March 1970 "perhaps the most far-reaching policy initiative of this whole period of the renovation of pacification." Ibid., p. 266.

10. *United States-Vietnam Relations, 1945-1967: Study Proposals by the Department of Defense*, 12 Volumes, U. S. Government Printing Office, Washington, D.C., 1971 (hereafter referred to as the *Pentagon Papers*), IV.C.8.

11. Ibid., IV.A.5, Tab. 2, pp. 22–24.

12. Ibid., IV.C.9(b), p. 5.

13. Ibid., IV.C.5, p. 20.

14. Cf. Chester Cooper, *Lost Crusade*, Dodd, Mead & Company, New York, 1970, pp. 275–276.

15. President Johnson raised this twice with the author in 1966–1967, but the author was strongly opposed. He felt as a matter of policy that the laboring oar in pacification should be strictly Vietnamese, and designed the "new model" program on this basis.

16. *Pentagon Papers*, IV.B.3, p. 73.

17. Ibid., IV.C.8, "Re-Emphasis on Pacification 1965–1967."

18. For two earlier views which stress local security as essential, see Nighswonger, *Rural Pacification,* and John C. Donnell, "The War, the Gap, and the Cadre," *Asian Survey,* Winter 1966. Both authors were U.S. civilian officials who served in Vietnam.

19. Thomas Thayer, in W. Scott Thompson and Donaldson D. Frizzell (eds.), *The Lessons of Vietnam,* Crane Russak & Company, Inc., 1977, p. 256.

20. *The Washington Post,* January 22, 1971, p. A-11.

21. For the most comprehensive account of the "new model" pacification program, see the extensive testimony of Ambassador W. E. Colby (Deputy for CORDS, 1968–1971) and his CORDS colleagues before the Senate Foreign Relations Committee, February 1970, and before the Moorhead Subcommittee of the House Committee on Government Operations, July 15–21, 1971. For an analysis of pacification impact, see R. W. Komer, "Pacification Impact on Insurgency," *Journal of International Affairs,* Vol. 25, No. 1, 1971, pp. 48–68 and Blaufarb, *The Counterinsurgency Era,* pp. 205–278.

22. Alain C. Enthoven and K. Wayne Smith, *How Much Is Enough?* Harper and Row, New York, 1969, p. 294.

23. Their activities are described in C. F. Romanus and R. Sunderland, *Time Runs Out in CBI,* Department of the Army, Washington, D.C., 1959, the relevant volume of the official history. Unfortunately, the work does not include total advisory strengths.

24. Ibid., pp. 15–16.

25. Ibid., Chapter VIII, pp. 231–261, 262–269, and 373–378.

26. Ibid., p. 378.

27. Ibid., pp. 359–360.

28. W. G. Hermes, *Survey of the Development of the Role of the U.S. Army Military Advisor,* Office of the Chief of Military History (OCMH), Department of the Army, Washington, D.C., 1965, pp. 59–60.

29. R. K. Sawyer, *Military Advisors in Korea; KMAG in Peace and War,* OCMH, Department of the Army, Washington, D.C., 1962, Chapters II–IV.

30. Ibid., p. 161.

31. Ibid., p. 170.

32. *Pentagon Papers,* IV.B.3, Summary and Analysis, p. 1.

33. Ibid., Part One, p. 6.

34. Ibid., p. 13.

35. Ibid., p. 16.

36. Ibid., p. 32.

37. Ibid., pp. 33–36.

38. Ibid., pp. 43–44.

39. Ibid., pp. 45–48.

40. Ibid., p. 49.

41. Ibid., pp. 50–51.

42. Ibid., Summary and Analysis, p. vii.

43. Ibid., Part Two, p. 70.

44. Ibid., pp. 109–112.

45. Tables in IV.B.3, Appendixes I–IX, pp. 125–133.

46. George McArthur article in *The Washington Post*, July 26, 1972, p. 14. See also report of Senate Foreign Relations Committee staff members Moose and Lowenstein cited in *The Washington Post*, June 29, 1972, p. 1.

47. *Pentagon Papers*, IV.B.3, Summary and Analysis, pp. viii–x.

48. Stephen T. Hosmer, et al., *The Fall of South Vietnam: Statements by Vietnamese Military and Civilian Leaders*, Crane Russak & Company, Inc., New York, 1980, p. 11.

8
WAS THERE A VIABLE ALTERNATIVE STRATEGY?

To many, a key lesson (or "mislesson") of Vietnam is that the U.S. realistically never should have expected it to end up as other than a catastrophe. Certainly it proved politically impossible to achieve our aims at acceptable cost the way we actually fought the war. Moreover, the range of environmental, policy, and institutional constraints already discussed in previous chapters suggests how difficult it would have been for us to act differently. Yet our twenty years of checkered experience in Vietnam also suggest that approaches other than those we adopted might have led to significantly different results. Indeed, developments in the field between the Tet 1968 watershed and U.S. withdrawal by end-1972 suggest that, if much of what happened then had happened earlier, the 1973–1975 pattern of events might have been different.

Many alternative strategic approaches were proposed at various times. George Ball's contention that we should not intervene directly with U.S. forces naturally looks much better in retrospect than it did in 1965. Other well-known proposals centered around the "enclave" strategy or advocacy of a larger and less restricted employment of conventional U.S. military power. "Victory through air power" had its advocates—the Air Force, Navy, and JCS repeatedly calling for more massive and less graduated air attacks from 1964 on. The U.S. military also proposed applying U.S. military power more effectively through attacking the sanctuaries in Cambodia and Laos or even amphibious thrusts against North Vietnam. General Bruce Palmer argues in hindsight that the U.S. should have concentrated its forces in northern I Corps and extended a defensive line across the southern Laos panhandle to the Mekong, thus cutting the Ho Chi Minh trail.[1] But Washington civilian decisionmakers usually opted against such forms of military escalation. We also repeatedly sought a negotiated outcome and compromised a great deal finally to get one, albeit it proved quite temporary.

Yet there was also an alternative approach which lay well within the political constraints imposed by the decisionmakers. In fact, its advocates were partly stimulated by a desire to avoid raising the military threshold. These advocates were an unusual mix of soldiers and civilians, some of whom had ready access to high policymakers.[2] In broad outline at any rate they favored with varying degrees of energy and persuasiveness what might be called a "counterinsurgency" strategy. Its intellectual antecedents lay as much in our own Philippine experience against the Huks and British experience in Malaya in the 1950s as in the French experience in Vietnam.

What was this alternative approach? It is hard to define precisely, because it was never all put down in definitive form and varied in content and emphasis from time to time. Nor was there ever an open confrontation between this and other alternative approaches, with the policymaker forced to decide among them. To the author's knowledge, there was never a clear-cut case of either/or. Instead, all approaches were almost invariably intermingled, though with sharply varying emphases.

Nonetheless, a more or less clear unifying thread ran through the views of many advisers and officials.[3] First was their emphasis on the primacy of political over military aims in the Vietnam conflict. They saw the greatest need as being to protect and win over the population on which the insurgency fed. This view often took the form of stressing the need to build a viable and responsive local government. It also underlay the stress on "winning hearts and minds" by providing a more attractive alternative to Communist rule. Land reform, rural aid programs, anticorruption measures, administrative decentralization, and representative government were seen as tools to this end. In security terms, this school placed greater emphasis on clear-and-hold by police and paramilitary forces to provide sustained local protection to the population than on conventional offensive operations against VC units. Thus, the counterinsurgency school laid greater stress on the CG/SDC (later RF/PF) and police than on constant buildup of conventional military forces.

An early exposition of the views of this counterinsurgency school was Assistant Secretary Roger Hilsman's final memorandum to the Secretary of State in March 1964. To Hilsman, the right strategic concept called for primary emphasis on giving security to the villagers. The tactics are the so-called oil-blot approach, starting with a secure area and extending it slowly. . . . This calls for the use of military forces in a different way from that of orthodox, conventional war. Rather than chasing Viet Cong, the military must put primary emphasis on clear-and-hold operations and on rapid reinforcement of villages under attack. It is also important, of course, to keep the Viet Cong regular units off balance by conventional offensive operations, but these should be secondary to the major task of extending security. . . .

Hilsman concluded by saying he believed we could win in Vietnam, but only if we did not "overmilitarize the war" and if there was "political stability in Saigon."[4]

Also implicit in this approach was that the main burden of carrying it out had to be borne by the Vietnamese; Americans could not do it for them. One corollary to this was that the U.S. had to use all available means (including if necessary all the leverage at its disposal) to ensure emergence of a GVN capable of executing the strategy. Another corollary was that both Vietnamese and Americans needed to organize sensibly to carry out such a strategy. As we have seen in Chapter 6, some Americans (though not always the same who pushed this approach) also advocated these things, but without much success, which is one reason why the alternative approach never got far off the ground during 1955–1966.

As noted at the outset of this study, we Americans early perceived these needs. The *Pentagon Papers* make clear that they were part and parcel of our Vietnam policy from the first. U.S. policy documents are replete with counterinsurgency oriented strategic guidance— whether it was termed internal security, counterinsurgency, strategic hamlets, revolutionary development, or pacification. The same held true of GVN planning.

Moreover, almost every element which might logically be regarded as part of a counterinsurgency-oriented strategy was called for repeatedly, and tried (often several times) on at least a small scale. Compared to the conventional U.S./GVN military effort, however, they were always "small potatoes." The weight of our effort was overwhelmingly conventional military from the outset, and became even more so after 1960. One weakness of the *Pentagon Papers* is that, being based so largely on policy documents, *they do not bring out the striking contrast between the amount of policy stress on counterinsurgency, or pacification, and how little was actually done—up to*

1967 at least. A look at the historical record amply illustrates the yawning gap between policy and performance.

THE EISENHOWER PERIOD—1954 TO 1960

From the very time that the U.S. took over from France as chief supporter of newly created South Vietnam, its major policy focus was on building a viable nationalist regime via elections, administrative and land reform, and the like. But not enough was accomplished toward achieving these ambitious aims, for reasons discussed in Chapter 3. For example, in 1956 Diem promulgated a land reform designed by Wolf Ladejinsky, but the program was delayed in starting and by 1959 was "virtually inoperative."[5]

A similar gap between policy and performance developed in our military assistance program, which initially was to be for "internal security" only.[6] By the late Fifties it was official doctrine that externally supported "subversion" was a major threat; in fact, in 1957 SEATO's second Annual Report stated that "subversion which has always been a major problem is the main threat we now face."[7] But, as seen in Chapter 4, this policy was converted in practice to overwhelming emphasis on building a conventional delaying force. Such internal security forces as CG, SDC, and police were neglected.[8] Little was done during 1954–1960 to develop an effective counterinsurgency capability, despite what policy prescribed. The *Pentagon Papers*, commenting on this failure, caution that

> This is not to imply that had resources been diverted from the creation of a conventional army to that of an effective counterinsurgent force the problem of Vietnam would have been solved, for the enemy has demonstrated both versatility and flexibility that would render such a statement vacuous . . . An effective counterinsurgent force, on the other hand, might have limited its choices; might well have prevented effective prosecution of the guerrilla alternative the Viet Cong and the DRV did elect to follow.[9]

Even during the late Eisenhower years there was much criticism from Washington and Embassy Saigon of MAAG preparing the Vietnamese forces primarily against an overt North Vietnamese attack when mostly indigenous insurgency was slowly growing in the South.[10] By early 1960 U.S. recognition that the insurgency threat was reaching crisis proportions led DOD and JCS to approve a CINCPAC plan emphasizing counterinsurgency-type operations under a new GVN central directing body.[11] The outgrowth was the Mission-prepared Counter-Insurgency Plan (CIP), which called for a comprehensive approach.

THE KENNEDY YEARS—1961 TO 1963

With the arrival of the New Frontier, the debate over what to do about the growing crisis in Vietnam was aired at the highest levels. Moreover, President Kennedy and his brother Robert were ardent advocates of coping with "wars of national liberation" by imaginative counterinsurgency techniques.[12] This effort received direct White House stimulus in such ways as creation of a high-level interagency Special Group-Counterinsurgency in 1961, upgrading of the Army Special Forces, and strengthening of police assistance programs abroad.[13] Kennedy was also taken with General Lansdale's report on Vietnam, which dissented vigorously from both MAAG's conventional-force emphasis and its complacency.[14] Paradoxically, however, the administration which most wanted a sophisticated approach to Vietnam, and tried hardest to get one, was also the administration which ended up putting the U.S. on an even more conventional military path.

One of the new President's first acts was to approve the Commercial Import Program and allocate $42 million more in U.S. aid for ARVN and the Civil Guard. But Diem evaded the reforms which were supposed to accompany this.[15] When Kennedy established an ad hoc Task Force on Vietnam under Deputy Secretary of Defense Gilpatric, its first (April 1961) report called for no increases in Vietnamese forces, but emphasized the need "to focus the U.S. effort in Vietnam on the immediate internal security problem."[16] Kennedy next approved a modest increase in the MAAG and authorized it to support the paramilitary Civil Guard and SDC.[17] The ad hoc Task Force Reports, the later Staley Report, and the Taylor-Rostow Report following their October 1961 visit to Vietnam all included elements of a comprehensive counterinsurgency strategy and program. Indeed, the President's October 13, 1961 letter of instructions to General Taylor emphasized appraising the threat to "internal security," noting that "while the military part of the problem is of great importance in South Vietnam, its political, social, and economic elements are equally significant. . . ."[18]

However, Washington debate in late 1961 focused mainly on the abortive issue of whether U.S. troops should be sent. By this time the policy record as to what strategic emphasis the U.S. was pursuing in Vietnam becomes quite confused. A mixed strategy seems to have been called for, though never carried out in balanced fashion on the ground. There was also growing controversy over strategic emphasis during 1962–1964, with various counterinsurgency-oriented officials in the State Department pitted against the more conventional Pentagon backed by the U.S. Mission in Saigon.[19] In what Roger Hilsman describes as a "search for a strategic concept," he and Averell Harriman and Michael Forrestal appear to have strongly advocated more unified U.S. field management, granting primacy to political factors, more military emphasis on clear-and-hold instead of search-and-destroy, and large-scale efforts to separate the guerrilla fish from the rural sea in which they swam.[20]

The next stage in the attempt to devise an alternative or complementary strategy was the abortive Strategic Hamlet Program of 1962–1963.[21] Many U.S. civilian officials in Washington and Saigon were strongly sympathetic to Sir Robert Thompson's proposals. They probably "were attracted by an argument which did suggest some hope for 'demilitarizing' the war, de-emphasizing U.S. operational participation, and increasing GVN's ability to solve its own internal problems using primarily its own human resources."[22] It received considerable high-level U.S. backing.[23]

Thompson strongly advocated a carefully planned and gradual effort focused initially on the rich Delta provinces. But his Delta Plan was perverted from the outset; it was even begun in the wrong place and for the wrong reasons in the notorious Operation Sunrise. And, regrettably, it got all too little concrete U.S. support. Again, a counterinsurgency program failed in practice, partly because Diem and Nhu conceived it too grandiosely and ran it poorly, partly because the CG/SDC were never far enough upgraded to provide the indispensable local security, and partly because it was generally attempted on what in hindsight looks like a shoestring. The major direct U.S. aid contribution appears to have been $10 million in piasters, a very modest sum for so ambitious a program. In any case, what had been done collapsed with the fall of Diem.[24] In retrospect, both the U.S. and GVN missed a major opportunity in not following the Thompson program as originally conceived.

Meanwhile, the controversy over strategy continued. According to John Stempel, "the State/Hilsman view pictured the war as going badly and advocated pressuring for political reform even at the risk of unseating Diem. The Defense/MACV position pictured the war as being successful, and suggested working for political reforms only if they would not promote governmental instability."[25] In March 1963, Harriman became Under Secretary of State for Political Affairs, and

Hilsman Assistant Secretary for the Far East, strengthening their roles. However, it is misleading to suggest either that there was a single State Department view or that Defense officials ignored political reform and pacification. Moreover, the whole controversy was soon submerged by the crisis leading to Diem's fall in November 1963.

Paradoxically, pacification became a constant preoccupation at the highest Washington levels only in late 1963 and after, when (as events were to show) there was no longer time to generate an adequate GVN effort. After learning during a September 1963 visit to Saigon how much the situation had deteriorated, McNamara and Taylor urged emphasis on clear-and-hold operations, consolidation of the Strategic Hamlet Program with emphasis on security, and better training and arms for the hamlet militia.[26] Right after the November 1963 coup, an emergency Honolulu Conference led to NSAM 273, which called for concentration of GVN and U.S. efforts in the key Delta area, where the guerrilla war was going badly.[27] Further disturbing reports from the field led to another McNamara visit to Saigon in December, which focused largely on pacification matters. It resulted in the first of McNamara's gloomy memoranda to the President.[28] More gloom was to follow.

In 1964 yet another attempt was made to stimulate a pacification program, this time under the auspices of the military junta led by General Khanh. His February 1964 Chien Thang plan, based on the "oil-spot" concept, was more modest than the nationwide Strategic Hamlet Program, being focused mostly on the eight key provinces around Saigon.[29] It was realized that "The political control structure extending from Saigon down into the hamlets disappeared following the November coup."[30] By March 1964, when McNamara again visited Saigon, Khanh had dressed this up into a nationwide National Pacification Plan, to be supplemented by national mobilization. Aside from an oil-spot expansion beginning in the key provinces around Saigon, stress was to be placed on land reform, higher rice prices to the farmers, and improved rural services and administration. Top-level U. S. support for this grandiose effort was approved in NSAM 288, which was replete with such pacification-oriented measures as strengthening and improving the paramilitary forces, increasing national police strength in the provinces, providing more U.S. advisers at district and province, and the like. The Americans also proposed a new GVN Civil Administration Corps to work in rural areas.[31]

But in reality, "Although VC successes in rural areas had been the prime feature of the downswing over the past half year or more, pacification was to receive less comparative emphasis, in fact, in the next year or so than it had before."[32] While Washington policy documents and the U.S/GVN dialogue in 1964 and early 1965 stress U.S. efforts to revive some form of pacification effort, all too little was done in practice by the GVN. As the *Pentagon Papers* remark, the limited U.S. measures during the hectic period between Diem's death and the introduction of U.S. combat forces turned out to be mere palliatives, largely because of continued political instability in Saigon. "Declaratory policy raced far ahead of resource allocations and use decisions."[33] The new team of Ambassadors Taylor and Alexis Johnson and General Westmoreland in Saigon was also preoccupied with the succession of post-Diem coups.

The last gasp before U.S. intervention was the modest *Hop Tac* scheme launched in September 1964 at U.S. initiative in three provinces around Saigon. The *Hop Tac* plan was produced by MACV, and given lip service by the GVN. But even this feeble effort collapsed in 1965 under increasing VC pressure, abetted by lack of GVN support and poor U.S. planning.[34]

Meanwhile both the U.S. and GVN, frustrated over their seemingly insoluble problem in the South, began looking at ways to relieve it by carrying the war to the North. Growing VC strength and the first signs of NVA infiltration helped reinforce this rationale. In effect, just as Washington was finally facing up to the needs of a counterinsurgency strategy, the deterioration of the situation led instead to growing emphasis on relieving the pressure on the GVN through direct U.S. military involvement.

PACIFICATION TAKES A BACK SEAT—1965 TO 1966

When the U.S. launched its "reprisal" policy of air strikes against the North, McGeorge Bundy at least clung to the hope that if this bought a respite for the GVN "the most urgent order of business will then be the improvement and broadening of the pacification program, especially in its non-military elements. . . ."[35] The object of the new policy was "to effect a visible upward turn in pacification, in governmental effectiveness, in operations against the Viet Cong, and in the whole U.S./GVN relationship."[36] This was duly enshrined in the formal Presidential decisions of February 13, 1965, the first of which was that "We will intensify by all available means the program of pacification within SVN."[37] The *Pentagon Papers* note "This stress on action in the South reflected a serious concern at high levels in the White House and the State Department . . . that a growing preoccupation with action against the North would be likely to cause the U.S. Mission and the GVN leadership to neglect the all-important struggle within the borders of South Vietnam."[38] They were right, though it is not clear what else the GVN could realistically have done in its state of disarray.[39]

At any rate, from this point there was hardly any stress on pacification in the policy documents relating to the growing U.S. military intervention in Vietnam. True, "Even during the dark days of 1964–1965, most Americans paid lip service, particularly in official, on-the-record statements, to the ultimate importance of pacification. But their public affirmation of the cliches about "winning the hearts and minds of the people" were not related to any programs or priorities then in existence in Vietnam, and they can mislead the casual observer."[40]

Instead the debate over ground strategy in 1965 revolved around the level and mission of U.S. forces. As described in the *Pentagon Papers*, three identifiable schools emerged: (1) base security—simply protecting the U.S. air bases involved in the bombing of the North; (2) Ambassador Taylor's favored "enclave strategy," aimed at denying the enemy certain key coastal areas while releasing ARVN to fight the war inland; and (3) a search-and-destroy strategy to seize the initiative, as pressed by Westmoreland and the JCS.[41] The base security strategy adopted initially was soon effectively superseded by NSAM 328 (April 6, 1965), which first allowed Westmoreland to use U.S. forces more offensively, as he desired.[42] In turn the enclave strategy had its brief day, but by June Westmoreland had full authority to employ his growing U.S. ground forces as he saw fit.[43]

> The difference between Westmoreland and Taylor was the former's insistence on using U.S. and 3rd Country forces to take the war to the enemy. Taylor was quite content to let RVNAF do that with the occasional assist from the Allied forces if they got into difficulty. Westmoreland did not think they could do it, and he was convinced that no kind of victory could be had unless some pressure were put on the VC/DRV forces in South Vietnam.[44]

RENEWED DEBATE OVER STRATEGY—1966 TO 1967

In 1966, after U.S. military intervention had averted GVN collapse, issues again arose over how to conduct the war. They arose from Washington's growing frustration over the demands of the U.S. military for escalation of the U.S. effort, from failure of the bombing campaign against North Vietnam to force Hanoi to desist, and from the dawning realization that continuing to grind up the enemy main forces did not by itself offer a way to achieve our aims so long as Hanoi could keep replacing its losses by infiltration and VC recruiting in the South. By this time, however, pacification was no longer seen as a preferred alternative strategy but merely as an indispensable corollary to the big-unit war against the growing VC/NVA main forces.

Other contributory factors were the August 1965 return to Saigon of Ambassador Lodge—a convinced advocate of a pacification-oriented strategy, and President Johnson's emphasis on the need to stress the "other war." While this emphasis may have stemmed largely from his perception of U.S. domestic political needs, at the February 1966 Honolulu Conference he pressed hard for reemphasizing pacification-oriented programs. This time, however, something new was added. The first steps were taken to create special U.S. machinery in both Washington and Saigon to give specific high-level focus to this effort (see Chapters 6 and 7). Thus for the first time pacification began to have high-level vested interests speaking for it.[45] In their new roles Porter in Saigon and the author in Washington began pushing practical measures, backed by the President, McNamara, and Lodge in particular.[46]

By 1966 small-scale counterinsurgency efforts began growing again— this time as a modest complement to the escalating main-force war. CIA and AID stepped up their attempts to generate rural paramilitary and developmental programs under the new rubric of Revolutionary Development. But the whole effort still added up to only a small fraction of the men and resources being invested in the main-force war. Since the U.S./GVN military still regarded such programs as essentially civilian business, they gave only modest support.[47] The GVN's many promises at Honolulu remained just that for the most part.

In March 1966 a detailed blueprint for a primarily pacification-oriented U.S. strategy came from an unusual source, a study group set up by the Army Chief of Staff. Done mostly by young field officers who had served as advisers in Vietnam, the PROVN Report proposed that the main weight of the GVN/U.S. effort be focused on territorial security, economic and political reform, and nation-building rather than anti-main-force operations, and be carried out on the U.S. side by a unified single manager system extending from Washington down to district level in Vietnam. While PROVN had considerable educational value, especially to the post-1966 pacification effort, its far-reaching proposals were initially rejected both in Washington and in the field.[48]

Having greater impact than PROVN was a prescient "Roles and Missions" study done by a talented study group under Porter in summer 1966. Agreeing with PROVN that RD (pacification) was the key to a successful strategy, it dwelt on practical steps by which both the GVN and U.S. should go about this task. For example, it focused more than any previous U.S. study on the critical need to get at the directing apparatus of the insurgency at all levels, noting that no task was given so much lip service yet so totally neglected in fact. It further urged analyzing whether the lavish use of air and artillery in populated areas was having counterproductive impact on village attitudes. While these proposals foreshadowed many of CORDS' later emphases, they were not accepted as policy at the time by either Lodge or MACV.[49] So the already mountainous stack of reports and recommendations continued to mount, but their impact remained minimal.

However, an unforeseen new element in the evolving situation was to give a powerful fillip to pacification. Since U.S. forces were increasingly taking over anti-main-force offensive operations, what role should RVNAF play? RD Minister Thang, Porter, and the author, arguing that sustained clear-and-hold operations were essential to successful pacification, proposed in June 1966 that a strengthened RF/PF be assigned this mission and be placed under the RD Ministry. This was turned down by Prime Minister Ky, perhaps under pressure from the ARVN generals. So the "Roles and Missions" study proposed instead that a radically reformed RVNAF, including most ARVN infantry battalions, be assigned this primary role.[50] MACV and the JCS came to a similar conclusion, leading Lodge to conclude prematurely that the Americans had finally achieved "giving pacification the highest priority which it has ever had—making it, in effect, the main purpose of all our activities."[51] The wish was father to the thought in this case. Nonetheless the GVN did pledge at the October 1966 Manila Conference that over half of ARVN maneuver battalions would be assigned to RD support.

A perceptive analysis prepared in the office of the Under Secretary of State in December 1966 forecast how weak a reed the ARVN was likely to be and how little a pacification-oriented strategy was actually being pursued. Basic counterinsurgency precepts "have survived in principle but have been little applied in practice." ARVN "has never escaped from its conventional warfare mold." Most GVN and ARVN leaders neither understand nor press a sensible pacification approach. Despite the claims of top U.S. and GVN generals, "the waging of a conventional war has overriding priority, perhaps as much as 9 to

1. . . ." Hence ARVN's basic weaknesses would probably undermine its effectiveness in pacification—just as in conventional warfare.[52]

Frustrated over military demands for more troops and bombing despite inability to relate these to a convincing strategy, and newly concerned over the inflationary burden being placed on the South Vietnamese economy, McNamara also focused heavily again on the pacification option. In a pessimistic report to the President following his October 1966 visit to Vietnam, McNamara concluded that neither a further major U.S. troop buildup nor bombing of the North would achieve our aims, and argued for settling down to a long-haul "military posture that we credibly could maintain indefinitely" via stabilizing the U.S. force level at 470,000, installing a barrier system along the DMZ, stabilizing the bombing campaign against the North, pressing for negotiations, and pursuing "a vigorous pacification program."[53] Calling pacification to date "a bad disappointment" (in fact it still hardly existed), McNamara granted that of all his recommendations

> . . . the one most difficult to implement is perhaps the most important one—enlivening the pacification program. The odds are less than even for this task, if only because we have failed consistently since 1961 to make a dent in the problem. But, because the 1967 trend of pacification will, I believe, be the main talisman of ultimate U.S. success or failure in Vietnam, extraordinary imagination and effort should go into changing the stripes of that problem.[54]

Commenting on this shift in McNamara's thinking, the *Pentagon Papers* note that "the increased emphasis on the pacification effort is apparently a result of the feeling that, since it represented the heart of the problem in Vietnam, and the main force war was only contributory to it, perhaps all that was needed in the main force war was to keep the enemy off the back of the pacification effort in a strategic defensive, rather than to destroy the enemy in a strategic offensive."[55] McNamara further developed this alternative to the attrition strategy in his Draft Presidential Memorandum of November 17, 1966. He argued that "the data suggest that we have no prospects of attriting the enemy force at a rate equal to or greater than his capability to infiltrate and recruit, and this will be true at either the 470,000 U.S. personnel level or 570,000."[56]

The new MACV/JGS Combined Campaign Plan for 1967 (AB 142), completed in November 1966, further "committed RVNAF to support pacification with the majority of its forces."[57] For the first time it gave pacification considerable prominence, reflecting input from the

Porter and Komer staffs and from General Thang. But again the primary focus was on the main-force threat. In fact too little effective military support to permit steady pacification expansion was given in 1967. Many ARVN battalions performed poorly in the RD support role and were constantly being diverted to other missions. Hence the pacifiers began looking more toward expansion and improvement of the RF/PF for this purpose.

The growing debate over how to fight the war became still more sharply focused in 1967. Again it was concern over new military proposals for more troops, more bombing of the North, and the like which drove the belated search for strategic alternatives. It was precipitated by General Westmoreland's March 18 request for around 210,000 more U.S. troops.[58] Several civilian critiques, including one by the author, disputed the need for many more troops and suggested various alternatives, such as greater efforts to jack up the Vietnamese contribution.[59] OSD/SA directly attacked the feasibility of a "war of attrition," pointing out that the enemy's capability to control his losses meant that more U.S. troops could not destroy his force. The DOD civilian leadership came down in favor of stabilizing the U.S. effort rather than escalating. The civilians won, and the President approved only a modest force increase from 500,000 to 525,000.

Again, the civilian arguments against troop increases and bombing were far more cogently spelled out than the strategic alternatives they advanced. Although a U.S. force stabilized at roughly existing levels was to provide the shield while the GVN pacified, DOD views on how the latter was to be accomplished were only vaguely spelled out; they added up only to getting the GVN to pull more weight and to get pacification moving. Since DOD at the same time kept stressing how the GVN was not doing the job and how poorly pacification was going, it is hard to avoid the conclusion that DOD civilian officials were more skilled at shooting down MACV, CINCPAC, and the JCS than at developing a viable alternative. Those who in 1966–1967 opposed the military view in the growing strategy debate were much more clear on why they didn't like the old strategy than on how to devise a new one. The crucial determinant was more the politically sensitive level at which U.S. reserves would have to be called up than strategic considerations in Vietnam.[60]

THE POST-TET REASSESSMENT

The Tet shock of February 1968, reinforced by MACV's controversial "request" for another 200,000-odd U. S. troops, was the final proof in Washington civilian eyes that the attrition strategy would not work.[61] To new Secretary of Defense Clark Clifford the real question was: Could [our present course in Vietnam] ever prove successful even if vastly more than 200,000 troops were sent?"[62] Whatever the validity of this conclusion, the *Pentagon Papers* reveal that it was based on bleak, even panicky Washington assessments of the post-Tet situation, which turn out in hindsight to have been largely wrong.[63] For example, the gloomy Vietnam prognosis in the February 29 initial draft of an OSD memorandum to the president proved off-base in almost every important respect.[64]

In the search for strategic alternatives which preoccupied Washington during February-March 1968, no pacification-oriented option was even seriously considered, since both the civilians and the JCS prematurely wrote off the new program as in a "shambles."[65] Among the plethora of strategic option papers prepared by various agencies apparently only one—an OSD/SA paper—even raised the pacification variant, only to reject it because "the enemy's current offensive appears to have killed the program once and for all (*sic*)."[66]

The civilian position which evolved, and was sent to the President, was that even with 200,000 more troops the existing strategy could not succeed. As the *Pentagon Papers* remark, these civilian officials

> finally came to the realization that no military strategy could be successful unless a South Vietnamese political and military entity was capable of winning the support of its people. Thus, for the first time, U.S. efforts were to be made contingent upon specific reform measures undertaken by the GVN, and U.S. leverage was to be used to elicit these reforms. South Vietnam was to be put on notice that the limit of U.S. patience and commitment had been approached.[67]

But all that the civilians recommended as an alternative was shifting to a defensive strategy of securing the populated areas and denying the enemy victory, while pressing the GVN and RVNAF to assume more of the burden. In any event no new strategic guidance was issued to the field. The JCS vigorously opposed a change, and even questioned the propriety of sending such guidance to the field commander.[68]

Nonetheless, the Tet shock did prove a turning point in a way which no one foresaw. President Johnson's decisions to restrict the troop ceiling to a modestly increased 549,500 and partially (later fully) to suspend bombing of the North marked the peak of the U.S. commitment and the beginning of U.S. disengagement. And this shock, coming on top of the Tet Offensive itself, did force the GVN and ARVN at long last to take such measures as manpower mobilization and some purging of poor commanders and officials. After Tet 1968, GVN performance improved significantly.

And for once attrition worked, though only because the enemy was consistently attacking us rather than our attacking him. The enemy's cumulative losses during his Tet and follow-on offensives of 1968 were a major factor in forcing him to revert to a protracted war strategy in 1969–1971. Not until mid-1972, almost four years later, had Hanoi rebuilt its forces sufficiently to launch another multi-front offensive of any size. By this time it had to be conducted mostly by NVA forces, and NVA fillers in nominally VC units. It had become an NVA war.

Another contributory factor was that the pacification program proved far less severely hurt than Washington had prematurely concluded. Instead it entered a period of rapid expansion in late 1968 which continued for the next two years. As a result, the GVN position four years later, by mid-1972, was far stronger than at Tet 1968, despite U.S. withdrawal of almost 500,000 U.S. troops and a substantial cutback in the air war.

WHY WAS THE PACIFICATION ALTERNATIVE NEGLECTED FOR SO LONG?

This brief review shows how from 1955 on counterinsurgency or pacification was a major if not dominant element in high policy thinking, both in Washington and Saigon. *But it also shows an immense gap between the policy prominence it was given and what actually happened in the field.* To see the full dimensions of this discontinuity between policy and performance we must look beyond GVN/U.S. declaratory policy at resource allocation in Vietnam. Even a cursory review of the bidding demonstrates that the GVN and U.S. actually devoted very little effort and resources to pacification programs, at least up to 1967. Throughout the 1955–1965 period these remained instead a very small tail to the large conventional military dog. Despite the recurrent policy emphasis on counterinsurgency-cum-pacification, and many abortive experiments, such programs never really amounted to much until quite late in the day.

The proof of the pudding lies in the feeble resources and manpower devoted to them, compared to the massive resources devoted to the conventional military effort (and the budget support and anti-inflation inputs which they required). We have seen in Chapter 4 how little

U.S. military aid was allocated to the paramilitary CG/SDC (later RF/PF). U.S. civilian aid inputs were of course far more modest than military aid. But even AID, for example, devoted far fewer resources to police and rural programs than to the economic stabilization effort required largely by the militarization of the war. Even in 1966, the year of so-called "re-emphasis on pacification," estimated GVN/U.S. pacification outlays amounted to less than $600 million (in dollars and piasters) out of a total of $21 billion in estimated GVN/U.S. war costs.[69] And since pacification utilized almost wholly Vietnamese personnel and largely local resources, it absorbed in 1966 little over 1 percent of what the U.S. itself was spending on the war.

So, whether or not a primarily counterinsurgency-oriented strategy was sound, *the fact is that it was never given a full-scale try*—before 1967 at least. Instead, it was swamped almost from the outset by more conventional approaches to the highly unconventional situation we confronted in Vietnam. In this sense, it is hard to fault Hilsman's conclusion as of 1966 that "If Vietnam does represent a failure in the Kennedy administration, it was a failure in implementation."[70]

If so many were advocating a multifaceted politico-military counterinsurgency strategy, why did it fail for so long to get off the ground? The reasons are many and complex. Most of them have already been alluded to in this study. Schlesinger, Hoopes, and Hilsman all attribute the failure to the reluctance of the military hierarchy to change. Hoopes claims, for example, that "predictably" the new concept of counterinsurgency developed in the early Kennedy years "met with determined resistance from the upper echelons of the U.S. military hierarchy—particularly in the Army—and was ironically and most unfortunately never applied in Vietnam."[71] Reviewing developments up through 1965, Hilsman finds that

> although many people in the Pentagon, in the Special Forces, and elsewhere in the armed services—especially among company and field-grade officers—became enthusiastic believers in the concept as a result of their personal experiences in the field, Secretary McNamara, the Joint Chiefs of Staff, and many general officers were never more than lukewarm. General Harkins, for example, the commander in Vietnam, always acknowledged the importance of winning the allegiance of the People. But he never saw that the central principle of the concept was the need to subordinate military measures to a political and social program. What he apparently believed was not only that a regular war should be fought in Vietnam, but that it could be fought parallel to the necessary political and social program without destroying that program—which was probably a mistake. In any case, General Harkins

was content to leave to someone else both the problem of pursuing the political and social struggle and the problem of seeing that military measures did not destroy it. As a result, the strategic concept was never fully implemented and military factors were emphasized over political.[72]

But it was more than the slowness of key officials like Harkins to comprehend. Most U.S. and Vietnamese generals felt as he did, and still do to this day.[73] The same holds true of many key civilians. And even though the civilians who favored a more counterinsurgency-oriented strategy could affect policy, they had far less of a handle on performance in either the U.S. or the Vietnamese government.

Thus we come back to institutional explanations. At least until 1967 counterinsurgency was not tried on a sufficient scale largely because it was not part of the institutional repertoire of most major GVN and U.S. agencies involved. It had plenty of supporters but no major organizational entity speaking for it. It fell between stools, and so was overshadowed from the outset by the more conventional approaches of the major GVN and U.S. bureaucracies which were playing out their own institutional repertoires. The military establishments in particular knew how to mobilize resources, provide logistic support, deploy assets, manage large efforts. So they employed all these skills to develop irresistible momentum toward fighting their kind of war, while the counterinsurgency advocates had a hard time even getting anything started. This changed only in 1967, when the military themselves were saddled with responsibility for pacification.

Moreover, whatever the merits of a counterinsurgency strategy, it was futile to stress such an alternative without developing a capability for carrying it out. Though many were advocating a more sophisticated counterguerrilla strategy, neither the U.S. nor the South Vietnamese developed tailored counterinsurgency *capabilities* on any major scale until 1967 and afterwards. Despite all the brave talk in the early Sixties (spurred by President Kennedy's genuine interest), the U.S. military services never made much of a real investment in them. The Army's Green Berets, the USAF "Air Commandos," the Navy's "Seals" were all small-scale efforts, never funded as their advocates desired. Service in them was rarely regarded as a desirable career pattern among professionals, which illustrates another form of bureaucratic constraint. There was relatively little R&D effort before 1965, except for ARPAs. Civilian agency counterinsurgency programs were even smaller. Police support programs were tiny and conventionally oriented, unsurprising since most of the U.S. advisers came from U.S. police forces with no constabulary type experience. Though AID and

CIA improvised several promising rural experiments, they had little existing capability for supporting major rural programs with paramilitary features in a chaotic wartime environment.

Another institutional constraint on any effective pacification effort was the lack for too long of any GVN or U.S. management structure able to give it proper stress. As we have seen in Chapter 6, both the U.S. and GVN attempted to manage a multifaceted conflict through essentially conventional government machinery. Indeed, if pacification is correctly regarded as necessarily Vietnamese business, the GVN of Diem and his early successors clearly proved incapable of administering much of a program, even with U.S. support. Not until 1966–1968 were effective steps taken to create special management structures to bring together pacification-related programs and to give them high-level focus. Nor was any consistent effort made at any point to unify interallied conflict management.

Finally, the escalating quasiconventional military conflict during 1963–1965 in itself acted as a magnet which drew U.S. and GVN attention toward conventional military responses. It led us to focus even more on the main-force war and Hanoi's support of it, to the neglect of the insurgency aspect. The beginning of NVA infiltration, and Hanoi's ability to match U.S. escalation, helped keep our eyes firmly fixed on the big-unit war. Paradoxically, the U.S. only returned to pacification, and started backing and organizing it seriously, when the cost of the war had risen to the point where the civilian leadership in Washington began to find it unbearable. By that time, pacification could no longer be the dominant strategic thrust, but merely a corollary to what had become a stalemated quasiconventional war.

WOULD A PACIFICATION ALTERNATIVE HAVE WORKED?

It is easy to conclude that for all these reasons the gap between policy and performance was inevitable—that, whatever the policy intent, there was no hope of carrying it out more effectively. Any other conclusion would be at best an historical "if." Yet there is considerable evidence that the U.S. and GVN could probably have performed more effectively—if only because in many respects they finally did. However spotty GVN and RVNAF performance was, there is no question that on balance they performed much better between Tet 1968 and the end of 1972 than in the period before. How else explain the improvement in the situation despite the progressive withdrawal of almost 500,000 U.S. troops and the sharp reduction in U.S. air support?

Of course, many other factors contributed to this improvement, not least among them the heavy VC/NVA losses in their 1968 offensives, which compelled Hanoi to revert in 1969–1971 to a strategy of protracted war. Particularly important, these losses were incurred mostly by the southern Viet Cong, who were always the chief opponents of pacification. Another important factor was Lon Nol's Cambodian coup of early 1970, which prompted a major diversion of North Vietnamese resources in 1970–1971.

But South Vietnamese performance during 1968–1971 was also in sharp contrast to what it had been before Tet 1968 (see Chapter 3). A larger, stronger, and better-equipped RVNAF managed to take over almost the entire ground combat role from the departing U.S. forces (though it still needed massive U.S. air support to cope with Hanoi's 1972 offensive). Overall GVN administrative performance also improved significantly. But in no important field did GVN performance improve so much as in pacification, a program which remained almost wholly "Vietnamized" even though extensively subsidized and advised by the United States.

Indeed, *it is on the role which the 1968–1971 pacification program played in the turnaround of the war during 1968–1971 that the case for a counterinsurgency oriented strategy must chiefly rest.* This is because the only large-scale and sustained test of what counterinsurgency oriented programs could accomplish came with this program, which began belatedly in 1967. It represented the first time that the GVN and U.S. allotted sufficient manpower and resources on a continuing basis to competing effectively with the VC in the countryside. For example, GVN/U.S. resources devoted to pacification rose from under $600 million in CY 1966 to around $1.5 billion at the CY 1970 peak.[74] The cumulative impact achieved during 1968–1971 is at least suggestive of what might have been accomplished earlier if comparable backing had been received. Despite the many weaknesses of the Hamlet Evaluation System, it gives a reasonable picture of the trend; at the post-Tet low point, in March 1968, only 59 percent of the population (and this mostly urban) was regarded as even "relatively secure." By end-1971 this had risen to over 96 percent, and the gains were mostly rural.

Aside from its larger scale and sustained nature, pacification after 1966 was different in several other important respects. It was the first time that either the GVN or the U.S. had developed a unified management structure for this program (see Chapter 6), and almost the first time since the Strategic Hamlet Program that it received sustained high-level GVN and U.S. support. President Thieu, who took office in late 1967, was the first top GVN leader who was thoroughly pacification-oriented and played a major continuing role in its implementation. In sum, many of the basic flaws which made pacification a shadow program in 1954–1966 were at least partly remedied in the subsequent period, with visible results.

On the other hand, pacification 1967–1972 was hardly a pure test of a counterinsurgency-oriented strategy as a preferred alternative. Since it did not achieve momentum until after the "big-unit" war had escalated, its impact is hard to sort out from that of the big-unit war. To what extent can the observed changes in the countryside during 1968–1972 be attributed to pacification, as opposed to (a) the "shield" provided by the allied anti-main force effort, which largely drove the VC/NVA from most populated areas; (b) the 1970 Cambodian diversion; or (c) the heavy VC/NVA losses in their 1968 offensives? Even the large-scale pacification effort generated after 1966 was at most only a modest complement to what had already escalated into quasiconventional conflict. The disparity between resources devoted to pacification and those allocated to the big-unit war remained enormous.

After 1964, as NVA infiltration grew, focusing mostly on a pacification-oriented, clear-and-hold strategy was no longer feasible. It now required a much larger military shield.[75] Indeed, it was the fortuitous circumstance that the U.S. took over most of the big-unit war and shouldered RVNAF to one side which led to a search for a new role for RVNAF. This more than anything else facilitated RVNAF's diversion to local security tasks and helped put pacification on the map.

Thus it seems clear that a *predominantly counterinsurgency-oriented strategy would have had its best chance for success prior to 1964–1965*, before insurgency escalated into a quasiconventional war. If the GVN and U.S. had pressed this approach on a suitable scale in 1955–1964, instead of putting their chief emphasis on conventional military responses, the Viet Cong might never have achieved the momentum that they did. This is certainly the lesson from the successful British counterinsurgency response in Malaya, though it is admittedly difficult to analogize from the 1948–1960 Malayan case to Vietnam.[76] Moreover, it was the failure to develop a counterinsurgency program worthy of the name which helped lead the U.S. irrevocably to the conclusion that the conflict could not be won in the South without greater pressure on North Vietnam as well.

But could the GVN, with U.S. backing, have created an effective counterinsurgency capability at that earlier time? In the event it did not, for many reasons already discussed, including the incapacities of the Diem regime, the lack of any viable politico-administrative framework, and the inability of the U.S. to bring about the necessary changes. Yet it must be acknowledged that the later Thieu regime did prove capable of carrying out a major pacification effort under even more adverse circumstances in the midst of an escalated war. It is at least conceivable that, if the U.S. had pressed the Diem regime far harder in 1955–1963, had allocated most of the aid it invested to counterinsurgency-type programs, had greatly strengthened U.S. management, and had insisted that the field conform to Washington policy, the insurgency might have been arrested.

By 1964–1965 pacification almost inevitably took a back seat to the growing "main force" war. NVA regular units came down in increasing numbers. From then on a substantial military "shield" for pacification efforts became indispensable. The conflict became a "strange combination of conventional and unconventional war. . . ."[77] But, as we have seen, the GVN/U.S. conventional military effort tended to become an end in itself, to the comparative neglect of pacification. Even though the latter remained a matter of major policy intent, in fact it suffered a near-hiatus during 1964–1965. Though a growing pacification effort finally got under way in 1966–1967, it remained to the end a modest complement to the conventional military effort— not the dominant strategic thrust. While it must also be noted that pacification finally had its inning under primarily military auspices, we never struck an optimum balance between pacification and the big-unit war.

In the last analysis, whether a pacification-oriented strategy would have proved a viable response must remain an historical "if." Naturally, it looks much more desirable in retrospect than what we actually did instead. But Hanoi would have retained the option to escalate via infiltration if the southern insurgency appeared to be crumbling. Sir Robert Thompson believes that Hanoi would have done so.[78] Moreover, a successful counterinsurgency effort would probably have required far greater U.S. success in turning around the GVN than was ever achieved. This is why those in the "counterinsurgency school" were generally stronger advocates of administrative reorganization, a more vigorous advisory effort, and greater use of leverage than their more conventional-minded colleagues.

Yet what was achieved belatedly (and temporarily) in 1967–1972 is also strongly suggestive of what might have been done. Even allowing for many other contributory factors, it suggests that vigorous emphasis on a pacification-oriented approach was feasible and might have led to a more satisfactory outcome—especially if applied much earlier. At the least, its even half-hearted execution would probably have resulted in less militarization and Americanization of the conflict, and in a greatly reduced toll in human life and resources as well as tragic side effects. And it is the very contrast between this enormous toll and the ambiguous results achieved that fed U.S. disillusionment with the war. Hence the very way in which we fought the Vietnam war may have been what foreclosed the "long-haul, low-cost" pacification strategy which in hindsight offered perhaps the best hope of achieving U.S. aims at politically acceptable costs. Samuel Popkin notes that "if America had fought the war . . . as if defending peasants was as important as killing Communists, we would have done better at both."[79]

The final irony is that the war ended as we Americans had thought it would begin—with a series of conventional NVA attacks employing artillery, tanks, and even air power. It was the collapse of the regular ARVN forces, weakened by withdrawal of the U.S. shield and congressional cutbacks in U.S. military aid, which brought the 20-year conflict to its ignominious end. By this time the indigenous Viet Cong insurgency had largely petered out. Pacification had not failed; indeed it had become a qualified success at long last. But it too was swept away in the final debacle.

In an ironic asymmetry, the Communists initiated the war against Diem in the late 1950s as a people's war and the Americans and the Vietnamese initially responded to it as a conventional military one; in the end the Thieu government was fighting a successful people's war, but lost to a military assault.[80]

NOTES

1. Bruce Palmer, *The 25-Year War: America's Military Role in Vietnam,* University Press of Kentucky, Lexington, KY, 1984, pp. 182–186. But even if this strategy had successfully cut off most NVA infiltration (except through Sihanoukville), Hanoi could still have just waited out the Americans.

2. For a discussion of the "two strategic concepts" considered in Vietnam, see Roger Hilsman, "Two American Counterstrategies to Guerrilla Warfare," in *China in Crisis,* Vol. 2, pp. 276–301.

3. Hilsman takes a similar view in ibid., pp. 276–277 and 289–290.

4. *United States–Vietnam Relations, 1945–1967: Study Proposal by the Department of Defense,* 12 Volumes, U.S. Government Printing Office, Washington, D.C., 1971 (hereafter referred to as the *Pentagon Papers*), IV.B.5, pp. 35–37.

5. Ibid., IV.A.5, pp. 24–26.

6. NSC 5429/2 of 8/20/54 cited in *Pentagon Papers* IV.A.3, pp. vi and 11.

7. Cited in A.A. Jordan, *Foreign Aid and the Defense of Southeast Asia,* Frederick A. Praeger, Inc., New York, 1962, p. 17.

8. John D. Montgomery, *Politics of Foreign Aid: American Experience in Southeast Asia,* Frederick A. Praeger, Inc., New York, 1962, pp. 64–70.

9. *Pentagon Papers,* IV.A.4, Summary, p. 51.

10. Ibid., IV.A.5, Tab 4, pp. 43–56.

11. Ibid., pp. 60–62.

12. For Kennedy's views, see Arthur M. Schlesinger, Jr., *A Thousand Days,* Houghton Mifflin Company, Boston, 1965, pp. 340–342. See also Roger Hilsman, *To Move a Nation,* Doubleday & Company, Inc., New York, 1967, pp. 578–579.

13. For an analysis of this period, see John Dallas Stempel, *Policy/Decision Making in the Department of State: The Vietnamese Problem, 1961–1965,* University Microfilm, Ann Arbor, MI, 1965, pp. 90–108. For the Kennedy emphasis on police assistance programs, see U. Alexis Johnson, *The Right Hand of Power,* Prentice-Hall, New York, 1984, pp. 338–339.

14. Schlesinger, *A Thousand Days,* pp. 340–341.

15. *Pentagon Papers,* IV.A.5, Tab. 4, pp. 95–99.

16. Ibid., IV.B.1, pp. 23–29.

17. Ibid., pp. 29–30.

18. Maxwell D. Taylor, *Swords and Plowshares,* W.W. Norton & Company, Inc., New York, 1972, pp. 225–226.

19. Stempel, *Policy/Decision Making,* pp. 170–175, 184–188, 201–204.

20. Hilsman, *To Move a Nation,* pp. 424–439.

21. Ibid., pp. 429–434. See also *Pentagon Papers,* IV.B.2.

22. *Pentagon Papers,* IV.B.2, p. 18.

23. Ibid., p. 21.

24. For a detailed analysis of the rise and fall of strategic hamlets, see ibid., IV.B.2.

25. Cited in Joseph Kraft, "Bureaucrats' War Over Vietnam," *Harper's Magazine,* May 1964, p. 110.

26. *Pentagon Papers,* IV.B.5, p. 33.

27. Ibid., p. 67; IV.C.1, pp. 12–15.

28. Ibid., IV.C.1, pp. 17–21.

29. Ibid., pp. 43–46, describe the plan.

30. Ibid., IV.C.9(a), p. 11.

31. Ibid., pp. 12–13; see also IV.C.1, pp. 44–53.

32. Ibid., IV.C.1, p. 52.

33. Ibid., p. ii.

34. See ibid., IV.C.8, pp. 1–7, for discussion of *Hop Tac.*

35. McGeorge Bundy's Trip Report to the President, 2/7/65, in the *Pentagon Papers,* IV.C.3, p. 33.

36. Ibid., p. 38.

37. Ibid., pp. 48 and 52.

38. Ibid., p. 50.

39. See ibid., IV.C.5, pp. 51–54, for the sad state of pacification in early 1965. Westmoreland's famous "Estimate of the Situation" of 3/26/65 hardly even mentioned pacification (ibid., pp. 84–88).

40. Ibid., IV.C.8, p. ii. Also interesting is the fact that COMUSMACV's year-end message on 1965 did not even mention pacification (p. v).

41. See IV.C.4, pp. 108ff., for discussion of these.

42. Ibid., p. 59.

43. Ibid., p. 104.

44. Ibid., p. 114.

45. See ibid., IV.C.8, pp. iii-iv and 1–45.

46. Ibid., pp. 55–61.

47. Ibid., IV.C.9(b), p. 24. When the JCS queried him about RD effectiveness, COMUSMACV replied that the program was primarily civilian.

48. Ibid., IV.C.8, pp. 74–79.

49. Ibid., pp. 83–88.

50. Ibid., pp. 84–85.

51. Ibid., pp. 88–89.

52. Ibid., IV.C.6(b), pp. 13–18.

53. Ibid., IV.C.6(a), pp. 81–89.

54. Ibid., p. 88.

55. Ibid., p. 93.

56. Ibid., pp. 105–119, especially p. 110.

57. Ibid., pp. 120–122.

58. Ibid., IV.C.6(b), pp. 61–67.

59. See Katzenbach, Komer, Bundy, and Enthoven memoranda cited in ibid., pp. 77–81, 85–89, and 105–110. See also ISA draft DPM of May 19, 1967, in ibid., pp. 146–165.

60. Ibid., p. 215.

61. An OSD/SA paper on "Alternate Strategies" stated flatly that "our strategy of 'attrition' has not worked." *Pentagon Papers*, IV.C.6(c), p. 28.

62. Ibid., p. 16.

63. See the JCS, CIA, OSD/ISA, CJCS, and OSD/SA assessments in ibid., pp. 1–76.

64. Ibid., pp. 33–34.

65. See CJCS Report of February 27, 1968, in ibid., pp. 12–13; OSD/SA Report in ibid., p. 28; and OSD/ISA draft report of February 29, 1968, in ibid., pp. 33–37.

66. Ibid., p. 26.

67. Ibid., p. 64.

68. Ibid., p. 63.

69. William Colby's testimony in Hearings Before the Senate Foreign Relations Committee on "Vietnam: Policy and Prospects 1970," 91st Congress, 2d Session, Government Printing Office, Washington, D.C., 1970, p. 708.

70. Hilsman, *To Move a Nation,* p. 578.

71. Townsend Hoopes, *Limits of Intervention,* David McKay Company, Inc., New York, 1969, pp. 14–15.

72. Hilsman, *To Move a Nation,* pp. 578–579.

73. For example, see Harry Summers, Jr., *On Strategy: A Critical Analysis of the Vietnam War,* Presidio Press, Novato, CA, 1982, Dave Richard Palmer, and Bruce Palmer.

74. William Colby testimony, op.cit., p. 708.

75. Robert Osgood makes the same point in *Vietnam as History,* University Press of America, Lanham, MD, 1984, p. 132.

76. See Komer, *The Malayan Emergency in Retrospect: Organization of a Successful Counterinsurgency Effort,* The RAND Corporation, R-957-ARPA, February 1972, especially Section X on "Malaya and Vietnam: A Comparison in Retrospect," pp. 76–87.

77. Robert Osgood in *Vietnam as History,* p. 132.

78. Sir Robert Thompson, in W. Scott Thompson and Donaldson D. Frizzell (eds.), *The Lessons of Vietnam,* Crane, Russak & Company, Inc., New York, 1977, p. 224.

79. Samuel Popkin, in *Vietnam as History,* p. 132.

80. William Colby, *Honorable Men: My Life in the CIA,* Simon and Schuster, New York, 1978, p. 286.

9

WHAT LESSONS CAN BE LEARNED?

The preceding analysis suggests that, whatever the wisdom of the various U.S. decisions to intervene in Vietnam, there is also much to be learned from the way we went about it. Indeed, the underlying conclusion which emerges from this study is the difficulty encountered by conventional government institutions—in this case both U.S. and GVN—in responding optimally to such atypical problems as they confronted in the Vietnam war. Though by no means the whole answer, this does much to explain why there was such an immense disparity between the cumulatively massive effort mounted and the ambiguous results achieved. It also helps explain why such a gap emerged between policy and performance—between the guidelines laid down by the policymakers and what was actually done in the field.

FLAWS IN GVN/U.S. PERFORMANCE

Among the many underlying reasons were the unique and unfamiliar conflict environment of Vietnam, the atypical nature of the conflict in which we became enmeshed, and the sharp contrast between the determined enemy we faced and the feeble regime we backed. However, even these reasons are insufficient to explain why we did so poorly for so long. As this study demonstrates, it was more than that.

To a greater extent than is often realized, we recognized the nature of the operational problems we confronted in Vietnam, and our policy was designed to overcome them. And whatever the gradualism of our response, we ended up making a cumulatively massive investment of U.S. blood and treasure in the attempt to achieve a satisfactory outcome. Yet the U.S. grossly misjudged what it could actually accomplish with the huge effort it eventually made, and thus became more and more wound up in a war it couldn't "win" the way it fought it. In this sense at least, the U.S. did stumble into a "quagmire" in Vietnam.

What needs to be added is how another set of real-life constraints—largely inherent in the typical behavior patterns of the GVN and U.S. institutions involved in the conflict—made it so difficult for them to cope with an unfamiliar conflict environment and greatly influenced what they could and could not, or would and would not, do. These institutional constraints helped render the U.S./GVN response to an atypical insurgency conflict unduly conventional, expensive, and slow to adapt. This added perspective—so often missing from critical analyses of our Vietnam experience—is essential to an understanding of why we fought the war the way we did.

The GVN's performance was even more constrained by its built-in limitations than that of the U.S. In the last analysis, perhaps the most important single reason why the U.S. achieved so little for so long in Vietnam was that it could not sufficiently revamp, or adequately substitute for, a South Vietnamese leadership, administration, and armed forces inadequate to the task. The incapacity of the regimes we backed, which largely frittered away the enormous resources we gave them, may well have been the greatest single constraint on our ability to achieve the aims we set ourselves at acceptable cost.

But to a great extent the GVN's failure was a U.S. failure too. Even in hindsight it is difficult to evaluate how much our inability to move the GVN was owing to the intractable nature of the problem and how much to the way we went about it. The record shows that U.S. officials often tried hard to get Diem and his successors to deal more effectively with the threat they faced. But for many reasons we seldom used vigorously the leverage over the Vietnamese leaders that our contributions gave us. We became their prisoners rather than they ours; the GVN used its weakness far more effectively as leverage on us than we used our strength to lever it.

Equally striking is the sharp discontinuity between the mixed counterinsurgency strategy which U.S. and GVN policy called for from the outset, and the overwhelmingly conventional and militarized nature of our actual response. The impact of institutional constraints is nowhere more evident than in the GVN and U.S. approach to Vietnam's military aspects, both before and after 1965. From the outset the preponderant weight of the U.S. and GVN military in the Vietnam picture tended to dictate an overly militarized response. The institutional background of U.S. and GVN military leaders helped shape the nature of that response. Molding conventional Vietnamese armed forces in the "mirror image" of the U.S. forces which were supplying them was a natural institutional reaction. We organized, equipped, and trained the RVNAF to fight American style, the only way we knew how.

Then, when the GVN and ARVN buckled, the U.S. in effect took over the "anti-main force war" and sought to do directly what the South Vietnamese had failed to do. In the process, as might be expected, it further Americanized the war—on an even grander scale. Trained, equipped, and organized primarily to fight the Russians in Central Europe, U.S. forces naturally played out this military repertoire. Instead of adapting our response to the unique circumstances of Vietnam, we fought the enemy our way—at horrendous cost and with tragic side effects—because we lacked much incentive and existing capability to do otherwise.

Our costly "search-and-destroy" or attrition strategy—ground and air—was also partly an outgrowth of these factors. It was a natural response of American commanders deploying forces hugely superior in mobility and firepower against an elusive enemy who could not be brought to decisive battle. But his ability to control his own losses by such means as evading contact and using sanctuaries frustrated our aims, as did his ability to replace much of his losses by further recruitment and, increasingly, by infiltration from the North.

The 1965–1968 U.S. air campaign against North Vietnam also reflects the way in which an institution will tend to play out its preferred repertoire. Airmen were eager to demonstrate that strategic bombing and interdiction would work even in a war of the Vietnam type. It was also a classic case of the availability of a capability driving us to use it—even though we soon recognized this use as having less than optimum effect.

Critical intelligence inadequacies which plagued the GVN/U.S. effort despite the huge resources invested in overcoming them are largely another product of institutional factors. The massive U.S. and ARVN military intelligence empires focused mostly on that with which they were most familiar, the size and location of enemy main-force units, to the neglect of such other vital targets as the opponent's politico-military control structure. We tended to see the enemy in our own image, one reason why we repeatedly thought we were doing better than we actually were.

On the civilian side the same tendency existed for the chief U.S. agencies involved to focus primarily on that with which they were most familiar. The State Department did not often deviate from its concept of normal diplomatic dealings with a sovereign allied government, not even when that government was falling apart. Similarly,

State clung to a traditionalist view of civil-military relationships, and made little effort to assert control over our military effort on political grounds—except with respect to limits on out-of-country military operations. State's concept of institution-building turned largely on encouragement of American democratic forms, a kind of mirror-imaging which proved hard to apply to the conditions of Vietnam. As for the Agency for International Development, though its operations were for the most part also quite conventional, the bulk of its resources went properly into a largely successful effort to prevent the inflationary consequences of the conflict from getting out of hand.

Even if our initial Vietnam responses were ill-suited to the atypical problems we confronted, why did they change so little over years of bitter experience? Again it seems that institutional factors played a major role. Especially significant was institutional inertia—the built-in reluctance of organizations to change preferred ways of functioning except slowly and incrementally. Another such factor was the shocking *lack of institutional memory*, largely because of short tours for U.S. personnel. *Skewed incentive patterns* also increased the pressures for conformity and tended to penalize adaptive response. And there was a notable *dearth of systematic analysis of performance*, again mainly because of the inherent reluctance of organizations to indulge in rigorous self-examination.

In sum, in an atypical situation that cried out for innovation and adaptation, a series of institutional constraints militated against them. For the most part, as Herman Kahn aptly put it, Vietnam reflected a "business as usual" approach. Bureaucratic inertia and other factors powerfully inhibited the learning process. In true bureaucratic fashion, each U.S. and GVN agency preferred doing more of what it was already used to doing, rather than change accepted patterns of organization or operation. All this helps explain why the enormous direct U.S. contribution to the war—almost 550,000 troops at peak, thousands of aircraft, and over $150 billion (in then year dollars)—had such limited impact for so long.

It also contributed to the failure of the huge U.S. support and advisory effort to generate an adequate GVN and RVNAF response to the challenges faced. Indeed, we probably did too much for the Vietnamese. We made them over-reliant on U.S. power, which impaired their performance when U.S. forces were withdrawn and then U.S. aid cut back. Hence Washington must bear its share of the responsibility for the 1975 collapse of the Saigon regime.

Nor was there any integrated conflict management to pull together all the disparate aspects of the GVN/U.S. effort. By and large, the

U.S. and GVN each ran their share of the war with essentially a peacetime management structure—in largely separate bureaucratic compartments. This had a significantly adverse impact on the prosecution of the war. Lack of any overall management structure contributed to its overmilitarization by facilitating the predominance of the GVN and U.S. military. It also contributed to the proliferation of overlapping GVN and U.S. programs—to the point where they competed excessively for scarce resources and even got in each other's way.

Meanwhile, counterinsurgency—or pacification—fell between stools; it was everybody's business and nobody's. Though many correctly analyzed the need for it, and it was from the outset a major component of GVN/U.S. declaratory strategy, the absence of a single agency or directing body charged with it contributed greatly to the prolonged failure to carry it out on any commensurate scale.

Last but not least, the lack of any *combined* command or management machinery seriously limited the ability of the Americans to exact better performance from the South Vietnamese. It deprived the U.S. of an institutional framework for exerting influence toward the solution of problems which it early recognized as critical. In retrospect, the diffusion of authority and fragmentation of command that characterized the efforts of both the GVN and the U.S. (and their interrelationship) provide yet other major reasons why it proved so hard to translate policy into practice or to convert our overwhelming superiority in men and resources into the results we sought.

Why did the U.S. and GVN settle for such conventional and fragmented management structures—in strong contrast to an enemy who exerted centralized control over every facet of his activities? Institutional constraints again bulk large, including bureaucratic inertia, agency reluctance to violate the conventional dividing lines between their responsibilities, and hesitation to change the traditional relationship of civilian to military leadership. Whenever combined command was considered, the chief argument against it was essentially political—that it would smack of colonialism. But also at work was the natural preference of any institution to operate as an autonomous, homogeneous unit.

While U.S. performance in Vietnam is most notable for its sheer conventionality, some adaptive solutions tailored to specific problems were attempted—and proved their utility more often than not. Unsurprisingly, such military adaptation as occurred tended to be either technological or in tactical means of utilizing new technology, e.g., helicopters or the sensors for the so-called "McNamara barrier."

Perhaps the chief example of large-scale institutional innovation was the major GVN pacification program begun belatedly in 1967. To back it, the U.S. created an integrated civil-military advisory and support organization, almost unique in the Vietnam war. The gradual expansion of the overall U.S. advisory effort was another attempt at adaptive response. Compared to any previous such U.S. effort, that in Vietnam was unprecedented in duration, extent, and comprehensiveness.

In assessing U.S. performance in Vietnam, it is also useful to pose the question of whether there was, *within the political constraints imposed by Washington,* a viable alternative approach to what we actually did. One such alternative—which might be termed primary emphasis on a counterinsurgency strategy—was repeatedly advocated, indeed was given prominence in our Vietnam policy as early as 1955. But there was an immense gap between this policy emphasis and what was actually done in Vietnam. Counterinsurgency (or pacification) did not fail in Vietnam. Whatever policy called for, it simply was never tried on any major scale until 1967–1971, which proved to be too late. Programs were overshadowed from the outset by more conventional approaches.

Before 1967 the U.S. and GVN devoted relatively little effort and resources to pacification programs; these were always dwarfed by the conventional military effort. Another constraint was the lack, for too long, of any unified GVN or U.S. management structure to pull together the many facets of counterinsurgency and give them proper stress.

Even after 1967, pacification remained a small tail to the very large conventional military dog. It was never tried on a large enough scale until too late mainly because it was not part of the institutional repertoire of the major GVN and U.S. agencies involved in Vietnam. In effect, the GVN and U.S. lacked an institutional capability to carry it out.

A predominantly counterinsurgency-oriented effort would have had its best chance for success before 1964–1965, when the insurgency escalated into quasiconventional war. Paradoxically, however, a reasonably effective pacification effort did not get under way until 1967–1968, when it belatedly became a modest complement to the raging big-unit war. Nonetheless, it is on the role which pacification played in the Vietnam turnaround of 1969–1971 that the case for a counterinsurgency-oriented strategy must chiefly rest. Even allowing for other contributory factors, it demonstrates that vigorous emphasis on pacification was feasible and might have led to a more satisfactory outcome—especially if undertaken much earlier. At the least, it is hard to see how it would have worked less well, cost nearly as much, or had such tragic side effects. But in the last analysis this must remain a historical "if."

THE REQUISITES OF ADAPTIVE RESPONSE

If this analysis is at least broadly valid, then many useful lessons flow logically from it. Insofar as they relate to the typical behavior of government institutions when confronting unfamiliar problems, these lessons of course have far wider application than to insurgency situations of the Vietnam type. However,

> The military lessons of the Vietnam War, while numerous, are by no means either self-evident or instructive about wars of the future. If the United States succeeded or failed in Vietnam because of its inability to adapt quickly to the circumstances of Vietnam or its penchant for conducting the war in Vietnam with capabilities and doctrines developed and tested in conflicts elsewhere, similar problems may arise in the wars of the future. Therefore, a learning of the military lessons of Vietnam, without regard for the unique characteristics of the Vietnam War and future wars, will serve American policy in those potential conflicts no more adequately than did the strategies and capabilities utilized in Vietnam.[1]

In fact Vietnam itself teaches us the dangers implicit in taking a past experience as an explicit model for the future. As we learned from attempting to apply in Vietnam what we learned in the Korean War, such lessons may not be applicable in quite different situations. Since the unique features of Vietnam are highly unlikely to be duplicated, we must avoid analogies which could lead to gross misperceptions about how best to deal with quite different contingencies.[2] The suggestions which follow are framed with these caveats in mind.

It is also tempting to suggest, as one key lesson of Vietnam, that "policy is easy to decide; execution is much more difficult." But this would be a grievous oversimplification. For sound policy formulation must itself take fully into account the capabilities of the institutions involved to execute it effectively. Our Vietnam experience amply illustrates the sheer enormity of the task of making much of a dent in the "system" and forcing it to adapt. It shows the difficulty of changing institutional behavior patterns, even in the light of frustrating

experience. Indeed, reflecting on our Vietnam failures, Stanley Hoffmann asks: "Are bureaucratic problems ones about which we can
do very much?" He fears that the government bureaucratic apparatus
is "thoroughly unreformable."[3]

But this seems a harsh verdict, perhaps overinfluenced by our
Vietnam experience. Vietnam was so atypical as to be a poor test
case. And this study has shown that even in Vietnam some institutional
adaptation emerged and much more was proposed. In fact, history
is replete with examples of institutional adaptation over time. Also,
some institutions seem to adapt better than others, perhaps private
ones more rapidly than public under the competitive pressures of the
marketplace. At any rate, the better we understand the nature of the
problem and the impact of the constraints involved, the more likely
we are to seek sensible remedies.

Moreover, large hierarchically organized institutions are a fixed
feature of the contemporary scene, indispensable to meeting the
complex needs of society. Since we can't do without them, we have
to pay the price of accepting their built-in limitations to the extent
that they cannot be altered. Thus, wise policy must take adequately
into account the institutional realities that will largely shape its
execution.

Lastly, it is always difficult to frame useful lessons in terms that
are sufficiently generalized to be broadly applicable, yet specific enough
to be operationally useful. What follows may not satisfactorily resolve
this dilemma, nor does it pretend to exhaust the lessons of Vietnam.
Moreover, the author is painfully aware that in every case they are
"easier said than done."

1. *Perhaps the key lesson to be learned from our Vietnam experience
is that atypical problems demand specially tailored solutions—not just
the playing out of existing institutional repertoires.* So baldly stated
this sounds almost banal. But as Vietnam shows, such adaptive
solutions are all too difficult to achieve in practice. Neither the U.S.
nor the GVN get very high marks on this score in the Vietnam case,
in strong contrast to the British in Malaya, for example.[4] Instead, our
approach was distinguished by its sheer conventionality. The reasons
for this, as discussed in this study, suggest several further lessons.

2. *Above all the policymaker must take fully into account the ability
of the institutions carrying out the policy to execute it as intended.* For,
whatever the nature of the problem and the policy adopted, the
institutions tasked to execute it will tend to contort this policy in
practice to doing what they are used to doing—playing out their
institutional repertoires. Vietnam provides overwhelming evidence

that existing U.S. and GVN agencies—including their field echelons—
were for the most part unable to perform effectively missions that
were different from those they were used to performing. And their
reluctance to adapt persisted, for largely institutional reasons, long
after it was patently clear that the missions were not being carried
out effectively.

3. *Adaptive response requires much more than well-conceived policy;
it requires adequate machinery at all levels for effective follow-through
to see that the policy is effectively carried out, and to force adaptation
where essential.* Such machinery was sadly lacking in most cases in
Vietnam, and its absence contributed greatly to the gap between
policy and performance. For what Vietnam suggests as to remedial
measures see the next section below.

4. *Where the U.S.—as in Vietnam—is largely fighting a war by proxy,
effective means of stimulating optimum indigenous performance are essential.* As this study suggests, the U.S. did not get comparable value
for its massive aid to the GVN. Means of narrowing this gap are
also discussed below.

WAYS OF FORCING ADAPTATION

As already suggested, it is much easier to draw such generalized,
and in hindsight obvious, lessons than to learn much from our
Vietnam experience how best to apply them in practice. Indeed, this
experience suggests instead the enormous obstacles involved. Insti-
tutionalizing flexibility and adaptiveness is no easy matter; it goes
against the bureaucratic grain. Moreover, changing institutional repertoires entails far more than a realistic appreciation of the nature
of the problem and clear policy guidance to cope with it—guidance
adapted flexibly to changing circumstances. It also involves balanced
programs vigorously and flexibly carried out with a realistic sense
of priorities, plus the management machinery to pull these programs
together and make sure they are effectively carried out.

It is also more than just a matter of providing the right leadership,
important as this is. Vietnam shows how even highly qualified and
experienced leaders, many of whom saw clearly the need for adaptive
change, were often frustrated in their attempts to get it. All the other
factors which influence how an institution will perform its mission
need to be modified as well. Doctrine, training, performance standards,
internal goals and incentive systems, and self-analysis capabilities
must all be made congruent with the mission to be performed.
Fortunately, some aspects of our Vietnam experience suggest at least

partial ways around these institutional roadblocks. What they add up to is the need for a deliberate effort to offset the inevitable bureaucratic tendency to keep doing the familiar and to adapt only slowly and incrementally, no matter how clear the necessity for change.

1. *First, and most obvious, we must select flexible and imaginative conflict managers at all levels.* It is depressing how so many of our senior and middle level officers and officials in Vietnam were picked on the basis of normal institutional criteria or even the convenience of the institution rather than because they were regarded as particularly qualified for the job. Vietnam also shows how many highly qualified people were available but how poorly suited U.S. and GVN personnel and incentive systems—military and civilian—were to bringing them to the fore. There was no more painful example of the inadequacy of conventional personnel and selection systems for coping with atypical needs. On this score, the military must learn that the best commanders may not be the most flexible and adaptive program managers, nor the best advisers to local governments or forces. Civilian agencies must learn that executives to run large programs, especially in wartime, may be quite different animals from those who normally rise through regular promotion systems which value quite different talents.

2. *Training and incentive systems need to be revised to place a higher premium on flexibility and adaptiveness instead of applying the "school solution," and on innovation and experiment rather than conformity.* Vietnam all too often showed the inadequacy of "doing it by the book"—a book which wasn't really very relevant. Again this is admittedly easier said than done, but Vietnam also shows how high a price we paid for not trying harder to do so.

3. Where specially tailored programs which are not in conventional organizational repertoires or which cut across conventional agency lines are required, *it may be best to set up autonomous ad hoc organizations to run them—with the requisite funding, resources, people, and other backing to do the job.* If the institutional constraints described in this study are such an impediment to adaptive response, then it would seem better to adapt the organizational structure to the need—in other words, deliberately break the bureaucratic mold—than, as so often in Vietnam, to try to meet the need through the existing organizational structure. In general, such ad hoc expedients proved successful in Vietnam (e.g., the Marine CAPs, the CIDG program, the RD Ministry, or CORDS under MACV) when given adequate support.

4. *Multidimensional conflict situations requiring integrated politico-economic as well as military responses can best be dealt with by unified management at all levels.* Vietnam suggests that in such a conflict we cannot afford to separate out its many aspects and attempt to cope with them in separate bureaucratic compartments only loosely coordinated in the normal peacetime fashion in Washington or in the field. Such normal peacetime machinery of government did not suffice in either Washington or Saigon. Diffusion of responsibility proved the enemy of adaptive response.

Interagency coordination and pulling all strands together only at the White House level may suffice for policy formulation. But in the Vietnam case it proved wholly inadequate to compel an integrated effort, responsiveness to priorities, and adequate follow-through to prevent the individual agencies involved from marching to their own bureaucratic tunes. Based on his Vietnam experience, Barry Zorthian sees integrated policy direction and program management as the first "bedrock requirement" for successful U.S. assistance to a local counterinsurgency effort. He defines it as "recognition by the U.S. that a successful effort depends on an integrated and responsive political/military program; and organization of our own considerable resources in accordance with this principle as a means of maximum effectiveness."[5]

If and when an exceptional U.S. supporting effort which cuts sharply across normal agency responsibilities is decided upon, it seems advisable to set up special ad hoc machinery at the Washington level to manage it. Several options are available, ranging from making a single agency the executive agent through ad hoc task forces to special machinery in the White House itself. Whichever is decided upon, it will need a clear grant of presidential authority and solid presidential backing to overcome the natural bureaucratic infighting which it will almost inevitably generate.

Unified management of the U.S. effort in the field is similarly essential to optimum response. The loose "country team" approach was a failure in Vietnam. The author would tend in most cases to share the view of Sir Robert Thompson that "to ensure a united effort, the ambassador must be a proconsul with absolute authority locally over all policy and agencies."[6]

This raises in turn a fundamental question as to whether the traditional U.S. separation between military and civilian responsibilities is optimum in multidimensional conflict situations such as Vietnam. Thompson regards civilian control as "imperative, though this does not mean that it cannot be exercised by a general in a civilian post."[7] In the author's view, the top field post could be either civilian or military, depending on the situation and on the caliber of leadership available. But, few U.S. ambassadors have had much experience in managing large enterprises; moreover, much would depend on whether U.S. support were to be predominantly military.

5. *Effective unified management takes more than just a "single manager"; he must also have his own staff.* As Vietnam experience demonstrates, the top manager cannot properly carry out his mandate without some kind of unified civil-military planning, operations, and evaluation staff responsible directly to him. He must have his own eyes and ears, and means of ensuring adequate follow-through. This staff need not be large, however; here is an instance when quality is far more important than quantity.

6. *A corollary lesson is the need to place a higher premium on thorough evaluation and analysis of performance.* Its relative lack was a critical flaw in Vietnam. By its very nature, this uniquely fragmented politico-insurgency conflict made quantitative as well as qualitative analysis indispensable to understanding. Yet Enthoven and Smith insist that "there was no organized critical analysis of the strategy and operations of the Vietnam war—cost effectiveness or otherwise." They conclude:

> One of the main lessons for government organization that should be drawn from U.S. involvement in Vietnam is that the President and the Secretary of Defense must have, but today lack, a reliable source of information and analysis of overseas operations that is independent of the military chain of command and Service interests, can get at the basic facts, is capable of self-criticism, and can give searching consideration to genuine alternatives without prior commitment to existing policies. . . .
>
> Another lesson of almost equal importance is that U.S. military commanders need, but for the most part either do not have or have and do not use, operations analysis organizations that provide them with a systematic method of learning by experience.[8]

ACHIEVING ADEQUATE PERFORMANCE FROM ALLIES

All the preceding lessons are, of course, as applicable to client states as they are to the United States itself. The fledgling GVN regime's response to the threat it confronted was even more constrained than that of the U.S. More surprisingly, most of the useful examples of adaptive response were U.S., rather than GVN-inspired. But Vietnam also suggests a series of ways in which the U.S. should act to secure optimum performance from the clients it is supporting.

1. *U.S. aid inputs, however massive, cannot be effectively utilized without viable indigenous institutions to carry out the programs the U.S. is supporting.* Lack of an effectively functioning GVN and RVNAF administrative structure to utilize it was one major reason why massive U.S. aid inputs to the GVN and RVNAF ended up largely wasted. However, Lyndon Johnson's suggestion that U. S. military government personnel take over this function would have been even more unworkable. As the author told him, we didn't even speak the language.

2. *Avoid mirror-imaging as a routine response.* When U.S. agencies are charged with helping shape and support local institutions, they almost invariably seek to shape these institutions along familiar U.S. lines, whether or not this is optimal (often this last question is not even addressed). In hindsight, we went much further in attempting to shape the GVN and RVNAF in our image than circumstances allowed. Thus much of our massive aid was misdirected, and too little aid flowed to programs which needed it most.

3. *When the U.S. is supporting local programs, it should not hesitate where necessary to use the leverage provided by this support to ensure that it is optimally utilized.* Despite the many obstacles involved, it is clear in retrospect that the U.S. failed to use sufficiently the enormous leverage its aid conferred on it to compel better GVN and RVNAF performance.

4. *Any U.S. advisory effort should be specially tailored to the needs of each situation.* Clearly, the U.S. advisory effort in Vietnam was too slowly expanded in scope and depth for optimum impact, not enough attention was paid to the selection of military or civilian advisers, short tours meant inadequate experience and limited institutional memory, and the emphasis was technical-assistance oriented to the exclusion of sufficient advisory focus on the deficiencies in individual leadership that proved South Vietnam's greatest weakness.

5. *When the U.S. is backing a major local government effort which cuts across nortnal interagency lines, e.g., counterinsurgency, it should press that government to create special machinery to manage it, if necessary by using U.S. aid inputs as a lever to this end.* Lack of such machinery was long a major handicap to effective GVN performance. Only when it was created in pacification, for example, did the GVN effort really begin to produce results commensurate with the investment.

6. *Should the local government prove so weak and ineffective that the U.S. decides on direct intervention, some form of combined command is probably indispensable to the optimum use of combined resources.* Among other things it will facilitate the use of such leverage as the U.S.

commitment provides. One can even envisage situations where the U.S. stops short of sending combat forces, but where the U.S. resource input is so large as to justify insistence on a form of combined command (or a Director of Operations on the Malaya model) as the price of U.S. aid. In retrospect, some form of combined command in Vietnam could not have helped but improve RVNAF performance, and have assisted in better selection of Vietnamese commanders. As we have seen, such devices as combined command or injection of U.S. officials into the GVN structure were considered (though rejected) even before the U.S. intervened directly.

7. Last but not least, if flexibly tailored response to the unique nature of each situation is the optimum, then it will not necessarily be best to follow in perhaps quite different circumstances what it seems in retrospect would have been the optimum in Vietnam. Indeed, we should consciously guard against what could become the new conventional wisdom. This too has numerous implications for our doctrine, training, incentive patterns, and the like.

* * *

If these rather generalized "lessons" and suggestions seem like restatements of the obvious, just recall what actually happened in Vietnam. Looking in hindsight at that tragic experience suggests that they were more honored in the breach than the observance. True, the variety of institutional and other constraints described in this paper are only part of the reasons why. Yet, as this study has served to demonstrate, they deserve to be included among the complex reasons behind our poor performance in the Vietnam war. If our failures in Vietnam help us to recognize this problem area, to clarify our perceptions of the costs of not dealing with it, and to encourage the search for ways of doing so in future, we will at least have a leg up on future solutions.

Unfortunately, this has not happened. Instead U.S. government agencies and American scholars have been turned off by a war we lost, and concluded that "no more Vietnams" would be the order of the day. Hence, in contrast to the spate of informed policy analyses of how we became entangled in this bitter conflict, all too little knowledgeable analysis of performance has taken place. On the contrary, as Douglas Blaufarb ruefully points out in one of the few first class analyses of counterinsurgency:

In the mid-1970s, very little if anything remained of the analytical structure which constituted the justification for the gravity with which, in the 1960s, the United States had viewed the threat of people's war and the urgency with which it sought to counter it. Rarely has there been so complete a reversal of strategic views and assumptions by a great power within so short a span of time. Many serious observers and analysts now look upon the brief preoccupation with counterinsurgency as an aberration stemming from cold-war fixations combined with the Kennedy style of policy development, a style emphasizing enthusiasm and faddishness at the expense of sober reflection.[9]

Of course, insurgencies did not stop occurring. Moreover, a decade after the fall of Saigon, there has been a modest revival of U.S. interest in counterinsurgency. It has been stimulated by the Reagan Administration's concern over the way the anti-Somoza revolution in Nicaragua was captured by the Marxist Sandinistas, who have been supporting another insurgency in El Salvador. But we still do not seem to have profited by many of the operational lessons so expensively learned in Vietnam. One is tempted to recall Santayana's maxim that those who do not learn from history are condemned to repeat it.

NOTES

1. Robert Pfaltzgraff in W. Scott Thompson and Donaldson D. Frizzell (eds.), *The Lessons of Vietnam*, Crane Russak & Company, Inc., New York, 1977, p. 277.

2. For a cogent symposium discussion of the dangers of misreading the lessons of Vietnam, see Richard M. Pfeffer (ed), *No More Vietnams?* Harper and Row, New York, 1968, pp. 1–5.

3. Ibid., pp. 100 and 210.

4. See R.W. Komer, *The Malayan Emergency in Retrospect: Organization of a Successful Counterinsurgency Effort*, The RAND Corporation, R-957-ARPA, February 1972.

5. Zorthian, "Where Do We Go from Here? *Foreign Service Journal*, February, 1970, p. 46.

6. *No More Vietnams?* pp. 161–162; also in *Defeating Communist Insurgency*, pp. 159–160.

7. Thompson, "Squaring the Error," p. 452. Also see his views in *No More Vietnams?* pp. 156–160.

8. Alain C. Enthoven and K. Wayne Smith, *How Much Is Enough?* Harper and Row, New York, 1969, pp. 290–291. See also their other trenchant comments in ibid., Chapters 8 and 9.